Course
Corrections

Course Corrections

Sharpen Your Edge through
Failure and Lead a Life of
Significance

Kevin C. Entwistle

Tampa, Florida

Course Corrections: Sharpen Your Edge through Failure and Lead a Life of Significance

Published by Gatekeeper Press
7853 Gunn Hwy., Suite 209
Tampa, FL 33626
www.GatekeeperPress.com

Library of Congress Control Number: 2023946705

ISBN (hardcover): 9781662942617

vi

The rivets and pivots we all face

Rules for being human handed down from ancient Sanskrit:

You will receive a body
You will learn lessons
There are no mistakes, only lessons
A lesson will be repeated until it is learned
Learning lessons does not end
"There" is not better than "here"
Others are merely mirrors of you
What you make of your life is up to you
Life is exactly what you think it is
Your answers lie inside you
You will forget all of this
You can remember it whenever you want

Author's Note

This book is a series of short stories about wrong turns, dead ends, breakdowns, and the course corrections taken thereafter. No matter where you are today, you are merely a course correction away from where you want to be.

This book is written to my children, but it is for my family and friends at all stages of their walk through life, especially those who are looking to make a change for the better.

Thank you, Mom and Dad, for everything you have given and taught me. There are no better role models I hope to emulate. Your love is everything to me.

Thank you to my more likable and fun sisters. You taught me how to let go and let live.

Thank you to those in the book who have made an impact in my life, whether they know it or not. Some call them friends; I call them angels.

And thank you to my powerful wife, who coached me to write this book, inspired me to embody these words, and who is intimately part of my everyday course corrections.

I had a dream one night that I would one day ask my kids at the kitchen table not what they succeeded at today, but what they failed at. Not only is this book about regrets and mistakes I have made, but it is also about opening yourself up to the idea that failure can be a positive driver for success. The idea is to dream big, put yourself out there, stumble, get up, stumble some more, check your compass, maybe change directions, cut through the bushes, discover a new path, and march on.

Life is a long process of dealing with everything, oneself, other people, one's circumstances, one's health, and one's mental agility or lack thereof. It's a beautifully arduous process, and my hope is that you, the reader, will find your voice and your own influence in the following short stories.

Foreword

Mike Tyson once said, "Everybody's got a plan until they get punched in the mouth." It's a sentiment that resonates with all of us at some point in our lives. We make grand plans, set ambitious goals, and map out our journeys with precision, only to find that the path ahead is fraught with unexpected twists and turns. My parents would remind me of this frequently, telling me on an almost weekly basis when I was a kid: "Vish, remember: Man proposes, God disposes."

Life reliably surprises us, challenges our resilience, and forces us to adapt. I've discovered that the truest life hack is the ability to pivot, both mentally and through our actions. As our environment shifts, as our circumstances evolve, as we face hurdles and crossroads, the art of 'finding another way' ironically becomes the only way.

For me, the seeds of this concept were sown early in life. When I was just twelve, my father introduced me to the practice of Kung Fu. Through my years of learning, I was immersed in Bruce Lee's philosophy of Jeet Kune Do. I learned that in order to maximize my chances of success, whether in a fight, negotiation, injury, or even in any venture, I was much better off being soft and yielding, rather than hard and unbending. I learned that a tree that sways in harsh winds will survive much longer than a tree that refuses to move with—and therefore accept—its environment.

Later, I learned that many optimized patterns are found in nature, and pivoting is no exception. It permeates the fabric of life, from the finding of biological niches in the grand sweep of evolution, to the steadfast albeit interrupted navigation of an ant in a labyrinth. Whether your horizon is long or short, the ability to pivot is the one constant cornerstone of success.

My own personal journey has been full of pivots so far, and I'm sure there are many to come. Against my will as a kid, I was moved from Jamaica to Canada with one week's notice, and had figure out life in a totally different culture. Even today, I still think about how hard that was for me. I later moved to Australia, the United States, and Switzerland—each move successively easier because of my constant practice in changing direction. I learned French, Spanish, and Japanese with reasonable proficiency, training to be a diplomat. Then I decided to be a detective. And then a doctor. I stuck with that one, mostly.

I was rejected from medical school three times before finally getting in. At first I faced these rejections like a stiff, unyielding tree. It was hard. But over time I remembered to be softer, to accept my reality and to graciously flow with it toward my desired direction. I finally earned my medical degree through the corridors of Melbourne and Harvard, and after a couple of years of full-time work as a medical doctor, I found myself at the threshold of another pivot. I ventured into the tech world, founding a company that would pivot not once, but twice, to become the leader in the domain of artificial intelligence-infused smart virtual workplaces: SoWork.

Kevin's book explores the essence of pivoting, not as a mere concept, but as a way of life. You'll learn to recognize your opportunities and have the courage to seize them faster. You'll understand the traits that enable swift and healthy adaptation: resilience, determination, and a relentless focus on your end goal. You'll introspect to find your 'what', while learning to be flexible in your 'how' and 'when'. You'll develop these skills, and become the master of your chosen destiny.

A fulfilling life, I've come to realize, is one of fluidity. It's the ability to dance with life, gracefully moving along with its rhythms. Sometimes, you lead, and life follows your steps. But that's rare. Much, much more often, it's you who will need to move to embrace what life presents. These pages will help.

As you embark on the journey of self-discovery in Kevin's book, you'll discover the profound impact that being skilled in this fluidity will have on your life. It's not just a survival strategy; it's the only way to thrive in our world of constant change. May you find inspiration and wisdom in these pages to help you dodge, flow, and pivot your way to all of your goals.

Vishal Punwani, MD
CEO, SoWork

Table of Contents

Introduction: Ask Good Questions

"The unexamined life is not worth living." (Socrates)

When all is said and done, the question of life's greatest mystery, which we humans are all forced to address, is this: "Who am I, and why am I here?"

Life is full of abstruse and difficult-to-answer questions that many of us would rather eschew altogether. But I caution you not to run from them forever. A good life—a meaningful life—is one in which the right questions are considered. A good question is one that stops you in your tracks, throws you off course, and makes you question everything that you took as fact. A good question is a hefty shove from your sibling, and maybe a kick or two to the kneecap. *Ouch.*

In truth though, asking these difficult questions requires deep mindfulness, practice, and patience. And in asking these powerful questions, we can learn to be still in thought, to sit with it, mull it over, and surrender our instinctual disbelief while cozying up to the possibility of greatness beyond limitation. Seemingly, the older we get, the less malleable our minds are and the more blinkered our perception becomes of what we can achieve.

Allow me to be clear: all humans must constantly redefine their limitations and expectations in order not to grow ossified in disbelief and limiting mindsets. After all, life is a mystery, and shouldn't we be open to exploring that mystery? Malcolm X has this to say about how adults lose their adaptability and willingness to be wrong or fail: "Children have a lesson adults should learn, to not be ashamed of failing, but to get up and try again. Most of us adults are so afraid, so cautious, so 'safe,' and therefore so shrinking and rigid and afraid that it is why so many humans fail. Most middle-aged adults have resigned themselves to failure."[1]

Before we begin a compendium of short stories to follow, let's put our world into context.

We are all born here on earth, this multilayered sphere of oxygen and carbon dioxide that mix perfectly together to bring us the exact ratio of air needed to fill our lungs, all the while trapping the good gasses and precluding the bad gasses from entering our world. Our earth is home to vast blue oceans and sky-high mountains that bring us playgrounds for exploration and food for nourishment, so we don't go hungry. This same earth is spinning gracefully around a ball of fire that heats our entire world so we can be protected from the cold and can see beautiful arrays of colors and smiling faces of children. Our earth is a tiny speck that exists within a galaxy full of likely uninhabitable planets, stars, and seemingly never-ending space that goes beyond imaginable distances. And here you are, at your exact coordinates on earth. Nothing is more brilliant. Truly, nothing is more brilliant. Admittedly, though, it can be frightening to think about where we came from or why we are here exactly, especially amidst the distractions of social media and the busyness of everyday life.

We are all required to walk our own life, acquiring bumps, bruises, and scrapes along the way, which is intrinsically unavoidable during our walk. We must learn to deal with our neighbors and learn to deal with ourselves. Who am I, why did this happen to me, where am I going, how do I fit into this world, how do I know I am on the right path, who are my friends, who are not my friends, when can I cry, and when can I laugh?

Life can be organized as a series of questions, and if you learn to ask good questions of yourself, you can better understand who you are, why you are here, and how you will make this world better than you found it. However, asking good questions is step one. Step two requires mindfulness and practice, which takes incredible patience, discipline, time, and experience. If asking good questions is the orange, mindfulness is the squeezing of the orange to bring about the good stuff: the flavorful nectar and the juice within. Mindfulness is the work that takes place in order to make sense of these existential questions. As Eugene Ionosco says, "It's not the answer that enlightens but the question."[2]

Ultimately, we humans all face the same fate: a ticking clock. Use this knowledge for good; allow it to inspire and move you. Design the life *you* want to live, and be around the people that fill *you* up. The moment you are born is the moment the shot clock begins.

Fact· Every day is not promised, but I still hope you choose to celebrate this beautiful mystery.

David Brooks wrote something life-changing for me in his book *The Road to Character*:

> "Many of us see our life through the metaphor of a journey, a journey through the external world and up the ladder of success. When we think about making a difference or leading a life with purpose, we often think of achieving something eternal, performing some service that will have an impact on the world, creating a successful company, or doing something for the community. Truly humble people also use that journey metaphor to describe their own lives. But they also use, alongside that, a different metaphor, which has more to do with the internal life. This is the metaphor of self-confrontation. They are more likely to assume that we are all deeply divided selves, both splendidly endowed and deeply flawed, that we each have certain talents but also certain weaknesses. And if we habitually fall for those temptations and do not struggle against the weaknesses in ourselves, then we will gradually spoil some core piece of ourselves."[3]

You see, it is not just about climbing up the corporate ladder or finding that cure that saves our planet from disease. Sure, these are noble ambitions worthy of pursuit. To me, life is really about the inner struggle against our own weakness, failures, and eventual course corrections in dealing with these setbacks and disappointments. As put in the book *On Being a Real Person*, "The beginning of worthwhile living is thus the confrontation with ourselves."[4] I believe that your happiness is contingent on how willing you are to engage with the failures and struggles in yourself.

And yes, there are moments I illustrate in this book to pick yourself up, dust yourself off, and use your own failing moments to discover and reinvent yourself. There are perhaps a few (hopefully only a few) cliches, which I still stand by, by the way. But really, these stories are all about framing our lives, our pursuits, and our shared struggles, as well as how we can rise above it all to cherish this gift we have been given. I don't pretend to believe every story will resonate as much as the next, but I do wholeheartedly believe you can learn something about yourself in each story if you are open to receiving the gift of wisdom gained through failure.

How to Read This Book

In the following chapters, I will share some of my most embarrassing and challenging moments in life to date. Most of the stories and memories represent ordinary and mundane experiences in my life. Spoiler alert: there are no NASA missions to space, no Olympic trials in my past, and definitely no Harvard degrees, but you will hear about my challenges addressing confidence, stress, leadership, friendship, family, faith, death, and pride, to name a few. When I look back on my life thus far, these moments delineate an unmistakable bread-crumb trail underscoring why I am the person I am. Just like you, I am on my own quest to discover who I am and why I am here, constantly changing course to make sure I am on the right path. I am constantly thinking of good questions with which to challenge myself so that I am the one who remains in charge of my being, and not someone else.

However, this book is not about me. This book is about you. Read this book like you are reading about yourself, and immerse yourself in the stories. Read this book while contemplating your own version of questions along the way. Was the narrator acting authentically? Why did the narrator make that decision? What would I have done in place of the narrator's action? Feel free to read this book chapter by chapter or to skip around to the lessons and stories you find most relevant. However you read it, find your own voice and life in it. Find who you are in the story.

I began writing this in 2022, so my views have likely changed since then, especially since we humans are constantly learning and unlearning. However, the actual experiences will remain immutable. Whenever possible, I left my voice and bias out of the story and only shared what lessons I personally gleaned from these experiences. Interpret them as you may.

We might feel one way about a situation now, only to find as we get older that our view or perspective has changed. Or we might later in life decide that what we took to be truth needs to be thrown out and relearned. I will be the first to admit that I am an unreliable narrator. I am of course biased by my own experiences, upbringing, and views. Moreover, the method by which I chose to tell my stories is not meant to speak to every individual, at least not every story. There are so many concepts and realities we all want to teach our kids or protect them from, though this is not an attempt to do so. Rather, I chose a method of humility and gratitude, so that someone reading might relate or find a way out for themselves. This is not about placing my views on others; this is about me challenging you to interpret your own views internally. This is about *you*.

As you will come to learn in the following chapters, I believe that "Life is full of individual, profound moments." Within these moments, we can learn a lot about ourselves and the course corrections we did or did not take. What I continue to come back to is this: All humans have stories and backgrounds to their lives. Take time to learn from them, become part of them, and ultimately remind yourself never to judge someone simply based on these backgrounds. Like Shrek says in the

Disney movie *Shrek*, "Ogres have layers and onions have layers." Take time to peel back the layers to see who someone really is, who they really are being. Your past is not who you are. Your achievements are not who you are. *You* are who you are. Your values, your character, what drives you, how you place yourself in the world—that is who you are.

Most importantly, though, you must find a way to raise your own banner in this life and experience your own stories of failure and success. Failing is a good thing, because it is progress toward success. Failure is a bad thing only when it means there is no forward progression or improvement, that you have stopped trying. Someone who is failing is excitingly on the road to success. The road to success, I remind you, is a tortuous and slippery slope, but if you can withstand these twists and turns, you will reach what you set out for. Just always be willing to correct course.

What do you want to be known for? What do you want to design your life around? What do you want to spend your time on earth chasing? There are a lot of really great dreams to chase to no end, but if you take the time to discover what is worth chasing, you will find that chase to be less onerous and more beautiful, more spectacular and more rewarding than any other chase. You might also consider the below question, on which my friend Dr. Vishal Punwani elaborates in the Foreword.

Question: Is it better to live an oblivious and blissful life or a more conscious yet potentially stressful life?

Read these stories through a lens of your own, and try not to be persuaded by my own spin. Throughout life, we all inherit concepts from those around us—our family, friends and even professors and teachers—so it is important to be careful with what you accept as true. You are tasked with designing your own life and your own model of what represents success and truth. You must take responsibility for this and not let others steer you.

Success is not derived by making Mom and Dad proud or doing what Mom and Dad want you to do. Perhaps success is making *yourself* proud and going after what it is *you* want to achieve. In other words, throughout this book and throughout your life, challenge your identity; find out what inspires you, what makes you tick, and how you will improve other people's lives. I encourage you to search for your own peculiar genius. What are you struck by? What is your technique and artistry for life? You. You. You.

Sometimes we get so set in our ways, we think it is too late to change. Life is for the living, so change one thing, change everything, or change nothing. But don't sit on the sidelines while life passes by. Consider your role on this earth, and be intentional about who you are and how you are showing up for yourself and for others. I believe in you.

You will find in your life that people will ask you this question over and over again: "Tell me about yourself. Who are you?" You will experience this question when making friends in school and when you are applying for jobs after school. The question is open ended, welcoming a variety of interpretations to answer it accordingly. When I boil it down, I think it is really a question of how you perceive the world. After all, as David Carr claims, "No one is going to give a damn about your resume, they want to see what you have made with your own little fingers."[5]

What values do you stand by, how do you behave no matter the circumstances, what are your non negotiables, how do you show up for yourself, how do you believe in yourself, what is important to you, and what drives you to do the things you do? In other words, who are you? Write your thoughts down in a notebook, or speak them into your iPhone, keep a scrapbook, take a lot of photos of your work at different stages in your process, scribble, scratch out, scribble more, whether in your diary, in your phone apps, or on your bathroom mirror. Be clear on who you want to be and what is important to you. Writing it and speaking it out loud will help bring your thoughts and imaginations to life. But it is not always easy to decide who you want to be, so how do you know your values and who you are?

I might suggest that the answer to who you are lies in three categories: your past experiences and upbringing, how those past experiences shaped some of your early life decisions, and how you want to use those early life decisions to pave a path forward for your future self and others. This is what some might call your origin story: where you came from, where you are, and where you are headed. In some senses, you can't change all of your story, like choosing where you will be born or into what family you are born, but you do have the choice to find the beauty in this mystery. In fact, you must make a choice. Embrace who you are fully, or waver through life without ever fully appreciating what makes you so uniquely you.

In keeping with the theme of transparency, I hope to evince an artless and straightforward account of my course corrections and the lessons I learned about myself and the world. Admittedly, a lot of the lessons to follow are what I endearingly describe as "borrowed wisdom," or lessons I have gleaned from other people in my life, some in my closest circle and others three degrees removed.

Importantly, the stories to follow are less instructive on how to live your life and more instructive on how life works, leading to an understanding that will stir in you a renewed inspiration to take responsibility for your life and your footprint.

Again, this book is not about me. Instead, this book is a series of short stories about wrong turns, dead-ends, breakdowns, and the course corrections taken thereafter. No matter where you are today, you are merely a course correction away from where you want to be.

Failure is humbling, and your willingness to be humbled determines how great you become. So, how willing are you?

"Life won't always make sense, it's not supposed to. We can't possibly know everything, and sometimes the truth will feel more like a lie. You aren't required to compromise the integrity of your heart to try and piece everything together, because you will always come back holding a picture filled with holes and missing pieces. Life is a mystery, sometimes we are detectives and other times we are part of the enigma itself. Give yourself grace, you are a part of all that is happening around you, not simply an observer—it is not your job to make sense to anyone, or make sense of anything. Just listen to how it makes you

feel and respond accordingly. How we respond is our power."
(Seyda Noir)[6]

* * *

I believe I am qualified to speak on failure because I am still
failing today, and I am failing in major ways.

Failure is something you should not fear facing. If you are
not failing at something, at least part of the time, you have likely
set your goals too low and are underachieving your true worth.
Harboring a worthwhile goal might cause you to fail not once but
twice before you finally achieve it, demonstrating the patience,
resilience, and tenacity needed to achieve a worthy goal. So
many of us become obsessed with going all in. Get into the best
preparatory schools, play or study at the best Ivy League schools,
get the best job out of college, go to the best graduate school,
have the best beachfront vacation home. It can be exhausting
chasing the next best thing one after another, and maybe I am
biased because I failed at all of these things too. But the truth is
this: many strive to be the best or bust, because when you think
you are good at something, you need to be so great at it that the
clouds part and the angels sing out from heaven. In other words,
you might suffer from the same paralyzing fear so many people
face, which is the fear of being mediocre at anything. If you are
scared to be mediocre, you likely won't uncover hidden talents
or be willing to show the world just how great and talented you
are. If you are scared to be mediocre, you will be scared to fail,
and because of this, you will not even try. Your talents will be
wasted, your brilliance never realized.

But if you have dreams, it is important to protect them, to nurture them, and to not let anyone tell you that you cannot achieve them. Jordan Kutzer tweeted on X Corporation, "Bryce Harper [the professional baseball player] was mentioned in the New York Times at the age of 13. The article was about unrealistic baseball dreams at too young an age. He made his MLB debut at 19 years old and just sent his team [the Phillies] to the World Series at 30 years old."[7] We get crowned with uncommon rewards only if we stretch beyond realistic expectations. Be unrealistic.

What might take you weeks, months, or years to achieve because you couldn't get over the hump, or because you were forced back to the drawing board, represent goals worthy of the chase. Just when you feel like throwing in the towel, you might think to yourself, "Oh, I am figuring it out. I am not there yet, but I see all the trappings of what a successful model or a successful step forward looks like." You start to feel it in your veins, right before you go out and accomplish this magnificent goal of yours.

As I walk through many of my own failures, missteps, and course corrections throughout life, I want to equip you with one final tool as you read through this book. If nothing else, this book is designed to get you off the sidelines and into the game. Remember to listen to your inner voice, to embrace your peculiarities, and to not be afraid to stick out and be different from the crowd.

As John Soforic puts it, "I learned that using my odd and peculiar traits was a necessary advantage for uncommon prosperity."[8] The more you can celebrate your uniqueness and embrace your curiosities in life, the more prosperous, self-aware, and fulfilled you will feel. Jim Carrey once addressed an audience about his own life advice, saying, "Don't let anything stand in the way of the light that shines through this form. Risk being seen in all of your glory. Our eyes are not viewers, they are also projectors that are running as second story over the picture we see in front of us all the time. Fear is running that script. And the working title is, I will never be enough. You can spend your whole life imagining ghosts, worrying about the pathway to the future, but all that will ever be is what is happening here, and the decisions we make in this moment, which are based either in love or out of fear. So many choose our path out of fear disguised as practicality, what we really want seems impossibly out of reach and ridiculous to expect so we never ask the universe for it. How will you serve the world? What do they need that your talent can provide? That is all you have to figure out. I can tell you from experience that the effect you have on others is the most valuable currency there is. You can fail at what you don't love doing, so you might as well take the chance of doing what you love. Relax and dream up a good life."[9]

Belief and Being

Putting most of the noise aside in life, it all comes down to a simple question: *Who am I being?*

I worked with a life coach once and decided I wanted to be the best in the world at many areas in my life. Best husband, best employee, best friend. The question became, "Who decides if I am the best at any of this?" It is completely subjective, but it was subjective to my own opinion. If I truly and intrinsically believed I was the best, I was more likely to act like the best, perform like the best, do what the best do, and exemplify and represent myself as the best. When Michael Phelps set the record for most gold medals during the Olympics, he won by nanoseconds, with his fingertips just scraping the wall in front of him while his opponent still had a speck of water between his fingertips and the finishing wall. The photo tells it all, however. Michael was fully extended and looking forward, while his opponent was turned to the side to compare himself to Michael. He was not focused on anyone other than himself, and it paid off in records and gold medals. For the next few chapters, I challenge you to think about who you are being.

We are all beings, living and breathing the same oxygen, and we all have a choice either to be the person we want to be or to fall victim to shrinking to the shadow of our own being. This is your life, and I urge you to stand up for yourself and make sure you are being the person you want to be. Don't use excuses about what you are missing or why it's not possible or how someone else or something else is prohibiting you from being that same person. Don't be someone else, don't try to change your being; lean completely into who you are, and you will find incredible enjoyment in life. When you align authentically with your own being, it will draw attention and excitement from others, and they will ask you, "What got into you? Something has changed, and I want some of what you've got going. You seem so sure of yourself, and I have been so unsure of myself; I want some of that!"

Consciously take the point of view that the universe is abundant, that life is trying to bring us what our hearts and souls truly desire—spiritually, mentally, emotionally, and physically. Almost everything you truly need or want is here for the asking; you only need to believe that it is so, truly desire it, and be willing to accept it. One of the most common causes of failure when seeking what you want is scarcity programming. This is an attitude or set of beliefs about life that goes something like this:

Shakti Gawain in *Creative Visualization* writes, "There isn't enough to go around . . . life is suffering . . . it is immoral or selfish to have enough when others don't. . . . Life is hard, difficult, a vale of tears . . . You must work hard and sacrifice for everything you gain . . . It's more noble and spiritual to be poor."[10]

These are all false beliefs. We need to realize that after our basic needs are met, the experience of abundance has more to do with expressing our creative gifts in satisfying ways and learning to give and receive in a balanced way. It has less to do with extravagant consumerism. The truth about this earth is that it is an infinitely good, beautiful, and nourishing place to be. It is not only acceptable to receive these gifts; it is natural and good. The universe is offering you gifts of abundance; don't reject these by playing small. Be grateful and be open to playing a big game.

Gawain then goes on to say, "The only evil comes from a lack of understanding of this truth." She continues, "Evil (ignorance) is like a shadow—it has no real substance of its own; it is simply a lack of light. You cannot cause a shadow to disappear by trying to fight it, by stamping on it, by railing against it, or by any other form of emotional or physical resistance. In order to cause a shadow to disappear, you must shine light on it. Take a look at your belief system and see if you are holding yourself back by not believing sufficiently in the possibility of success, prosperity and a good life."[11]

God, Please Help Me Pass This Test

When I took the Charter Financial Analysis (CFA) examinations, we were packed into auditoriums, with thousands of other obsessively focused and talented individuals competing against one another to make the passing marks on a bell curve and move on to the next level. One person's failure was another person's gain.

I began studying for the CFA when I was about one year into my first corporate job. Studies would take six months of hard work. I knew it required a lot of time and diligence, and when I decided I would go for it, I said I would fully commit. Full body yes and go for it. I even had some doubt in my mind of my capabilities. After all, I didn't do so great on the SATs, so *I must not have been a great test taker*. Well, that was totally not true. And I am glad I stuck up for myself against my subconscious misbelief.

The night before the exam, candidates barely sleep, and they have to show up to the test center extremely early, wait around for hours, listen to thirty minutes of instructions once everyone is finally seated, take a grueling three-hour exam, and then do it all over again for the afternoon session. It was stressful and neurotic; during the exam, people would run to the bathrooms so as not to waste any more time than absolutely necessary. Judges paced the aisle to make sure we could not cheat, and instructions were yelled over a loudspeaker to all of us at once. It felt rigid and sterile, like the Hunger Games:

Candidates, begin.

Candidates, stop.

Candidates, put your pencils down.

It was a grueling, all-day experience that takes every ounce of energy out of you. The environment was hostile, not friendly. It was isolating and very stressful.

After the exam, there was a dreaded three-month waiting period for results. Just enough to drive you crazy, but also just enough time to forget about how important the results were to you. By then, you had already moved on in life. Allegedly.

I ended up passing Level 1 in the summer of 2017, and I passed level 2 in the summer of 2018 (which they say is the hardest level, with a nearly 60 percent fail rate). But right when I felt like the door was wide open to just slip on by, I found out three days before my wedding, in the summer of 2019, that I did not pass level 3. It was also on my wife's birthday. *Impeccable timing.* It was a slap to the face and very shocking. I knew I didn't feel too confident after the test, but that was usually a good sign, because if you felt confident, you likely fell into the traps or didn't think through the questions carefully enough. I was pretty devastated, mostly because I was ready to put all the sacrifice and time commitment behind me. Move on with my life. Become more sociable and enjoyable to be around again. Sorry, family!

I remember the advice my mom subsequently gave me: "Treat it like a game." Get back on the horse, and figure out a way to get inspired and motivated again. So I did. I dug in and got ready for the next offering of the test, which would be summer of 2020, an entire year away.

Two months before the test, as I was really finding my groove and ramping up practice tests, I found out the test was canceled indefinitely, due to a pandemic we were unprepared for as a world. I was crushed; my dream was put on hold again.

Rather than dropping my studies, I decided to stay in the game. I studied on the side to keep it going in my head so I wouldn't lose my working knowledge. The next date for the test was slated for December of that winter, another six-month haul away.

Well, as November approached, the test was canceled again.

Are you kidding me?

They're joking, right?

I could easily have given up at this point. I was now two years into my marriage, working full-time at my dream job, and I certainly didn't need another six months of studying the same material over and over again. Besides, I wanted to enjoy my summer this time around. I had even promised my wife more vacation days together. Eventually, almost two and half years later, I was able to sit for my retake of level 3, after a myriad of reasons to just let it go and move on. But even after finally, and I mean finally, sitting for that test, I still had the dreaded three-month delay in test results.

I hadn't told anyone which day of the week I would find out the results, but I knew that it would be this morning. At 6:30 AM, with barely a few hours of sleep due to the stress of nearly two-and-a-half years of work on my last level, I crawled out of bed and into my apartment gym. It was best to get all my anxious energy out beforehand, if for nothing else then as a distraction. I was on the bike, pedaling fierce strides as I pulled up and pushed back down. The rhythmic push and pull on my feet was somewhat calming and distracting. I stared into the mirror in front of me, lost in a blinking contest between myself and my reflection. *Think you're better than me?* I almost smirked as I realized the insanity of talking to myself. Once I had produced a reasonable puddle of sweat below the bike, I hopped off and headed back up to my bedroom to check my work email and make some breakfast. Heart still pounding from my workout, I squinted as I leaned over to reach my phone charging by my bedside. Results wouldn't be out for at least a few more hours, so I could get some emails down beforehand. Pass or fail, this day was going to be an emotionally long and draining one. It sucks that one test, one result, one day can drive so many other emotions and feelings throughout the year, or in my case, years. It all boiled down to this, and I couldn't tell if my hands were sweating from the workout or if my "patience wheels" were coming off the bus. *If I don't pass, I will have to wait another year to retake this test. My family will hate me, my wife will leave me, and I will have no friends because I will be spending my weekends in coffee shops studying the same material until my eyes cross.* A strong dose of negative self-talk to go with my post-gym shake.

Scanning my phone unsuspectingly, I could suddenly feel my stomach rise into my throat. My heart even stopped for a second. I shivered, even though I was sweating a few minutes ago. My hands were shaking as I tapped into the email that was waiting for me, The subject line read, "Your CFA Results Are Ready." It is like inadvertently opening a closet a few days before Christmas and finding the presents wrapped with a slight tear in the wrapping paper. Once you see it, you can't unsee it. And your curiosity overtakes any discipline you might have to just walk away and move on. I immediately thought back to over a year ago, when I received this same email while at a car repair shop. That same stomach-in-the-throat feeling, with all the excitement of such a promising moment, on my wife's birthday and three days before my wedding. *Alas, the finale has arrived,* I had wrongly assumed. I still remember like it was yesterday: "Fail." Devastatingly unmistakable verbiage from the CFA Institute. Not "Better luck next year." Or "We hope you try again." Instead, a brutal dropkick into space like a scene out of *Game of Thrones.*

Just then, my wife called out from the other room, "Kevin, I am making some post-workout smoothies; want one?" I couldn't focus, so I just let out an indecipherable grunt. She didn't seem to question my incoherent babbling, or she was just used to it after all these years of me writhing in pain every morning as I began my two hours of studying before work like some kind of CFA zombie. My finger hovered above the email as I took one last second to process the weight of the next few sentences I was about to read. *Wasn't this supposed to come later in the day?*

Upon reading the email further, my body produced a sound of exhaustion, like an Ironman contestant reaching the finish line and crumpling to the ground. It was an immediate feeling of disbelief, what I imagine doctors would call shock. It was no longer about a 24 × 24 certificate that could have easily been replaced by a piece of art, any piece of art, for that matter, on my wall. This was about my own journey from self-doubt to self-belief—although it wasn't linear. When I first signed up, I told myself if I failed level 1 I would give up, and if I failed the infamous level 2, I would give myself one last try. But having built a well of confidence passing through both levels on my first attempt, falling flat on my face for level 3, waiting an entire year to retake the exam, then to have the exam delayed not once but twice, all put a huge dent in my confidence. I went from doubtful to extremely confident to "Oh no, what is two plus two again?" My wife in the other room cried out, "Kevin, are you okay?"

This time I didn't let out a sound of exhaustion; instead, I let out an emphatic scream that likely would have woken up the entire apartment, if they hadn't been up already. The email read, "Passed"! I dropped my phone on the floor and started running around the apartment with my dog chasing after me. I fell and extended my entire body like a snow angel. I might have even pretended to row my invisible kayak, like Teemu Selanne after scoring a game-winning goal in hockey. I had finally closed a chapter in my life that had haunted me for years. The chapter of "what if." What if I didn't pass, what if I had to study another year, what if I wasted five years and never crossed the finish line? I escaped my mental prison of what if and was finally awarded the results I had hoped for.

Almost every day before I began studying, I would write at the top of my paper, "Kevin Entwistle, CFA," so as to start pretending like I already earned my charter, like I had already achieved my goal. I would see my name with the acronym and believe that it would come true. It made waiting more tolerable, and physically writing it down almost fools your mind.

I probably wrote my name out over a thousand times. But you need disciplined effort to instill confidence. Self-belief does not exist without some elbow grease. Self-belief is not cockiness. Instead, it is an endless resolve—a willingness to overcome your doubts. You have to teach yourself and feed your mind the operating instructions that this dream of yours can truly happen. I believe that this game I played, this mindset change, this flip-the-script mentality truly kept me focused and kept me sane, as crazy as it may seem. It reminded me why I was doing this.

There is a story of a Navy Seal, Marcus Luttrell, who was trapped behind enemy lines. He was separated from his team and had been in some heavy gunfight battles. He also suffered major injuries and was left crawling through the foothills of enemy territory, alone and without radar. His resolve was remarkable. As the story goes, Marcus would draw a line in the dirt twelve inches ahead of him and would crawl to that line. Once he arrived one foot ahead of where he had been, he would repeat this line in the dirt and crawl another twelve inches ahead. He shortened the game. Safety and hospitality were many miles away, but he used the "shorten the game" mentality, or what some call the "quick win" mentality, to eventually make it out safely. He could see and believe in the success and progress he was making.

Short wins, short goals, keep moving.

My CFA exam is nothing compared to what Marcus went through, but the same type of technique can be used to make a faraway goal seem more approachable.

The other type of visualization is creating imagery. The aforementioned style above speaks to the mechanics of writing something down to will it into your brain, to see it with your eyes, to move your hand to teach your mind to believe it as truth. It is a reminder in the form of visualization.

The night before my final CFA exam, I came up with a few affirmations. I leaned on my own personal faith and would simply repeat the following words, "I cast this burden upon Christ within me." This was my God and my faith, but it can be any kind of spirit or belief system you want to call on. But I called upon a higher God to guide me through the next grueling eight or so hours of test-taking. It was not about giving in but about giving over.

I then pictured myself walking into the test center. I would remove all stress from things I had no control over, such as what everyone else was wearing, doing, or studying, and instead, I focused on myself. I had a smile on, I was pumped, there was motivating music in the background as if I were walking into the test in a movie, or like it was opening day in baseball. There was excitement around this. I created this positive environment by flipping the script from what most think of as a negative environment. I fooled my mind through imagery and visualization. I kept creating. I had all of the people in my life lined up on both sides of the aisle as I walked through them and into the room. Old teachers from grade school, high school, college, tutors, my parents, siblings, wife, and friends, hockey and lacrosse coaches, neighbors and coworkers. They were clapping; it was emotional. And loud. And they were all smiling back at me and patting me on the back. They were with me the whole time. They wanted to see me win. They wanted to see me get this done. I felt empowered. I felt guided. I felt I could let go and just focus on the questions. One question at a time. Break the test down into sixty seconds as opposed to six hours. After each question, I would picture myself physically leaving the last question and arriving at the doorway of the next question, helping to visually erase any doubt about whether I answered the previous question correctly so I could focus all my attention on the next question at hand. I could feel the love and presence of everyone, and I felt myself floating into the test room. When I walked into the exam, I was in the best possible headspace, due to the overwhelming peace and calm I visualized the evening before. It stuck with me, and from there, I went on to perform at one of my greatest levels.

Not only did the visualization form my self-belief, but the momentum of the "cookie jar mentality," developed by Navy SEAL David Goggins, helped keep me motivated. The cookie jar technique, as explained in an *Impact Theory* video, "Is something I've made up of all the failures of my life. All the things that I failed at and later went back and finally succeeded at. All the things that kicked my ass, well, I put them all in the Cookie Jar. Because in times of suffering, even the hardest men (and women) forget how hard they are. Suffering is just a test of life. Whenever I get pulled into a 'woe is me' or 'life sucks' mentality, I step off and pull out something from my Cookie Jar and remind myself what a badass I am. It's a reminder of who you truly are at the core of yourself."

But those who are willing to play the game, foster crazy belief in themselves, and who embody Nike's "Just do it" mindset, with the right attitude and gameplan to go along with doing it, can achieve astronomical feats. Don't settle for good or even excellent. Go all the way; reach for astronomical success, crazy success, however you want to define that.

I had such little self-confidence when I started the CFA certification that I had already developed an exit ramp in case I failed. I gave myself permission to fail and even expected myself to fail. Even though many have gone on to become Chartered Financial Analysts, it was a dream come true for me, and I had no intention of downplaying the effort and discipline that was required to accomplish this. In some ways, I believe that by giving myself the permission to fail, I was able to get off the sidelines and step up to a test that was intrinsically terrifying to me. I was not a great test taker, and with no guarantee of passing this test, despite the extraordinary time commitment that would be required to study, it would have been far more normal and comfortable to take a pass on it all together. The anecdote about Greek soldiers burning the boats upon arriving on shore enemy territory, so as to eliminate in their minds any ability to retreat back home, makes for a nice motivational theme, but would not have helped me in this case. By keeping the boats at the shore's edge, I gave myself the confidence to go after something that I would have never attempted in the first place. While no one strives for failure, too often the fear of failure restrains us from going after that which we truly desire.

Lesson: "It is impossible to live without failing at something unless you live so cautiously that you might as well not have lived at all, in which case you have failed by default." (J. K. Rowling)

Try Out for the Best Team, Not the Weaker Team

I played ice hockey for about two decades under the Hackensack Ice House Avalanche program. When I was younger, my dad took me skating, and I hated it. I cried the whole time, and I swore I would never play again. I was able to grow around that and try it again, and of course, I fell in love with it. Upon falling in love with the sport, my dad had asked, "So, Kevin, what team would you like to try out for? Do you want to play for the Ramapo Saints or the Ice House Avalanche?"

I thought about it for a second. "The Saints," I replied. Simply put, I thought it was an easier team to make; it was more familiar, and it was likely a more reasonable and approachable team to go for. It made sense in my head.

That was one of my earliest memories of really coming to grips with limiting beliefs. Why did I even think that? I barely put any thought into that decision. I just immediately and without intention believed I should go for the seemingly easier team. Because I believed it had a better coach? Better teammates? More room for improvement? A better rink and facilities? No, because with a blink I decided inside me that I would limit my potential. It doesn't make me a bad person; it makes me like most people. We all do it. And it is nasty. It's nasty because you don't even know it's happening if you are not paying attention. We make so many decisions every day without even thinking. If you are not attuned to this inner voice, this inner perception, this inner belief, you become susceptible to auto shortcuts your brain takes by deciding you are not worthy.

I have found that you have two sides to your mind: the conscious and the unconscious. There is a guiding force in life—call it a spirit, God, movement in the universe, or anything you want to call it. But it is powerful and real. The more you learn to tap into this, the better off you will be. Some call it manifesting, where you control and actually bring to life something because you thought about it or prayed about it or simply brought it into existence. This falls under the idea that where you focus your attention, you will see results.

I like to think of it as asking. Asking a higher power to grant you something. Asking to bring it in front of you so that when it is in front of you, you can realize it. You can be prepared and open to this blessing or this gift. Your conscious mind is the controlling factor, and your unconscious mind listens to it. It does not recognize truth or falseness. The unconscious mind only knows to believe exactly what the conscious mind tells it.

For example, you tell yourself coffee keeps you up until 3 am, and then when you drink coffee, your unconscious mind is wired to keep you awake until 3. When you tell yourself you are scared of rollercoasters, or that you always get sick, your unconscious mind takes this to be true.

What I am saying is that it is critically important to feed yourself healthy thoughts, to reinforce your health, safety, and power. You need your conscious mind (the mind you actually control) to give proper directions to your unconscious mind so that you can build a strong infrastructure of who you are, not who you think you are. This is why I love affirmations and positive statements. We need to constantly be rewiring, adjusting, and getting ourselves back on track. As the saying goes, success costs something every day; you must wake up and pay the rent. It is not owned; it is rented. You are either improving or getting worse, but you never stay the same. Similarly, we need the discipline to recognize we need to fill our mind with positive affirmations, not just yesterday, but also today.

Be deliberate with your words. Your tongue is your rudder. Most don't realize this power. They say things like this:

I'm tired.

This is hard.

I'd rather be somewhere else.

It's too hot outside.

I can't.

What you say dictates what you see. When something sucks, think about replacing your negative language with the language of some of the most disciplined human beings in the world: Navy SEALs. Try saying, "I am tired, but wow, this is a full benefit." Hiking in pouring rain? Full benefit. Lost the draft to your project? Full benefit. Driving and your car breaks down? Full benefit. Silver linings are everywhere, so think about how you can reprogram your subconscious by making conscious efforts to feed it positive self-talk to draw from in the future. Because I had taken the time to recognize my limiting belief, I have been able to course correct in my life today to consciously take on challenges, even when I am scared or don't feel worthy of it. Sometimes it is simply a matter of repetitions (reps) and getting the practice in, but mostly, it is about choosing to try rather than shying away. While my hockey career had its own bumps along the way, I am proud of myself for sticking with the Ice House Avalanche, rather than following my low-hanging goal of playing for the Saints (sorry to all the Saints players, whom we typically beat every year).

Lesson: "The master has failed more than the beginner has tried." (Stephen McCranie)

Wrongdoings

In *The Go-Giver*, Bob Burg and John Mann remind us, "No matter what your training, no matter what your skills, no matter what area you're in, you are your most important commodity. The most valuable gift you have to offer is you. Reaching any goal you set takes ten percent specific knowledge or technical skills—ten percent, max. The other ninety-plus percent is people skills. And what's the foundation of all people skills? Liking people? Caring about people? Being a good listener? Those are all helpful, but they're not the core of it. The core of it is who you are. It starts with you."[12] You are not always going to be your best self; that is a given. But you can always be mindful of who you are, and you can make the necessary changes in your being along the way. You might not be acting like the best sibling, child, or friend, but you always have the choice to apologize. You will experience anger and frustration, and sometimes, in the heat of the moment, you might lash out. But you will be judged more so on your ability to course correct and learn from your mistakes than on your mistake itself.

In some of the following stories, I take control and accountability of my moments of weakness, while at other times, I am simply surrendering my life to grace. David Brooks posits, "Should you stay in your suffering or move on from it as soon as possible? Should you keep a journal to maximize self-awareness or does that just lead to paralyzing self-consciousness and self-indulgence? Should you be humble or self-expressive? Should you take control of your own life or surrender it to grace?"[13] Admittedly, I don't know all the answers to these questions, but I find them to be useful when thinking back on some of my own stories. The point of self-reflection is not to become obsessed with our mistakes but to acknowledge them and take from them meaning and lessons so we can become better versions of ourselves, rather than repeat the same mistakes. Despite conventional wisdom, we can truly be redeemed by our weakness by struggling against that weakness and using that as a problem to grow a beautiful strength. If you are willing to course correct and rise to new heights of self-respect, you can overcome any wrongdoing you have committed.

Brooks goes on to say, "There is something heroic about a person in struggle with themselves, strained on the rack of conscience, suffering torments, yet staying alive and growing stronger, sacrificing worldly success for the sake of inner victory."[14] The purpose of the struggle of failure, suffering, weakness, and shortcomings is not to win, because that is not possible. Instead, the purpose is to get better at waging it. It doesn't matter if you work at a hedge fund or a charity serving the poor. There are heroes and schmucks in both worlds. The most important thing is whether you are willing to engage in this struggle of inner confrontation.

Getting comfortable with inner confrontation is important, because you are going to commit wrongdoings against others. You are going to shame someone, whether on purpose or accidentally. At times, you will find yourself in a position in which you need to apologize, to ask for forgiveness, and to be sorry. This is not a position of weakness; it is one of strength. You cannot prevent hurting someone's feelings in all situations, but you can have the emotional awareness to identify when such a disconnect occurs. Taking the high road is usually putting the needs of someone else above yours, especially after those moments when you forgot to do so. Those redeeming moments after you put someone down or put yourself first are the ones that matter. We all make mistakes, but how we acknowledge to others that we made a mistake is what we should be judged by.

Time heals old wounds, space provides possibility for eventual reconnection, and opportunities present themselves in serendipitous ways in life, as if God put two people back on the same path in a game of divine checkers. It might seem almost too coincidental that you bumped into that old colleague from the company you quit or the old family member you stopped speaking with. An olive branch or open hand is a good first step, but it is the willingness to change that can rectify any past messiness. As Rich Roll, the author of *Finding Ultra*, says on his podcast, "Change isn't for those who need it. It's for those who want it. It's all about willingness. While in many ways pain makes the process of change easier, the truth is you don't have to hit rock bottom to make a transformation. Change is always within your grasp if you can summon the willingness to ask for it—and most importantly receive it. It's your birthright to grow, it's in your DNA."[15] We can't change our past actions, but we can change our present attitudes. We can always change our being and who we are, despite who we have been.

The Cold-Caller

"Kevin, don't ever do that again, okay?"

A wave of shame washed over me like hearing your name called to the principal's office. At one time in my life, homes included a landline telephone. Most calls would actually arrive through your home phone rather than your cell phone, which is obviously very different from how calls are directed these days. When the home phone rang, it was an unwritten rule that someone would answer, especially in those days predating caller ID.

One day when the phone rang, I was in the kitchen where the landline was connected, so I ran over to answer the caller.

"Hello?" I answered, waiting to see first who was on the other line before offering anything more.

"Hello, this is James from such-and-such company, and I wanted to let you know about a deal we have going on through the summer. If you have a few minutes, I would love to share more about it."

Immediately and sarcastically, I went into teasing this polite caller on the other line. After all, I had seen it on TV before. An unknown caller trying to sell something calls the home line, and the person who picks it up is frustrated and impatient and decides to confront the caller in an impertinent manner. Maybe even subconsciously, a scene flashed before my mind of a person selling cutlery at the front door and the person answering the door slamming it in their face. Either way, my mind was wired to quickly belittle the caller, to put myself above them, and to ridicule them. It was shameful and embarrassing, but here is what happened next.

"Why don't you hang up the phone and try to find a real job? Why don't you just grow up?" *Click.*

Well, devious little Kevin, who had just returned home from his third-grade classes and was ready to dive into a sleeve of Oreos and a tall glass of milk for dipping, thought he was all alone. In his mind, he had just killed two birds with one stone: told this guy off so he would never call again, and had a good laugh.

Except I was not alone. In fact, my mom had been standing over my shoulder the whole time, and she was horrified by what she had heard.

"Do you have any idea what you are doing?" she asked. "You have no idea what that person's situation is, or what is going on in their life. You could have really hurt someone's feelings, really crushed someone's soul. That is so not right, Kevin. Think about it. You immediately turned this man into a monster and assumed the worst of him. You couldn't even look him in the eyes, but instead you were able to hide behind the phone and say whatever you felt. Tell me you understand why I am mad, and please don't *ever* do that again, okay?"

Just like that, I lost my appetite for those Oreos and milk. Suddenly, the cold caller whom I just told to go kick rocks was not the monster in my mind; rather, it was abundantly clear that the monster was me. In the movie *Goodfellas*, Henry Hill describes his friend Tommy by saying, "Tommy was the kind of guy that actually rooted for the bad guy in movies."[16] Most of us are not like Tommy. We don't grow up hoping to be the bad guy. Moreover, I don't really believe in bad people. Making bad decisions is simply part of life. Whether through a lapse in judgment or an uncontrolled emotional outburst, good people make bad decisions. Far more than any cotillion class could have taught me about etiquette, I learned that day an important visualization tactic when interacting with anyone in life, not just cold callers: Don't treat others how you think they want to be treated; treat others how you want to be treated. Imagine you were them, talking to you. Think about all the things that could be affecting them and how they might be feeling. It is the same visualization that gets people to sit with lonely strangers at restaurants or coffee shops or park benches. We identify something in someone, a feeling or an emotion; We place ourselves in their shoes and minds, and we listen to and act on that emotional connection. Whether it is a cold caller or anyone else in life, using this technique, I have found it easier to find the good in someone before I immediately assume the bad. Remember, there is no such thing as a bad person, just bad decisions. Choose to see that good, and you will never be a monster.

Lesson: What you say has serious consequences on how people feel about themselves. Be mindful and purposeful with what you say to people, especially when you don't know them or how their day or life is going.

The Seafood Paella Woman

The summer after college was mine to enjoy. My first company gave the five of us newly employed associates a summer to recharge so that when September arrived, we would come in with fresh experiences, ready to roll up our sleeves and get down to it. As will be discussed later, I did take some time to travel with friends, but I also took time to move into the North End of Boston early, settle in, and fish in the Charles River. After about a week of fishing and no fish, I realized it probably made sense to find a summer job to keep up on my rent payments and start saving some money—the empty fishhooks weren't paying any bills. That is when I reached out to my dad's college buddy, who owned a boating company out of Rowes Wharf in the Boston Harbor. These boats went out on hour-long tours around the harbor and also held nighttime parties with full bartending services and snack concessions. For anyone interested in unobstructed water views of the Boston city line, this activity was a must.

I was excited to do something with my day, make some extra money, and learn how to bartend. I was also excited to be on the water in the fresh air with views of my favorite city in the world, Boston. It was a fantastic illusion, and I soon found that working on a boat was not the same as enjoying a restful day on a boat. My daytime shift consisted of serving a mere five guests, with at most $10 to $20 spent on concessions, leaving the tip jar mostly empty. I also did not experience that sea breeze I anticipated, as I was told to work behind the bar only, on the first floor in the dark room that smelled of an unwashed kitchen floor. To top it all off, when we docked after every hour shift out at sea, there were toilets that needed to be cleaned, and the sides of the boats needed a hose down. If I had to do it all over again, I would recommend to anyone the position of deckhand, as opposed to the position of bartender, as the job description of bartender was certainly ambiguous.

One summer night shift, we had a party of about one hundred guests, which was not bad compared to the daytime shifts of about five guests. We were hosting a group of friends who insisted on an island breeze theme. It usually took me about an hour to set the bar up for these larger scale events, and I was tasked with lugging cases of liquor from the bottom of the boat up the narrow and steep staircases from the hull to the main deck. Once all the bottles were upstairs, I began attaching pouring caps over each bottle spout, lining the liquor bottles up in the most efficient way against the bar, stacking plastic cups, starting the cash register, and making sure we had enough juices and mixers available. Once set up, there was usually a few minutes to loaf around and get in the way of the other deckhands preparing the boat.

On this particular evening, I wandered up toward the top of the boat to breathe in any of that summer air breeze I could from the harbor, as if one big gulp of air coming off the water, endearingly known as dirty water, would compensate for the stale and dry air inside the boat. That is when I met the woman making seafood paella. Naturally, two convivial and outgoing personalities hit it off. We were discussing summer plans, favorite foods, and mostly cracking jokes and laughing at one another's stories. I let my guard down because of how well we were getting along, but unfortunately, my next statement was anything but redeeming. When she asked me about bartending, I skirted the question by saying that this was not my "real job" and that I actually started my "real job" in September, when the start date for my corporate job began.

Suddenly, I could tell something in that temperate sea breeze changed. The pleasant salt air was now suffocating.

She hesitated but then spoke. "Um, well, you do know that what you do now is a real job, right?"

Trapped, I thought to myself that not only had I sounded foolish by presenting myself as "too good" for a boat bartending job, but I also came off as boorish and rude by insulting this nice woman by indirectly telling her I also thought I was too good for her, since her job was a similarly lower paid one. She was not pleased, and I could sense her frustration.

I had somehow found myself back in that same awkward place as I had been in the past. I wasn't using my head, and I definitely wasn't using my heart. She went on to explain to me that she had worked in this role for many years, and it had provided her a great life. That a real job was not one that "had to be spent at a desk or in an office," and that not everyone can be afforded an opportunity to work a desk job, for that matter. While many people in my social network have a college degree, not everyone does, and nor does everyone need, want, desire or have access to a "real job," at least according to my flawed standards of a "real job."

We all have different skills, talents and crafts to offer the world, and the value of your personal worth has nothing to do with the value of your checking account, college degree, or job identity. Quite contrarily, I believe it to be an inverse relationship, in that the more you can humble yourself to show humility and compassion, the greater your personal worth really is. Richness is not about material goods. You can build yourself up with all the luxury goods in the world, and you can still live in a hollow home. My family has a saying: "We are rich in love," which underscores the value we place on our love for one another. That is not something that money can buy. But in this momentary lapse of judgment, I certainly was not showing the love to the seafood paella woman that day.

While I have yet to perfect the art of empathy—and don't expect ever to perfect it—I have improved upon my understanding of life outside my own bubble. Regardless of your origin story, such as where you grew up, what you were sheltered from, where you were educated, and who you hung around with, you, too, have your own bubble. Bubbles are created by communities and can bring a lot of positives to the lives of those living inside them. However, left unchecked and unexamined, a bubble can thwart the ever-important search for outside-the-bubble thinking to escape from unquestioned uniformity. This story is a metaphor for the bubble I was living in. My bubble provided me many gifts and blessings, all of which I was grateful to accept. However, my bubble misled me in thinking that when parents work, they work as doctors, lawyers, real estate agents, or financial experts. In other words, they work at corporations or institutions. It was an unconscious bias that was surfacing, and it was a direct factor of my lack of consideration for the many other people in the world besides Kevin Entwistle. This might seem like an obvious lesson, similar to the cold-caller story, but I can assure you the devil is in the details. As we age, we are less intentional about getting outside our bubbles, and many times, we have a more strained relationship with society as a whole. We become too defensive and feel forced to pick sides. Our knowledge of the other's weakness makes it difficult for us to get along. Instead, we will be left to our inner circles, constantly being pushed down and confined to our routine bubble lifestyle. Michelle Obama says this on success: "Success isn't about how much money you make, it's about the difference you make in people's lives."[17] Success is finding that escape hatch and getting outside your bubble so you can better pay attention to the people around you. Now, I try to speak with those who are least expecting of my conversation. In fact, my family took a boat trip in Turks and Caicos one winter, and I was so fascinated by one of the deckhand's life story that I spent the entire trip back to the island speaking with him rather than with my siblings in the front of the boat. This is not to say that spending time with family is unimportant, but I was so locked in and present with this man, I wanted to continue sharing in a moment of vulnerable conversation. I could tell he really felt heard, as he told his story of his dying brother and his pursuit to chase his dream of becoming a singer. There are dreams and inspiration all around us; we just have to get outside our bubbles and pay attention to the hidden beauty beneath the surface.

Lesson: Don't be impressed by people's jobs; be impressed by how well they treat other people.

The Undefeated Princess Peach

My oldest friend and I were around seven years old when we started playing Mario Kart, the video game on Nintendo 64 with animated characters racing go-carts with balloons attached to their rear ends. Your character starts with three balloons, each representing a life. When a competitor hits you with one of their specialty attacks, like a banana peel or a hard-shell missile, your character loses a balloon or a life. When you are on your last balloon, it is wise to play more cautiously, because without that last balloon, you will be eliminated completely. We would play for hours and would always beg my friend's dad to come play with us. Eventually, with enough jabbing and insults, his dad would give in to meet his final fate.

Only he had plans of his own. He was not going to give in to our machinations so easily. In fact, his dad had strategically picked Princess Peach as his character. We would laugh and tease him for his pick, as if to suggest his character was a reflection of his own self, a self that we thought was worthy of ridicule. Kids are great at finding ways to tease and provoke someone into an all-out Mario Kart battle. But we would soon discover how wrong our imagination had been.

Princess Peach was a fanciful kart driver, equipped with the panache of a Netflix Bridgerton character, but she also embodied the strength and bravery of a powerful woman. We had grossly underestimated the playing potential of Princess Peach, as well as the motivation behind his dad to kick our butts in this video game. We thought this would be a lay-up, an easy win over

Princess Peach. After all, we had mistakenly thought Princess Peach was a princess, and this was an all-out balloon fight; there was no world we could imagine in which Princess Peach would conquer the formidable duo that we put up against her.

We couldn't be further from the truth. Princess Peach would win, not once, not twice, but almost every other round that we played as well. It was a tough pill to swallow. We would be screaming and laughing as we slid our karts across the different maps on the screen, up the ramps and over the crevasses, incessantly chasing down Princess Peach but never fully eliminating her three balloons. Princess Peach played with reckless abandon, not just keeping up with the other characters but even spinning circles around them. It was not only an impressive feat; it was straight up sobering.

Years later, after all those Princess Peach showdowns, I remember an equally important lesson my mom made sure I learned. I had come home from school one day with great excitement to let her know how much I really enjoyed one of my classes. When she asked why that was, I had told her that the class was full of fun, cool, and smart guys, just like myself. "And, Mom," I doubled down, "the best part of the whole thing is that it is like a 'boys' club.' It is going to be so fun." While I did not intentionally do so, I had neglected a very important consideration that my mother, thankfully, made sure to correct right then and there.

"Kevin," she said. "I don't want to ever hear you use that term again. I have been working for over twenty years in a male-dominated industry, and while there is much improvement still to be made for women in the workforce, I will not listen to you speak like this is the sixties. Please don't use that term ever again, but mostly, please do not believe that a boy's club is a worthy coterie to begin with."

A boys' club is insular, narrow-minded, and full of arrogant men. She wanted me to know that not only is it entirely impudent to exclude women from having a seat at the table or in the classroom, but also that it was utterly embarrassing to myself to demonstrate that kind of thinking and belief, whether I really meant it or not.

Now, at surface level, I was not intentionally out to exclude women. In my mind, I was simply finding joy in being around my male friends in the class. However, there is an important lesson in a situation like this.

It does not take only direct and sardonic language against a group of people to be considered inconsiderate. Most times, I would argue, and certainly in this situation, it is the neglectful language of not even mentioning or thinking about another group. It is only in reading between the lines can we truly decipher the underlying root of exclusion, because at surface level I already knew women were amazingly powerful beings capable of feats equal to anyone else's. As far as I am concerned, there is nothing wrong with men, especially a group of men. Men can do incredible things together, but not at the expense of excluding others for the sake of their own "boys' club." Many people will have their own opinion on this—in fact, there is an entire section of literature called feminism that I am sure I have not fully upheld in my storytelling, nor would I imagine I am the consummate feminist. But it doesn't matter. What matters is that I try to understand other perspectives. I try to get outside my own bubble and challenge my views, even some of my most rooted and seemingly incorrigible.

I had made a mistake by failing to realize the gravity of the words I used, and for that reason, I was rightly put in my place by my mother. Thanks, Mom. You have made me so much better over the years, and I still am working on using appropriate and inclusive language, not for the sake of being politically correct but for the sake of bringing the best out in everyone, including myself.

Furthermore, never judge a book by its cover, and whenever you can, take the time to get to know people and what matters to them. If you can learn to celebrate the fact that we are all capable of amazing feats, you will find yourself far more successful and happier than you could have ever imagined. You will find yourself surrounded by incredibly thoughtful people who will help you challenge your own belief system, which, in turn, will make you such a better person. When my kids ask me to play Mario Kart, I know who I will be choosing as my character: Princess Peach.

Lesson: Inclusivity is about considering groups of people or individuals that would not normally be considered in your immediate network.

Brotherly Antics

It was only seven o'clock in the morning, but the sun was already brightly shining through the hotel window, warming my back as I sat on the edge of the bed interrogating my older sister. Despite the warmth of the morning sunrise, there was ice in my blood. I had a fight to pick, and no level of heat in that hotel room was going to calm me down. My friend and I decided to visit my older sister in Park City, Utah, for a week of snowboarding while experiencing her newly created lifestyle out west. Too immature to focus on anyone but myself, I lacked even the tiniest grain of gratitude to express for her hospitality, free lift tickets, or just her willingness to spend time with us. I had lost sight of the bigger picture, and now I was going to take it all out on my sister.

I had seen enough over the last few days, and there was not much to like, I had thought. Quick to compare her relationship to my own, I was not impressed with the difference in our values hierarchy, or what we prioritized in our separate relationships. I judged her for lacking what I thought were necessary aspects to a strong connection, and took it upon myself to wipe that big, beautiful smile off her face because of my own judgments, unfounded as they may be. I had a lot of growing up to do, not yet fully appreciating the different kinds of relationships and ways that people express love. I was agitated by what I perceived as a threat to my sister's happiness, defined by my own standards and not hers. Rather than seeing the bigger picture, like the fact that she loved this lifestyle she created, I compared my own lifestyle to hers, and was ready to air out all the dirty laundry before breakfast was even served at eight o'clock in the lobby.

As I begrudgingly announced all the perceived faults of my sister's relationship directly to her, I could see she was upset, but she was still willing to defend herself. She was confused why we didn't all hang out the night before, which was supposed to be a big celebration in town, and was wondering if any of this anger I was showing had to do with the fact we were separated throughout the night. But I kept going, evading her defenses, and like a flank attack on an unsuspecting line of soldiers, I took her down. The battle was over before it even began. Quickly her expression went from defensive, to sad, to disbelief, and finally, complete despair and tears. Having the last word never leaves a good taste in your mouth. Though I had completely torn her down, disrespecting every aspect of the life she had created— her life, not mine—I had felt torn down myself. *Who the hell was I? Why did you push so hard on the topic? Couldn't you just have swallowed your tongue? Did you have to make her cry?* Victory of this kind is never sweet; it is always sour. Choice words for a cocky kid like myself. But I didn't have time to lament my wrongdoing, because before I could begin consoling my sister, which, to be honest, I am not sure would have happened, her boyfriend had walked into the room using his own key card. Unbeknownst to me, he was waiting outside, like reinforcements against my flank maneuver. The surprise counterattack was on, so everything would have to be left on the line at this point—no turning back.

He was wearing his sunglasses, not because of the sun shining through the hotel window but because he wanted to intimidate me. His tone of voice told me he wasn't backing down, and his arms hanging by his side with clenched fists was an easy giveaway that either I was going to explain myself or there would be repercussions for my actions. Sarah was now yelling at me through her tears to just leave, to get the hell out of the room, and never talk to her again. Two against one. I lost. I mumbled a few sarcastic words, grabbed my jacket, and left the room, without looking back to see if any punches were headed in my direction. The door slammed, and that is when it hit me. Damage control was out the window. My adrenaline was pumping, and I had just realized nothing would ever be the same again. I had single-handedly been responsible for putting my sister down. She was right, and she would probably never talk to me again. Here I was, hiding behind my own pristine house of safety, comfortable with and protective of my own relationship, jaded by the idea that if her relationship didn't look like mine, it must not be good enough. *Good enough?* How about: *It is good, Kevin, so enough already. Let it be.* It was the loneliest chair ride up the mountain that morning, and no amount of fresh mountain air could shake me from my stupor. I had committed the most egregious foul of all by not sticking up for my family.

Back when we were kids, I would do almost anything my sister told me, as I looked up to her as my older sibling. As an example, she was notorious for being tardy to class, despite the fact we lived right behind the high school, only a two-minute walk away. And when the school would send letters of notice to our parents about her tardiness, she would have me pull those envelopes from the mailbox so they never found their way inside. Perks of having two working parents at the mail delivery time of three o'clock in the afternoon. But mostly, I genuinely cared about her. When she got in trouble with my parents, my younger sister and I would sit at the top of the staircase to listen in on the "kitchen table" conversations she would have with my parents. They were more like soliloquies, because only one person was doing the talking, and that person was not my sister. We would worry for each other as siblings, which is a sign of love. But throughout life, we took different paths, focused our attention in different areas, and eventually, the love and care slipped away. I had mistakenly allowed that to happen for a short time, but after a few years of living across the country from each other, we were able not to forget that moment but to forgive that moment.

Rather than remember the bad, I choose to remember the good. And I will always remember the speech my sister gave at my high school graduation party in our backyard. There were a hundred young adults gathered in and around the pool, not because I intended for there to be so many, but because as soon as you tell my mom you were having a small gathering, she would ask, "Well, did you invite this person? How about that person? You can't not invite this person if you are inviting that person." And this line of thinking compounded with more and more kids attending my party. What started with a few beer cans turned into an epic high school summer party, and because kids were showing up with gifts as if this was a formal graduation party, my mom made the decision to run out and get a cake. Perceptions are everything, after all. Without incriminating her, she also called up my older sister's friends, in hopes of bumping the average age of the party well north of twenty one. She has always been an innovative thinker. When the cake and the twenty-year-olds arrived, my sister called everyone into the kitchen, squeezed elbow to elbow, some of us in towels and bathing suits. With college lingering in the near future, many of us wondered what would happen to our relationships with one another. *Was this it?* Sometimes, in moments of importance, people rise to the occasion and deliver the greatest speech they have ever given, and for my sister, this was her moment. She got up on a chair, corralled a bunch of wild high schoolers, and went on to say, "Listen, y'all. I love all of you. I am so happy you are here to celebrate graduation. You will go on to lead amazing lives, make new friends, and experience the ups and downs of life, no doubt. Just never forget the friends in this kitchen side by side. Because you have been through it all already, and each and every one of you can lean on one another. Now raise your glasses, and let's get the music back on." Simple and straightforward, but in less than thirty seconds, she made her salient point about the importance of friendship. And with that, beer, wine, and whatever else went flying all over the kitchen like a World Series championship locker room scene. Except, instead of the ski goggles, a few were wearing swimming goggles; oh well.

It wasn't just my older sister who received the infamous brother treatment; my younger sister did too. We were walking to grade school together, and like most days, I was a few steps ahead of her and her friends, far too cool to be caught walking my sister to school. My sister had just tripped, and I heard her backpack hit the pavement, with her pencils and notebooks spilling out.

With a cursory response to this embarrassing moment, I had cheekily told Emily to get up and dust herself off. The fall could not have caused much more damage than a scab or a bruise; she was close enough to the pavement that it was unlikely she would reach a velocity to severely hurt herself. Besides, I had a reputation to uphold, and every minute my sister was down for the count was another moment my friends might hold against me.

"Get up; you are fine, seriously."

"No, Kevin, my arm really hurts." Tears were coming down her face.

"It really hurts, Kevin, what should I do?" She was desperate for help as she winced in pain. She trusted her older brother and was looking to him to do something, anything.

"I don't know. Just rub it a little and get up; we are going to be late for school."

My sister's pains and hurt feelings would have to be sidelined, I had thought. And boy, did I think wrong.

"You definitely broke your arm," the nurse had instructed. "Call your parents and let them know they need to pick you up and bring you to the emergency room for an X-ray and cast for your arm." I can only imagine what was going through my sister's mind at this time, but I don't think she was reeling about how helpful, caring, and loving her older brother had been.

I am positive she wasn't telling the nurse about how incredibly brave she felt because her brother walked her to school and told her everything would be okay. As I have gotten older, I have become more aware of the moments I have not shown up for my sisters, and it makes me realize how much more I want to show up for them now. I used to think that my actions did not affect others, until I realized that not only do they affect others, but they can also have a significant longer-term effect.

I have found you can repair most relationships in life. The past is the past. But I can tell you that we are all humans, and we all need to feel love. Show your siblings love, show your family love, and I promise it will be worth it. No family is perfect, so swallow your pride and show someone love in your own way that is meaningful. You only hurt yourself by letting relationships dry up. And when you feel like hurting your siblings' feelings, just remember my sister's speech: nothing comes between friends and family.

Lesson: You can always show your siblings love, no matter what has happened in the past.

Snowballs and Regrets

"Kevin, my dad just built this igloo for us to play in! Do you want to come play in the snow?"

My neighbor had knocked on my backdoor with sleds full of snowballs that we could stash in the newly created igloo. "Sure, I'll be right out." I grabbed my winter hat, gloves, jackets, and boots, and ran out into the backyard—the same backyard in which we played our fictitious game, rescue heroes, during Hurricane Floyd and Wiffle ball during the Fourth of July parties. While I played my fair share of video games, nothing compared to getting outside and having fun.

"I just heard my mom pull into the driveway. Quick, hand me a snowball," I said to my friend as we started joking about throwing snowballs at our family members. My mom had a cup of coffee in her hand, and for all I know she was having a bad day to begin with. I was ten years old and was no longer the cute, innocent child that she probably remembered. All she wanted to do was get out of the car and find the warmth of the inside after a long day. Mom was surprised, though, when before she reached the back door, she saw me wind up with a snowball out of the corner of her eyes. What must have been going on in her mind in that split second?

Back when I was younger, Mom would take me biking on the boardwalk in Spring Lake before the sun came up. She would make snowflakes with me out of paper and glitter when my older sister was at school and I was not attending preschool yet.

She would take me to Burger King before kindergarten, and she would set up playdates for me so I had friends to hang with. She was such a fun mom to be around growing up. She always gave us attention, fed us our meals, spent time with us, and showed us love. But at some point, a son starts to grow up and must come to grips with his coolness and manliness. However, I had yet to learn a very important lesson about being a man. A man's coolness comes from how he treats his family. And treating your family poorly is not cool.

Don't believe me? Then take it from Don Corleone from *The Godfather*, who says, "A man who never spends time with his family can never be a real man."[18] I was only ten, and I had not had a chance to watch *The Godfather* yet, sadly. Unfortunately, as soon as the snowball had already left my hand, I immediately regretted the decision. It is like missing a hoop, or throwing a ball instead of a strike, or tossing a football too far from the receiver: as soon as it leaves your hands, you already know you missed your target.

The debate in my head? Look cool in front of my neighbor, or choose to show my mom love and put the snowball down. I chose to look cool, according to my misconstrued version of what *cool* meant. The snowball sailed through the wintery air, collecting shame and guilt all through the fifteen feet it traveled before finally pelting my mom right in the face. Coffee spilled, and redness was already filling her face. Was it from her anger or from the shavings of the ice that fell from the snowball? Who knows? All I remember was that the guilt was building, and the next thing that came out of my mom's voice was the cherry on top of a shameful sundae. "Are you [bleeping] kidding me, Kevin?" except she didn't say *bleep*. She said some other word that felt like a gut punch. In many of our mistakes in life, we end up feeling guilty after getting caught, sometimes hours, days, or years later. But in these types of mistakes, the really bad ones that can hurt someone's feelings for many years, that type of guilt sets in before the snowball even hits your mom's face. It is an immediate reaction before anyone even has time to catch you.

Although this was one of the most embarrassing moments of my life—throwing a snowball at my mom's face—it would not be the last time I failed to show my mom love.

There was also the time I told my mom I was embarrassed by the way she dressed when she came and picked me up at the ice rink, and there was also the time I told her how angry I was that she received a promotion at work because I had thought all she cared about was her career and her own success. You must be feeling pretty good about yourself at this point, right? Who throws a snowball, tells their mom the way she dresses embarrasses them, and discourages them from succeeding in their career? All-time low, I know.

If I could go back and change a few things in my life, I wouldn't change much. But the first stop I would go back to is the ice rink, to tell my mom she looks beautiful and that I love how she shows up for me at these ridiculous hours of the day to come pick me up. The second stop would be the igloo, so I could instead walk over to the car and help my mom into the house while keeping her from slipping. And the third stop would be when Mom and I were walking down my hometown street, where I first told her that she didn't care about me or the family because she was too focused on work. I would tell my mom this: "You are beyond inspiring, and you deserve the level of success you have reached, and I can't wait to see what else you will accomplish." In my eyes, my mom is the best dressed, most successful, and most loving mom there is, and everyone should feel the same way about their mom.

If you also haven't been your best self in the past, that is okay. I don't think you can do worse than I have, and yet, I still know how much my mom loves me. It is important we tell each other how we feel, even if we have done wrong in the past and are embarrassed to repair those relationships. Things left unsaid rot your insides; they weigh you down and become stones in your life.

Lesson: Don't carry stones. Apologize to those you need to apologize to and remind yourself of the love you are capable of showing.

Sometimes Being the Tough Guy Is Not Being the Tough Guy

As a junior in college, you are no longer the lost freshman or the sophomore who takes advantage of still finding themselves in the first half of their college career. Rather, a junior has crossed into the semi-adult category, which comes with its own set of responsibilities and, hopefully, shedding some of the cockiness and immaturity. I had just started seeing someone, my wife-to-be, and things were clicking between us. I was even acting more responsible, at least more responsible than the reckless abandon I carried through my first two years at school. *Maybe I was getting the hang of this whole semi-adult thing.* My friends and I were enjoying a party at my girlfriend's apartment, with some of her tennis friends and roommates. We were not causing trouble but were instead minding our own business, and we were likely on the way out to the bars in only a matter of time. It could have been like any other night, except it wasn't. We received a knock at the door, and when we opened it, we were greeted by the hallway's Resident Assistant (RA). She was not happy. She told us that we had to shut the party down and that everyone was going to get written up, which meant documented and punished.

Stepping into my apparent hero shoes and cape, I decided to stand up for the group. I was thinking I could be the leader and help do the right thing. Control is what I do best, for better or worse, so why not make this yet another moment of overstepping. It is usually easy to do the wrong thing, but it takes guts and discipline to do the right thing, especially when it goes against your emotional pull. To me, this moment to shine was about an honor code, about respecting and sticking up for my teammates and friends. It came from a very loyal place in my heart with some of the best intentions, but in this setting, in this moment, for this person at our doorway, this show of "leadership" was 100 percent misplaced.

Here is what I thought I said: "Good evening, thank you so much for letting us know that this pregame party is not something you want us to continue. I appreciate you giving us the heads up and coming to talk to us personally. We are all adults and can clean up our act and move forward in an agreeable manner. In fact, we are on our way out the door, and I think this is the perfect time to cut the party. Thanks for your patience with us, and we hope you have a great night."

Except it sounded more like this: "Oh, really? You think we are all mad right now? You don't want to see us all get mad." Mistake number 1. Showing all my cards on the table right there. Not the tough guy I thought I was, I sounded more like I was putting on the full court press. It's interesting too; I was never much of a trash talker in hockey, and yet here I was sounding like someone instigating a fight after the whistle blows. Engaging with the RA was mistake number 1, but mistake number 2 happened after being asked to leave the apartment. I went downstairs and outside for some fresh air. *Think, Kevin, what did you just do?* In a second instance of momentary judgment lapse, I saw four trash cans lined up perfectly, and I felt called to kick them all down like a World Cup soccer team striker. Trash littered everywhere, and finally a moment of clarity dawned. *I know what I just did. Not only did I make a series of mistakes, I lost my composure while sticking up for my friends. I had misplaced my loyalty because I wanted to defend my friends from getting in trouble, which led me to feel empowered in righteousness.* And just like that, my stream of consciousness led me back to the right course of action.

Like an immediate course correction, I began leaning over and picking up the trash from the ground, right as a campus police officer pulled up with his lights on. Out came the officer to ask me what in the world I was doing. I explained everything, confessed I was kicked out of a party, for which I was underage, and that I exchanged words with an RA and subsequently came downstairs and kicked all the trash cans over in frustration. I lifted my two forearms for him to strap on the cuffs and take me in. What else do I have to lose at this point? The officer looked at me, measuring me from top to bottom while deciding how he would react. He looked me in the eyes for a few more seconds, started chuckling, and then bent down and started picking up trash with me. He immediately patted me on the back and said, "Sorry to hear all of this, but don't worry, I am going to help you out. This will not be your last song, and you are not alone." His handcuffs remained strapped to his belt, and the trash was picked up completely.

One thing I've learned from this experience was that in any moment of frustration, anger, or confusion, it never hurts to fit a good cleaning session in. I have a friend who gets to cleaning, making beds, washing dishes, folding laundry, and organizing when he is upset. And this was my first experience with the cathartic nature of applying my emotions to something productive and useful. This wasn't the end of the story. I did have a hearing and community service to fulfill. In my hearing, I would have to explain myself and my actions. That meant facing the possible judgment of others and reliving an embarrassing moment, serving as a reminder that I was not the hero I thought I was.

But before the hearing, I would reconnect with that same officer who helped me pick up the trash that night. I remember I was running through downtown Providence when he called my cell. I didn't know who it was, but I picked it up anyway.

He said, "Kevin, when you go to your hearing, this is what I want you to do."

I interrupted, "Sure, I'll do anything."

"Kevin, I want you to just ask for grace." He paused again for emphasis; he was good at making his point. He continued, "Grace is a gift from God. All you need to do is ask for it, but it is extremely powerful. Here is the thing about grace, Kevin: no one can give it to you but God. And it doesn't matter what you did; you don't need to explain yourself or worry about what anyone else thinks about you or your actions. Just ask for forgiveness by the grace of God. I am not better than you, and you are no better than me. Got it?"

I was flooded with relief, and after hanging up the phone I began running with much more bounce in my step now that the fog was lifted. This officer was like a guardian angel, arriving at my worst moment and making sure that I was back on my feet afterward. Like other guardian angels I have heard about through friends and family, he did the same thing. He came into my life, and then he was gone. But I have never forgotten the message from that day.

No one is immune to mistakes, and to know that someone is always waiting with open arms to bring you back to a path of good intention is truly a miraculous gift. There are no strings attached and no bargains to be made. You, too, can feel the unconditional love—and priceless love, I might add—by asking for grace. It costs you nothing but will reward you everything.

"Only the one who descends into the underworld rescues the beloved," Kierkegaard says in *Alice in Wonderland*. "In the valley of humility you can learn to quiet yourself. Only by quieting yourself can you see the world clearly. Only by quieting yourself can you understand other people and accept what they are offering. When you quiet yourself, you open up space for grace to flood in. You will find yourself helped by people you did not expect would help you. You will find yourself cared for by others in ways you did not imagine beforehand. You don't have to flail about, because hands will hold you up."[19]

When you get knocked off course, either by an overwhelming love, or by failure, illness, loss of employment, or twist of fate, grace is what gets you back on course. The U-shape form of grace works like this: advance, retreat, advance. In retreat, you admit your need and surrender your crown. You open up space that others might fill. And grace floods in. It may be love from friends and family, assistance from an unexpected stranger, or a spiritual embodiment. But the message is the same: you are accepted. You just have to accept the fact that you are accepted. Gratitude fills the soul, and with it, the desire to serve and give back.

Will Smith writes in his book *Will*, "People often say ignorance is bliss"[20] He later goes on to dispel this myth. He continues, "We punish ourselves for not knowing. We always complain about what we could and should have done, and how much of a mistake it was that we did that thing, that unforgivable thing. We beat on ourselves for being so stupid, regretting our choices and lamenting the horrible decisions we make."[21] But as Will came to acknowledge, that is what life is. Take it or leave it. "Living is the journey from not knowing to knowing. From not understanding to understanding. From confusion to clarity. By universal design you are born into a perplexing situation, bewildered, and you have one job as a human: figure this sh*t out. Life is learning. Period. Overcoming ignorance is the whole point of the journey. You're not supposed to know at the beginning. The whole point of venturing into uncertainty is to bring light to the darkness of our ignorance. I heard a great saying once: life is like school. With one key difference—in school you get the lesson, and then you take the test. But in life, you get the test and it's your job to take the lesson. We're all waiting until we have deep knowledge, wisdom, and a sense of certainty before we venture forth. But we've got it backward; venturing forth is how we gain the knowledge."[22] In my own course correction, I made sure to call that resident assistant and apologize to her directly. While you can always receive grace, it doesn't excuse you from acknowledging and addressing a mess you made. Just like I had to clean up the trash I kicked over, it was important that I also cleaned up the mess I might have caused in someone else's day. Lesson learned.

Lesson: Get mad, then get over it. Getting mad is a natural and healthy emotion we all experience, but staying mad isn't useful. And ask for grace, because no matter how good of a person you think you are, we all have moments when we say something we wish we could retract or behave in some way we wish we never did.

Leadership

It has been my experience that most people choose not to follow leaders who don't know what they want or where they are going. How do you want people to see you as a leader? Maybe you are a corporate "hi-po," meaning someone with "high potential," and on track for a corporate-level position. Perhaps you were named captain of your travel sports team by your peers, or maybe you are the leader of your household. You likely want others to see you as someone who respects others' opinions, as collaborative, strategic, decisive, and driven by the organization's or team's best interests instead of your own.

I have heard Carla Harris say countless times that the best leaders give their power away.[23] Leaders don't just assign the difficult work away and put up their own feet; rather, they understand the importance of trust and of elevating those around them. Giving your power away helps empower others, so let them know you think they are better than you. By doing so, you will likely create meaning for the team supporting you. Not to mention, giving away power is a great way to build your influence and overall power. Leaders should make sure they are not focused on executing something that someone else could be doing, because you will want to be focused on problem solving so that you can come up with the best solution for all shareholders involved.

It is also difficult to let go of a responsibility. Again, it's often a matter of ego. People convince themselves that they can do something better than anyone else, or they are afraid that if they give up a task or responsibility they will be perceived as being less essential to the company. It takes confidence for a leader to overcome these ego problems. Daniel Kahneman writes, "We have an almost unlimited ability to ignore our ignorance."[24] Humility is the awareness that there's a lot you don't know and that a lot of what you think you know is distorted or wrong.

It is human nature to want to see the fruits of your labor, to feel the dirt between your fingers, to perform tasks that not only produce tangible results but that are themselves tangible. Leaders must seek a different kind of satisfaction. They have to be able to build up people and give them responsibilities, to find ego gratification in training, directing, and overseeing others. Sell your team. The smarter you make the people who work for you look, the smarter you are going to look as a manager. It's also less masochistic.

A leader must make every difficult and mostly uncertain call, and not only that, he or she must also commit to it and stick by it. The leader bears the brunt of the responsibility and, as Dwight D. Eisenhower was reported to do, give the credit away to the troops when successful but assume full blame when the mission fails.[25] Carla Harris puts it this way: "I made the call, it happened on my watch, and I am ultimately responsible."[26] The Navy SEALs call that "extreme ownership," a defining trait of any fledgling or experienced leader. Another leader, the ex-CEO of Morgan Stanley, John Mack, once said, "The essence of leadership is making decisions under pressure, whether you're running a business, raising a family, or simply living your life. Making the hard calls when you have no idea of the outcome, taking the risk, putting yourself out there, that's when you prove your mettle."[27] John Mack later went on to detail in his own memoir that during his more than four decades on Wall Street, he learned about managing, and mismanaging, people both in times of crisis and the ordinary day-to-day operations.

Leaders ~~Eliminate~~ Welcome Mistakes

If you examine our military hierarchy, soldiers are taught to give orders in their own name rather than their higher-ranking official. Though the orders may have been passed down from the commander-in-chief, the sergeant knows not to say, "The general said," but instead to delegate the order using their own authority and thus take full responsibility for the resulting outcome. The difference between a great leader and an exceptional leader is in making decisions. It is a paradox that leaders are faced with, in that they need to make decisions rather than drag their feet in over-analyzing, but they also must remain accountable. Decisions are what make great leaders; they are judged on their track record of decision making. As an example, nobody wants to be known as a "do-nothing president," especially since the price of inaction is greater than the cost of making a mistake. Leaders instill confidence in their team by giving away their power and creating action in their decision to do so.

A leader is challenged to keep their head on their shoulders in uncertain times. These are the moments when charisma is not only built but shown. It is in times of toughness that loyalty, discipline, and accountability shine clear. And a leader must remember to remain calm in front of those whom they are leading, like a duck pedaling furiously under water but calm on the surface above water. Or like a flight attendant who looks calm regardless of the amount of turbulence, because as soon as he shows any signs of discomfort, it will alarm everyone else.

A leader should be measured on how much they love, not on whose love they win. Leadership takes many forms, but I will say this: I have never come across a servant leader I have not wanted to follow. Leaders who serve relentlessly, giving more than they take, are leaders who inspire. They say that leaders go the way and show the way. When no one wants to raise their hand in class and answer the first question, or no one wants to shoot the last basket in the game, that is when a leader shines and steps up to the plate. It can be an exacting position, demanding tenacity, discipline, and bravery, but being a leader could make the difference between the team winning and losing.

Colin Powell is a great example of a leader who garners trust, accepts failure, and remains optimistic. Powell has said, "When you trust your people . . . they trust you."[28] Great leaders intentionally create an environment for people around them to give their honest opinions and to not be afraid to speak truth to those in power. Hardly anyone is willing to tell their boss—or their team captain—the hard-hitting truth. But if you can make it clear to them you are not going to shoot the messenger, you will create a much deeper layer of trust and communication.

Powell was also known for giving his aides "rules cards," detailing the way he preferred to communicate and his preferred procedures, like never hiding any information from him or never signing his name for him. Powell's type of leadership was one of transparency, as most people tend to hide the ugly information from their boss, parent, or teacher. He would tell his team, "When anything is going wrong, tell me about it. I'm not going to chew you out. We're going to solve it."[29] He would even go so far as to have trusted colleagues within his circle who would intentionally offer him feedback on where he messed up or even that he needed to use the dry cleaners more often.

But I especially admire Powell's position on failure as a leader. Powell underscored how imperative it is to move on from our mistakes. "You've got to learn to move on and remember that your life is not spent because you had one failure. It's just beginning, because you've learned something about yourself."[30] He even had a method for getting over his mistakes, by rolling up a piece of paper into a little ball, throwing it over his shoulder, and never seeing it again. This is not dissimilar from President Eisenhower's method of dealing with failure by keeping a drawer in his desk full of all his mistakes crumpled up into little balls. While they both have similar careers in the military and in politics, I don't find it a coincidence that these two leaders share one other sentiment, which is that it is never as bad as it seems and never as good as it seems. In other words, both leaders took the moderate pathway and found ways to strike balances with differing opinions and differing outcomes. After all, few leaders make sound or sustainable decisions in an atmosphere of chaos.

As laid out in Alex Banyan's book *The Third Door*, when Warren Buffett, American investor and philanthropist, was working as a stockbroker, he decided he wanted to hone his skills and go to business school. Alex writes, "He applied to Columbia University because he knew Benjamin Graham—the Wall Street legend known as the father of value investing—taught there. Buffet got into Columbia, took Graham's class, and eventually Graham became his mentor. When Buffett was about to graduate, he decided not to take a high-paying corporate job, which most MBAs did, but to try to work directly for Graham instead. Buffett asked Graham for a job, but Graham said no. Buffett then offered to work for free, and Graham still said no. So Buffett went back to Omaha and worked as a stockbroker. But he continued writing letters to Graham, visiting him in New York, and in Buffett's own words, after two years of pestering him, Graham finally gave him a job. Buffett was married and had a child by this point, but he still flew to New York as soon as possible to begin. Buffett didn't even ask if there was a salary. He worked at a desk outside of Graham's office, learning firsthand from the master. Two years later, when Graham retired and closed his firm, Buffett moved back to Omaha to start his own fund, and when Graham's old clients were looking for a new place to invest their money, Graham referred them to Buffett."[31]

What Warren understood, as do many other leaders, was that it takes empathy to make decisions. If you didn't work your way up the ranks to understand how those you are leading think and view life or their job, then you better take the time to listen and understand. Be willing to humble yourself and find a mentor or a sponsor that is going to show you the ropes. Have patience, learn, and be open to other opinions. Use this information to make decisions that incorporate a broader scope. This is what exceptional leaders have proven to do.

The bottom line? Leaders must make decisions. Exceptional leaders have a short memory, they remain calm in uncertainty, they lean on others for critical feedback, and they harbor a fierce love and trust for their team. One important caveat to decision-making is this: As paraphrased from Morgan Housel, decision-making also requires humility, not in the idea that you could have the wrong answer, but with the understanding of how little of the world you have experienced, and especially in knowing how those you are affecting think and make decisions themselves. Most of the time, not all the time, it is the academically smart people who quickly advance into roles with responsibility for others. But because these academics experienced a different career path than those less intelligent people, they lack the emotional intelligence to relate to how others think, what they have experienced, how they see the world or solve problems, or what they are motivated by. A leader, though, usually makes decisions hardly with all the time they would want, and he understands he needs to go out of his way to listen and empathize with others who have different experiences than him.

Once you have the trust of your team, selling your vision is one of the most important and defining parts of your evolution from individual contributor to leader. Moving from individual contributor to leader is probably one of the toughest transitions for anyone to make. If you are like most of us, you have been focused on your personal benefit, risks, and potential losses for a number of years. But as a leader, you can't get caught up in the false productivity narrative. The check-the-box mentality of completing the daily tasks and routines does not make a leader any more impactful; in fact, it likely decreases their leadership impact on others. Whoever said being anxious and more busy gets more accomplished anyway?

The best leaders know to give their power away. Typically, the more successful a leader is, the more willing they are to share their secrets with others. Forget about a 50/50 mentality, because 50/50 is a losing proposition. The only winning proposition is 100 percent. Leaders put to the side what they need and focus 100 percent on making the win about the other person. Your influence will be determined by how abundantly you place first the interests of other people. This is not a strategy for leadership; this is a way of life. And when you do this, you will find unparalleled success in your endeavors. Your true worth in life is determined by how much you give in value rather than what you take in payment. The insecure leaders are the ones who can't provide security for the people they lead and are constantly seeking validation, acknowledgment, and love. Insecure leaders cannot celebrate their people's victories and limit the recognition they give them. It is only the secure leaders that believe in others, give their power to others, and have a superior respect for themselves to be able to do so.

Lesson: "Your candle loses nothing when it lights another." (James Keller)

Mount Rainier

We had just completed "snow school," a two-day training program at the foothills of Mount Rainier on its snowy patch, despite it being the middle of summer. Snow school was about making mistakes at the bottom of the mountain so that when you made mistakes at the top, you knew how to handle them. In the military, this concept is called *wargaming* and is a way to take visualization out of your mind and into real life. As teammates, role-playing potentially dangerous situations helps keep the objective front and center. The military also calls this *theater objective*, and any decision made needs to be made in the context of whether it helps or detracts from this objective. Simple as that.

To paraphrase Nick Saban, the head football coach at Alabama, "We don't practice until we get it right, we practice until we can't get it wrong."[32] Snow school was all about getting as many reps in as possible, not only so each reaction was built into muscle memory but also so we could execute any maneuver knowing we had done it several hundred times over. In a team environment, whether on the field, on the ice, in the classroom, or in the boardroom, players have to be able to take risks, and if the target is the bullseye, consider that a 10x. But if a player hits the outside black numbers that is not a bad thing; it is when you miss the dartboard completely that you might want to reconsider your training regimen.

No team is going to be operating at perfection all the time, which is why you role-play for stress inoculation. When things inevitably go sideways, you have the training to lean on, you can retain your poise, and you can regulate your emotions before acting out sporadically. Peak performance requires luck, practice, recovery, little headwinds (if at all), and usually a few tailwinds. But if your team is focused on optimal performance versus peak performance, you can incorporate into your wargaming and role-play uncertainty, missteps, dead ends, wrong turns, and what I like to call course corrections. Hardly everything goes to plan 100 percent of the time, so preparing for these unexpected bumps greatly increases the chances of success when obstacles abound. Things are caught, not taught, so it is very important you attend snow school, learn the proper step techniques, and understand how the ice axe feels in your hand or what it feels like to accidentally cut your leg if you handle the axe improperly. You need to feel the soft snow and the hard snow to know the difference in safety, and you need to feel the rope slip beneath your oversized glove while the sweat builds below your oversized coat, your breathing picking up and eyes fogging. In other words, you need practice being uncomfortable and making judgments based on feel.

If you are in a captain position on a team or in any type of corporate leadership role, your leadership starts with you. Snow school forced us to have a team lead on the rope team, or someone who directed the team through the course and up the mountain. This leader is supposed to model the behavior for the rest of the team: the exact step, the exact breathing technique, and the pace everyone else should follow. Most people tell leaders to fake it until they make it; however, my snow school instructor told us that most people are smart and can sniff that out. He was the leader of a handful of Mount Everest expeditions, so anything he said was like gold. But as a team lead, when the going gets tough, not only are you expected to say you don't have all the answers, but you are also expected to gather information and marshal resources as well as to be frank and solicit opinions and feedback, even if you don't apply all of it. People need to share their ideas, concerns, and thoughts to feel engaged, and that helps build trust on the rope team. But as rope team leader, you are there to make decisions—that is your main role. And your theater objective is to bring your team to the summit and back down safely, despite the many external and unexpected risks that lay ahead.

We had made it to Camp Muir—the base camp—at 10,000 feet, around 6:00 p.m., after an entire day of hiking. All we wanted to do was cheer for one another and kick our feet up to watch the eventual sunset. Instead, our climbing guides asked us to get to our cabins for some shut-eye. It was difficult to sleep; after all, Mount Rainier has a 50 percent summit rate, and there was a lot out of our control. Thankfully, it was pitch black in the cabin, but outside, it was still bright out, and others were enjoying big dinners, drinks, and laughs. Our team, however, was going to make our summit attempt in the morning, so we had our ready-to-eat rice bags and headed to bed early with our game faces on.

"All right, wake up, everyone. We checked the weather patterns, and we have a window. Green light." It was 12:03 a.m., with a full moon illuminating the ice paths ahead. We took thirty minutes to pack up, change our gear, and rope up as a team.

For the next six hours, we would look like an ant trail of bright lights staggering back and forth across the dark landscape of the mountain until the sun rose.

"Remember, you have practiced this hundreds of times before. Stick together as a team, make decisions with all the information you have, and commit. We will see you at the top." As our team began ascending the Disappointment Cleaver, a tricky segment on the mountain, we started building our confidence with each step forward. But as we arrived at our first break point, we were asked to wait an additional twenty minutes to link up with the team behind us. This was a huge risk, as twenty minutes was enough time for our temperatures to drop significantly, as well as for blood clots to form with our blood pressure pumping at such high altitudes. I was the rope team leader, and so I had to make a decision: wait for the team, or forge ahead without them. I surveyed our team, thinking about the current weather patterns as well as our team morale at the moment. After surveying the group, I decided we would wait. I wanted to keep moving, thinking that was the right call for the team. But as I allowed for others to speak up and share their true feelings, it became apparent that they cared more about not leaving anyone behind. As Adam Grant says, "The true leader in a group is rarely the person who talks the most. It's usually the person who listens best. Listening is more than hearing what's said. It's noticing and surfacing what isn't said Inviting dissenting views and amplifying quiet voices are acts of leadership."[33] Even though I was the team leader, I was amazed at the leadership of everyone else.

We were wearing avalanche beacons in case snow buried us, we had puffy extreme-cold parka coats on to protect us from wind piercing our bodies, and we wore helmets with headlamps to keep us from walking off the mountain during the dark hours of the morning. We had to remain quiet to listen for cracks in the snow or for large snow chunks breaking off the walls of the mountain ahead. We stepped slowly, one foot in front of the other, with what felt like minutes in between each step.

Step, pause.

Breathe, step, pause.

Breathe, step, and pause continued to be the cadence.

But like runners from Kenya are taught in track races, let the lead car pace, and everyone else, watch your legs. Don't think; just do. Being on a rope team requires teammates to move as a unit, not allowing too much rope to space them but also making sure the rope is not too tight, restricting the other climbers from moving forward. Teammates have to work together, grind it out, and remain calm. Sometimes, the leader needs to strategically be at the end, pushing the team up the mountain, and at other moments, the leader needs to take the front position to properly guide by example. I personally have always thought the leader's positioning is situational.

I decided to wait for the team behind us, which caused my team to burn some energy in the cold, and we lost time in our tight window to make a summit effort. But as a leader, you have to stick by your decisions, so I didn't let that weigh us down. We moved past Emmons Glacier on the northeast flank of the mountain, up the Disappointment Cleaver and into the avalanche fields. We began to space out amongst ourselves, almost ten yards apart, with the rope dragging between us, vanquishing into our own sloshy thoughts. The repetition and isolation of being on the mountain soon begins to drive anyone crazy. We were faced with the last hour of ascent, but we still had some major crevasses to cross, and without careful attention, any minor slipup could bring the whole rope team down. This is an extremely dangerous situation that can occur, and has occurred, many times on Mount Rainier.

The brochure didn't include crevasses, ice axes, avalanche beacons, or headlamps in it. Instead, it was a group of smiling teenagers—go figure. Here we were, teenagers, sure. Smiling? Absolutely not. With our legs tired from the nearly six-hour, forty-five-degree ascent, we had one last stress-induced moment to overcome as a team. I went last, encouraging others that I was right behind them if anything happened. I wasn't sure what the other side held, or if there was loose snow that would result in me falling even if I cleared the crevasse. It was at least a hundred-foot drop, with jagged ice and a dark cave tunneling at the bottom. It was a moment that tested my will. We had overcome so many obstacles already throughout our climb; why not tackle yet another? It was a pivotal moment as a team, because though we had not reached the summit, this last little victory of crossing possibly the deepest hole in the mountain led us to believe we would make it to the top. It was like a monumental battle of

Bunker Hill or a key last-season victory for a team just entering playoffs. We were sure destiny was on our side at this point.

Our team did summit the mountain, and on our way down, we still had our work cut out for us. All I could think about on the way down was how much fear I carried the day or two leading up to our summit attempt. At the foothills of Mount Rainier, the cloud-suffocated and snow-capped top, towering over all of Seattle and beyond, felt like an indomitable monster. *You want me to do what?* To me, it felt like entering a fun house as a kid, with terrifying popouts and actors creeping around every corner waiting to scare you out of your pants. I remember our group even airing out our anxieties the night before in our campground, discussing what we were most frightened about. Some said not coming home; after all, people die on Mount Rainier every year (just look up the book *The Ledge*). Others brought up their fitness; it was a hefty climb, no doubt. But as for me, I was most concerned with letting my fear block me from getting to the top. You know, that endless film in my mind projecting the doom and what-if scenarios that could occur, playing in my mind all the imaginable situations. I had one goal in mind, and it was to bring my team to the top and back. But even though there were moments to turn back, like when we had to make a crucial decision about waiting for other rope teams that were cutting teammates loose on their summit attempt, or whether we should cross the unexpected crevasse in the first place, I found an inner strength to power through. I think back about my journey on Mount Rainier all the time, and I pull so much confidence from that summit day. I learned something about dealing with my fear by putting myself to the test on the mountain and walking one step forward at a time, breaking the climb down into smaller feats and manageable outcomes. If nothing else, I learned how important it was to get outside, to push through fear, to get out of my head, and to put myself in situations that are uncomfortable, because the confidence you can draw from it later in life is immeasurable. Put another cookie in the cookie jar.

Lesson: The T-shirt I bought at the bottom of the mountain read, "Mind over Mountain." Don't shy away from fear; harness it, grit your teeth, and go for it.

Commitment and Attitude

"Do what you say you are going to do, long after the mood you said you would do it in." (Bear Grylls)

I love this quote because it exemplifies the discipline needed when your motivation runs out. Sure, you popped the champagne bottles on New Year's Eve, and you are feeling extra inspired to get that first run in tomorrow—but what about in a month, when it is cold and raining and you are a little sore, you haven't seen the results you expected yet, and your friends want you to stay at their party a little longer? You won't be successful if you only do what you need to do when it's convenient or when you feel like it. High-functioning athletes know to remove how they feel from their mindset. Michael Phelps, the Olympic gold-medal swimmer, may not feel warm and cozy while in his jumpsuit before plunging into a 60-degree pool at 5:30 a.m., but he has the commitment to separate his feelings from his routine and discipline.

One of the most important skills to constantly polish in our lives is that of commitment. Commitment to our family, our friends, and our passions. Choosing where to direct your attention in life will help eliminate any lack of commitment. When you don't know where to direct your attention or have the motivation to keep that attention, it is easy to give up on your commitments and turn away. However, in order to choose where to focus your attention, you will likely need to decide on where *not* to focus your attention. Embrace the necessary course corrections by trying a range of different hobbies, making a range of friends, studying a range of curriculum, and shuffling through a range of jobs.

Become Obsessed with Developing Your Toolkit

Become obsessed with being the rookie or the newbie at something outside your comfort zone. I was always enamored with the idea of being a "renaissance man." This is to say, I wanted to be someone who is versatile and can be useful in many different situations or has many different skills. I do believe in the importance of strengthening your strengths and applying a concerted effort on mastering a particular expertise, especially a strength. But even more so, I sincerely believe that a happy and fulfilling life, at least for me, requires having my hands in many different things. Sports were always my go-to, but as I matured, I realized how cool it was to have different talents and hobbies. I became more interested in becoming interesting. I wanted to garner more experiences so I could expand my perspective in life and grow my interests in other areas. I was never the best at anything, but I grew more interested in learning to speak about other topics outside my normalized baseline domain.

I found that brilliant people in my network could speak to many different subjects. They had range. I was never fully interested in sports talk and sports betting, as much as I love to play sports and watch them. I never found much use from following all the sports analysts' blogs and podcasts. I didn't feel the need to surf social media and digest every play and statistic that occurred the night before. However, I have a lot of friends and colleagues who do, and I don't think that it is inherently a bad thing. All I am arguing for is finding multiple channels for inspiration, not just one sole area.

As an example, I always told myself I would have my kids learn another language. My mother-in-law is from Rome, Italy, and I have been working for ten years now to learn Italian. While I have improved my conjugations and sentence structure, I still am not fluent. But how cool would it be to speak with Nonna in Italian, as opposed to typing out messages to her every week on WhatsApp? I always think about how fascinating you become when you can speak different languages, connect with more people, and better understand cultures simply because you can relate through language. Did my year-round hockey schedule help me improve my game? Absolutely. Was it important for me to put my focus and time on improving on the ice? Of course! But part of me thinks it would have been so cool if I could have spent some of that time working on my Italian, or French, for that matter.

It's the same reason that I took up guitar my freshman year in college, thanks to one of my best mates who taught me how to play my first few chords, or how to hold the guitar properly, for that matter. It's true that when I play air guitar I still play as a lefty, even though when I play guitar now, I hold the guitar right-handed.

But I didn't find a guitar until I was nineteen years old. Before that, I played saxophone in the fifth grade. I even played on a street corner in Ridgewood with my friends with an open case, until one of my parents' friends saw me and let my parents know (thankfully). That was an awkward dinner table conversation that night. I thought I was being entrepreneurial; my parents thought I had lost my mind.

After playing the saxophone, I was drawn to percussion. I had a friend who could play the kit like a pro. In middle school on my birthday, I was surprised to hear my sister, who was in our basement, hitting the high hats, symbols, and snare drums, which is how I ended up taking lessons from a teacher for a year. I even had a good little garage band going with my neighbor, who was a great electric guitarist and still is to this day. We played AC/DC and Led Zeppelin, like every other rock band those days. I worked hard on my paradiddles and paradiddle-diddles (yes, it's a real thing).

Sampling different interests, different studies, and different career paths is not just a way to understand what you like so you can lead a life of purpose. Critically, it is a way to ensure eventual success in whatever you choose. In fact, you can be "set free by failure," which will force you to try work that better matches your talents and interests. As David Epstein explains in his book *Range,* "Match quality is a term economists use to describe the degree of fit between the work someone does and who they are—their abilities and their proclivities."[34]

The same ability to have breadth can make for successful academics and careers. Morgan Housel says, "Someone with B+ intelligence in several fields likely has a better grasp of how the world works than someone with A+ intelligence in one field but an ignorance of that field just being one piece of a complicated puzzle."[35] The idea is to think differently, to not follow the herd, and to find a new way to look at something or solve a problem. Perhaps my greatest failure is that I am simply mediocre at a lot of things and not spectacular at one thing. But by adding to my experiences, I am improving the way I relate to others and possibly view the world, as opposed to having a narrow view. There are certain muscles, both physical and mental, that need exercising, and exercising them brings you the adaptability and flexibility that many of life's situations require, such as thinking outside the box.

My dad told me while driving me home from hockey practice one night, "I am always willing to support you and your dreams if you continue to show up and work on your craft." He wasn't promising me support only if I succeeded, he simply appreciated and wanted to see me commit to something, to work hard at my craft, to give it attention. I have carried this lesson with me a long time and try to apply it to other commitments in my life. As the Navy SEALs say, anything worth doing is worth overdoing. Don't half commit; make it a full-body yes, a full-body commitment. One important detail is that specialization and commitment should come later in life. True, we should commit ourselves to worthy causes, but only after we have taken the necessary time to determine our match quality toward that cause.

Seth Godin speaks to the idea of quitting and failing early, and that we shouldn't even feel badly about it. I don't think Godin wants us to evade our problems or quit just because the going gets tough. Godin is not advocating for us to quit something simply because the going got tough, because persevering through difficulty is a competitive advantage for any of us. Instead, knowing when to quit is a strategic advantage. It's the idea of failing fast. The key is understanding whether you are quitting because of a lack of perseverance or because of a lack of possibility. What you are doing may not be a fit for you, and therefore, it may not be possible. We are always changing in life, and so is our self-knowledge. With growing self-knowledge, we have growing goals and passions. The idea that we should pick and stick to something is unfounded. We can and possibly should all respond to our lived experience with a change of direction, Godin argues, which involves a particular behavior that improves your chances of finding the best match. Godin controversially terms this "short-term planning."[36] Aha! We can finally do away with the dreaded five- and ten-year plan and focus on the now. Specialization is not required up front.

We receive the advice to think long term all the time, but it is within the short-term planning that we can apply pivot after pivot, eventually leading us to build a spectrum of experiences that will help us fulfill our long-term vision. When it comes to commitment, you don't need to sacrifice the coveted and proverbial Millennial and Gen X rite of passage—that is, endless self-exploration—in order to immediately commit to one rigid goal. Many successful people do end up pursuing a long-term goal, at least eventually, after they have spent time deciding what that worthy goal entailed. Like those who have experimented, you, too, should learn to lean into your strengths to become successful, but only after you have taken advantage of a period of exploration. Additionally, as you age, you change. Some of the most important personality changes occur between your teenage years and twenties. Thus, going after what you think you want at an early age can often backfire, both because you changed your interests and also because you neglected to grow or explore other areas and skill sets. You neglected to expand your domain of knowledge in obtaining the narrow skill set you thought you desired.

Do I think you need to be all things to all people? No. But is it helpful to learn new skills and develop other facets of your life, especially since the varying skill sets can cross-pollinate and lever your already existing skill sets. I spent a great deal of time in cold locker rooms, with 5:00 a.m. winter morning wake-up calls. I spent countless days on the cold ice rinks, and many summers competing and training to improve my hockey prowess. I wouldn't trade those experiences, because I gave a full-body yes. In my mind, playing hockey with my best friends, scoring goals, competing, and living the lifestyle of a hockey player provided me with lessons in leadership, teamwork, failure, and success. Yes, I wanted to play college hockey (I used to dream of scoring the national championship goal for Boston College), but it was equally the journey and the process of imagining, dreaming, and feeling motivated to pursue these things that was so special. The chase was easily enticing. However, as I got older, there were moments I would think to myself, "Suppose I had started practicing Italian earlier in life, or suppose I spent more time on my golf swing, or on skis, or mastering debate skills on the debate team?" You can't do all things, but you can build a portfolio of skill sets and interests throughout your life. And you are never too old to build something new into your repertoire.

When I attended Providence College, we didn't have fraternities and sororities, but we did have different clubs you could join as a student. While I loved my hockey buddies, I also loved my other friends from other clubs. For instance, I played in the church band with one of my best friends, the same one who had taught me how to play in the first place. I also worked on Student Congress, and I remember sitting in my first meeting listening to our group run through the political agenda and having no idea what was going on. Students were following a strict pattern of agreements, formalities, and voting, and I was completely lost. I even joined the sailing club, which did not last very long. I had no idea even how to tie a knot! And of course there were intramural sports and the not-so-occasional bar nights with friends, always pulling me in multiple directions.

The point is, I am proud of all the things I tried, even if I was mediocre at best, and I would encourage anyone to try as many hobbies as possible. It is proven that deep work that focuses exclusively on your strengths is a very successful method, rather than also working on your weaknesses. However, I have found a life of fulfillment through the trial and error of my journey through both success and failure, thanks to my willingness to branch out. Curiosity is filled with recreating yourself, trying things, meeting different people, and understanding what you like and don't like, so you don't end up wasting so much time in life with blinders on chasing one goal. Chasing one goal can be admirable, but if you can imagine other goals in life because you had taken the time to learn and think about what you like and don't like, perhaps you might find even greater success, because you have identified your true passion and purpose through trial and error.

Bobby Orr, the famous Hall-of-Fame NHL player and Booton Bruins legend—they don't put statues up of every player—once said, "I don't believe that summer is the time to train for winter sports. If you want to play your sport more, that is great. But I see parents ship kids off to camp all summer thinking that will turn them into a player. The fact is no one can make a kid into a player if that is not the kid's passion. My preference would be to see kids play other sports, especially during hockey's offseason, be it lacrosse or soccer or rugby, or any other activity they enjoy. There is something to be said about cross-training, which helps a person become an athlete and not just a player of a specific sport. Youngsters in multiple sports get the opportunity to experience a broader range of skills development, and that will only help them when sport specialization starts later in their teen years."[37] Bobby is not the only hockey player who carries this sentiment; Wayne Gretzky has said very similar words.

In the book *Range*, a study of music students aged 8 to 18 and ranging in skill from rank novices to students in a highly selective music school found that when they began training there was no difference in the amount of practice undertaken between any of the groups of players, from the least to the most accomplished. The students who would go on to be most successful only started practicing much more once they identified an instrument they wanted to focus on, whether because they were better at it or just liked it more. Furthermore, it was apparent the students who had a large amount of structured lesson time early in development fell into the average skill category and not one was in the exceptional group. Researchers believed that too many lessons at a young age may actually not be helpful. These less-skilled students tended to spend their time on the first instrument they picked up, as if they could not give up a perceived head start.

Psychologists highlight a variety of paths to excellence, but the most common was a sampling period, often lightly structured with some lessons and a breadth of instruments and activities, followed only later by a narrowing of focus, increased structure, and an explosion of practice volume. The more contexts in which something is learned, the more the learner creates abstract models, and the less they rely on any particular example. This can be linked to the concept of interleaving, where instead of having math students solve repetitive questions with the same traps, the teacher can weave in slight nuances so students must apply a lesson to different patterns and trends, giving breadth and scope to their problem-solving skills. Learners become better at applying their knowledge to a situation they've never seen before, which is the essence of creativity. Want to increase your interleaving skills? Increase the unstructured play in your life, and add more breadth to your routine.[38]

Take time to develop yourself, make yourself interesting, grow your network, learn something unique, and dig in once you find that thing that motivates you. Now, at thirty, my learning has adapted. My curriculum is no longer pushed by adults and school systems. I create it. I listen to what friends are reading and thinking about. What questions are they solving? What inspires them? I use the holiday season for deep-work reading and learning something completely new to me. I use the summer for reading inspiring books at the beach, looking for good stories, and I try to fit in non-fiction because I believe it is important to keep my imagination strong. I also find the fall to be a great self-improvement time, so I read books on leadership. Fall always brings that renewal season, the excitement following the lulls of summer. I encourage you to find your rhythm and what works for you. Roll up your sleeves and get 1 percent better every day, whether on a passion project or some new fun or interesting hobby. I like to think that not only am I a collection of my thoughts, beliefs, and experiences, but I am also a reflection of the literature I have consumed and the minds of those I have entered through literature.

What am I committed to outside of my work and my family right now? Well, ever since I was in high school, I started doing something considered "not cool," even on my own. I lived down the street from an open field that included a bandshell, and in the summers I could sit in my backyard and hear live music being played. So, I started riding my bike down the street with a lawn chair to watch these mom-and-dad bands play music on Tuesday and Thursday nights in the summer. It was really a perfect American summer dream. Water park, baseball diamonds, fresh-cut grass, stars in the sky, bright stage lights, normal people like you and me playing music, and a big group gathering of children, parents, and of course, massively romantic elderly love birds, still dancing in front of everyone even at the age of ninety. No cell phones, no distractions; pure bliss. Over time, my family started to join me, and we even brought a few sodas with us too. It has been about ten years since I learned to play guitar, and about eight years since I played live music every

Sunday at our 10:30 evening mass, sprinkled in with a couple open mic nights in McPhail's, the local Providence College bar. But there is a feeling I still get when I pick up a guitar, a familiar childlike wonder. Music was a latent passion for me, and while I did not go on to a professional career, I know that over the next few years, I will be chasing a new goal of mine: to create my own mom-and-dad band to play at the bandshell. It is my commitment and dream to have a mom-and-dad band and to play at the bandshell. Not all dreams are about making it to the big stage. You can create your own big stage right where you are today.

Keep a commitment to remaining interesting. Oftentimes, the part of you that is least expected is often most respected. Austin Kleon, quoting Lawrence Weschler, encourages us "to be curious and attentive, and to practice 'the continual projection of interest.' To put it more simply: To be interesting, you have to be interested."[39] I would take it a step further and say if you want to remain committed, you should start by being interested. You need to take the time required to understand what you love and what drives you and inspires you. Too many of us claim we don't know what we are passionate about and that we can't start until we are 100 percent convinced and are a master of it. The reality is that passion is a product of action, so don't wait around to get struck by inspiration; begin by committing to the consistent effort of discovery and exploration. Try new things, make observations for yourself, and don't let a lack of knowledge preclude you from making the necessary steps forward in following your brilliant curiosities.

Lesson: You are never too old to try something new. Childlike wonder is not just for children.

The Ship Has Sailed on My Naval Academy Dreams

"When you want to succeed as bad as you want to breathe, then you will be successful." (Eric Thomas)

My legs grew heavy as I reached the doorway, and before opening the door to face my fears of what was on the other side, I placed my hand over my chest to make sure it wasn't obvious that my heart was beating out of my shirt. I was visibly uncomfortable, not accustomed to wearing dress shoes and formal clothing every day, but it was mostly my facial expression that had this seriousness to it, like a CEO testifying before Congress. Sure, they have a boatload of confidence, as their industry knowledge might be far and beyond what the congressional leaders' knowledge consists of, but at the end of the day, it was their courtroom, not the CEO's. And when playing their game by their rules, nerves and uncertainty will come with the terrain for any CEO in that position. The door swung open, and I was greeted by fifteen decorated military veterans, whose seriousness in their faces made my own seriousness now look more like pathetic desperation, something Kevin Spacey in *Horrible Bosses* would sniff out in seconds. I'll never forget the one question, from the mostly quiet General, sitting in the back-left corner of the executive-style conference table holding all sixteen of us. It felt like the situation room at the White House, where key military decisions could be made in the blink of an eye. I remember the question, though, because of the critical feedback I received following my answer. "No, Kevin, the answer is to never leave a man behind." That was obviously the feedback to my response on what the most important mission was, which I had mistakenly thought was execution of the mission critical objective.

Almost two years before this all-important interview for the Naval Academy, I was completing the various other requirements of my application for candidacy. There was the doctor's appointment in Yonkers, where I was measured from my waist to my head—too tall, there goes naval aviation—put in a sound box for ten minutes, and studied by doctors for almost an hour before getting the green light of approval. Then came the day-long interview process with New Jersey's senate and congressional leaders, questioning and not-so-politely poking holes in my every word and answer. After that was my Blue-and-Gold Officer meeting, in which my parents hosted an alumni sponsor, with which every candidate is required to meet before receiving a potential letter of recommendation from them, that lasted hours in my living room. And how could I forget the fitness test that my coach led, which tested my one-mile run, following consecutive tests in the number of pull-ups, push-ups, and sit-ups I could complete in a two-minute series. There were all the days I wore my Navy sweatshirt to school, and the buzz haircuts I gave myself, all in preparation for the path I felt destined and called toward. But all the work and time I put in, all of the emotional significance I placed on serving my country, all the support and help along the way from coaches and sponsors, and all the sacrifices I had made by putting the Naval Academy ahead of every other school choice, was summarized in a brief two-sentence letter I received in the mail. A simple, unembellished, and remarkably unapologetic letter describing the fate of my seventeen-year-old being, with no mistaking the tone and gravity of the verdict. Letters have a funny way of making an outsized impact on a life event. "It's just a letter"? Try telling that to a kid with a dream. I had spent thousands of words, emails, and conversations with those in the military, and I was utterly unprepared for the two sentences that would follow.

I grew up abnormally obsessed with Bear Grylls, the youngest person to summit Mount Everest and member of the British Special Operations team. He was a badass, and he was just launching his TV career on *Man vs. Wild*. But it was well before his show taught me how to count the minutes until sunset on my fingers, or what types of berries you can live off in the wilderness, that I was drawn to the military. My dad and grandparents had backgrounds in the military, and I was very keen on watching all the classic war movies, including *Saving Private Ryan*, *We Were Soldiers*, *Tears of the Sun*, *Pearl Harbor*, *Black Hawk Down*, and various other films. I even created a game with my neighborhood friends, which we would play all the time, called, "The gun game." We would split up into two teams; one team would hide out, and the other team had to go find them and "neutralize the enemy," as we'd say. We were very creative and passionate as kids, and we loved playing make-believe. In reality, it was a glorified game of tag and manhunt.

My dad helped me understand the importance of duty, honor, and country as a young kid. He would take me hiking in the woods behind our first home, encouraging me to pick up sticks and pretend to chase imaginary enemies throughout the trails. As I got older, I attended West Point Army lacrosse camps in the summer, and I would show up to their hockey games in the winter. Our family would tailgate for the football games in the fall, where I would witness the helicopters and fighter pilots cruising around the skies before kickoff. They were so low and made so much noise, my senses were always on overdrive when I stepped onto campus, which was anything but a typical college campus. In fact, it was a fort, a military compound, and it brought some of the most disciplined, honorable, and high-performing individuals together in order to groom our country's next military leaders.

There is a higher call—and higher level of purpose and duty—that some feel naturally and others don't. It doesn't make one person better than the other, but it is as clear as can be when it is coursing through your veins. I had attended a lacrosse camp in Annapolis, Maryland, with my dad as a high schooler, but the tournament was completely rained out when we got down there. Because we weren't about to get in the car and drive five hours back home, we decided to check out the U.S. Naval Academy, which was only a few miles down the road. Blown away by the campus, the geography, and being right on the water, I had made up my mind right then and there that this was going to be my path, that I was going to be a Naval Officer. There was a particularly visceral experience of being on campus that reminded me of my early days admiring West Point. It offered routes to so many options: Navy SEALs, marines, surface warfare officers, submarines, naval pilots—I could go on. It was like a latent dream of mine, always in the background, but now as obvious as tripping over a traffic cone. The Navy was where I wanted to be, even if I didn't know how to get there.

I didn't fully understand how I would make such a dream come true, but I believed deep down that it would work out. The U.S. Naval Academy takes about twenty thousand applications every year, while only offering about a thousand students scholarships. I say "scholarships" because the U.S. taxpayer (you and me) pays the government to bring these kids to military academies in exchange for their commitment to serve in the military after their four years of education and training. Some of the smartest, most devoted, most talented, and most hardworking humans come through these academies, many of whom learned the pledge of allegiance before nursery rhymes.

Though I believed in my candidacy, I knew I had one glaring challenge to overcome: I was not the world's best test taker. In fact, I had taken the SAT three times and the ACT one time. On a separate occasion, I even took the GMATs in case I one day decided to go to business school. It's like throwing paint against the wall; maybe one of those tests would go well. Except, none of them went well. The ultimate reason was not that I didn't have a tutor (I did; I had two separate tutors), and it wasn't that the questions were too complex for me to solve or that I didn't have enough time on the test to arrive at the correct answers. It was because I failed to prepare. I failed to commit. I failed to take extreme ownership and accountability that this was my life and if I wanted to achieve my goal, I would have to go beyond reasonable measures of preparation. Instead, I chose not to.

But here is the problem: I believed in the U.S. Naval Academy path, and I was willing to do anything to get in, so I thought:

Do you need me to do more pushups at 5:00 a.m.? I'll do more of those.

You want me to be a captain on my hockey team? I will work on leading others.

But the one task that was required of me by my Blue and Gold Officer—responsible for leading me through the two-year application—was to retake the SAT, yet again. My Blue and Gold Officer had sat in my living room for three hours with me and my parents and had told me he was going to help get me into the Academy, that he believed in my story and my determination, and that if I followed his instructions, we'd get it done together. And his instructions were simple: "I don't care how many times you have already taken the test; I just want to see you take it one more time."

In hindsight, taking the SAT one more time seems so simple and so straightforward, I can't imagine not listening to my Blue and Gold Officer. Unfortunately, I didn't have hindsight when I was seventeen; instead, I was so focused on everything right in front of me that I neglected to think about the bigger picture. I failed to grasp that he was testing my resilience, and instead, I thought it was more a test of intelligence. Sure, the Naval Academy has rigorous standards for their candidates, and attitude alone does not grant you acceptance. But my lack of confidence when it came to test taking and lack of preparation proved devastating to my candidacy. For a seventeen-year-old kid, high school hockey warranted a lot more attention than some stupid test that I knew I wasn't going to do well on anyway. And so begins the tracing of exactly where I went wrong with the Naval Academy. One of my biggest misses in life, the college application process.

I was a very average hockey player with pretty good mitts. I had an average stride and a few quick steps, but nothing that Boston College was paying attention to on their recruitment trips. I had one of the slowest wrist shots, although I did have a formidable habit of taking the puck to my backhand and flipping it over the shoulders of goalies. While I might have been average, some of my teammates I skated alongside were incredible players, some of whom went to the National Hockey League (NHL). We all have those stories of friends, linemates, and peers that go on to highly competitive leagues. But what is so cool to me about these past experiences is that at the time, these games were more important than any other. As a team, you are focused on that season, that month, that week, and that game. Nothing seems as important in life as the present competition or task at hand. And for me, that task was Ridgewood ice hockey.

The Ridgewood Maroons, my high school hockey team, was playing a hockey game against Bayonne late at night in Bayonne, New Jersey. I was supposed to take the SAT again the next morning. But for some reason, hockey subconsciously weighed heavier on my mind that night. I "felt" like I needed to rest, and I "felt" like I was coming down with a cold. And therein lies the issue: I gave more priority to the way I "felt." Rather than roll out of bed to prepare for battle—a battle with the SAT—I avoided the battle altogether and skipped the test. *It was one lousy test,* I thought to myself, *what difference does it make if I take this one day off?*

For most of my SAT scores, I underachieved in the mathematics sections, which was always a little surprising to me because I am diligent when it comes to numbers and calculations. To this day, I'll never know if I was just a bad test taker and I just had bad test days, but something was very discouraging and demotivating about having to take the test again. I had essentially forgotten the reason I was doing all of this in the first place. I lost sight of the "why" behind my struggles.

I have made a lot of judicious decisions in my life and stepped up at the right times, but this was regrettably one of the worst decisions I ever made. I am convinced that not showing up to this test was the reason I did not get into the Naval Academy.

On the one hand, I thank God because I would never have met my wife, but on the other hand, the regret hit my confidence and left some scar tissue in my mind because of my underperformance. I knew I had more to give, and I did not ultimately give it. I knew that I had potential, which is sometimes the hardest step in accomplishing goals: believing in yourself. What I originally harbored as a dream, to attend the Naval Academy, soon became a fleeting wish. But as my mom likes to say, "Man plans, and God laughs." You have to be willing to course correct as new information becomes available to you. When I had read that letter in the mail detailing in two sentences that I was formally being notified I was not accepted into the Naval Academy, with no deepest regrets, sincerest apologies, or better-luck-next-year sentiments, I was crushed. I didn't believe it was real. *Don't they know that my coach told everyone at my school I was going to the Navy already? Was this a mistake?*

Putting my military goals aside, the process of applying to college is one of excruciating pain if done incorrectly. But luckily, you can learn from my monumental mistakes, whether you are applying to undergraduate programs or graduate programs, or whether you are helping someone do the same. The first important truth I discovered is that no matter what college you go to, it will not guarantee you anything. There are many elite schools that promise the prestige and social status exclusive to those granted access within their four walls, but admittance does not guarantee a life of financial success, abundant love, or unbreakable friendship. Many kids end up in the school their parents always dreamed of attending, or applied to the schools that had the best name recognition. Sure, some kids do genuinely desire the education they will receive from a specific program. I had a friend who was offered acceptance at every Ivy League school, and she landed at Brown University because she felt the cultural fit was strongest. But the simple truth is that you still have to willingly seek out, and struggle with, success, love, and friendship no matter what university you attend or don't attend.

The second truth I discovered is that while many people attach their identity to their college or university, you do not have to. I remember the day I received my only college acceptance letter; it was a few weeks after I received my remaining rejection letters from Middlebury, Boston College, Holy Cross, and Villanova. The letter was a large envelope, which was a dead giveaway that it was an acceptance letter—as I was told—since I had never actually received an acceptance letter before, but could take my friends' words for it. Providence College, the same school my parents, my aunt, and my grandfather had attended, was offering me a seat in their next fall semester. *Great, can we just eat dinner already?* I nonchalantly threw the envelope of a smiling friar on the couch, unenthused by the acceptance. To me, it didn't feel earned; it felt expected. And my personal issues of judging myself for not attending a school of high enough caliber, misunderstanding my identity as a would-be Navy Cadet, and comparing myself with friends who all appeared to have made it into their "top choice" schools, was one of the biggest course corrections I needed to face up to. I had mistakenly assigned so much of my own identity to my school that as soon as my fate was sealed with Providence College, I had lost my sense of who I was. *What's the point? I might as well just settle.* While there are usually many options after failure, I decided to move forward and accept my offer to Providence College, and I eventually learned to take extreme pride and gratitude in my alma mater. It was an active choice, something I had to practice and retrain my brain. What I then realized, and only after coming to grips with my own reality and my own self-identity, was this: No one cares. No one cares enough to judge you longer than maybe a few seconds, because they are likely so busy judging themselves and worrying about what others are thinking of them, at the exact same time you were worried about them judging you. The moment you realize that no one really cares is the moment you will liberate yourself to your true identity, not the identity you attach to a diploma. And that identity is entirely free and your choice. Who you are is not where you went.

Finally, the third truth I realized was that you are responsible for your choices. I had internally blamed so many people who didn't provide me the right guidance, and I had made a handful of excuses as to why I didn't get into my top choice schools. As an example, for many years I considered that I didn't get into my other top schools because I was unable to apply early-decision to any other school, because the Naval Academy prohibited candidates from doing so. *Had I just been able to apply early-decision to one of those schools, I would have surely been accepted.* Ultimately, after years of reflection, I was reminded that it's not only about realizing no one else cares but also that you have to care. As Charles Horton Cooley says, "I am not what I think I am, and I am not what you think I am. I am what I think you think I am."[40] You have to independently take action, perform the research on different schools and state cultures, and decide on what it is you want. As I grew up, I met more people from schools I truly admired, but I never took the time to learn more about them. You can't expect your parents, or anyone in your life for that matter, to tell you exactly what to do. Even if you did, it wouldn't be a great idea to take their advice without weighing your own priorities. You have to own your decisions and choices and not put the excuse on anyone but yourself. I decided to apply to the schools I did, I decided not to retake the SAT, and I decided that I would have to sacrifice the chance to attend a top school in order to place the Academy at the top of my list. But only after taking responsibility for myself was I then able to proudly embrace, cherish, and thrive at my school. Only after coming to grips with my own choices did I feel the overwhelming amount of gratitude for the path on which I found myself. It just took major self-reflection beforehand, a course correction I am forever grateful for.

Lesson: Leaders don't let their feelings override their purpose. Instead, they do what they say they are going to do, while remaining open to new possibilities and course corrections.

Retesting My One Mile in Fifth Grade

We had just finished the one-mile beeper test in elementary school, and I was fairly satisfied with my seven-minute mile. I figured I could rest on my laurels and go hang out with my friends on the playground at this point. My gym teacher had let me know it was the fastest time out of all my classmates, but it was my classroom teacher who was anything but complaisant. "Kev, I think you can actually do a lot better; you should take the test over again. I want to see you run faster this time. I know you have it in you."

I took his challenge and retested my one-mile run that same day, while all my friends and teachers watched. There was no pressure or stress around it; in fact, I remember singing in my head and listening to the sound of my feet hitting the pavement. I was always a very independent kid; I woke up early, made my own lunches before school, even got my morning exercise in by the bedside with pushups—but I was also very impressionable and coachable. Sometimes in life, we all need someone to recognize our talent and to push us out of love and support. We need someone to believe in us.

I remember sprinting the last leg of the track, and I could see all the faces and hear the cheering at the finish line. I galloped past my gym teacher, and his thumb immediately and emphatically clicked the beeper to stop.

"Six minutes and thirty seconds!" he yelled out. Not only did I beat my seven-minute mile, I beat it convincingly. They were all proud of me, but mostly, I was proud of myself. We all have the choice to sit it out or dance, as the song lyric goes, and when you get the chance to sit it out or dance, I hope you dance. I am not saying that you should push yourself at every opportunity, but doing so at different points in your life, while also including this attitude of self-improvement, is very healthy. It will also reward you with a confidence boost you can always look back at so you can say to yourself, "Hey, remember that time you dug a little deeper and found what you were really made of? That was pretty cool, huh? Hm, I wonder if you still got that good stuff in you today. Maybe we should test our chops again and see where we stand."

I had an anonymous quote on my childhood bedroom wall that read, "You either get better or worse every day; there is no staying the same. Every morning, a winner must wake up and pay the rent, because success isn't owned, it is rented." Our achievements of the past are in the past, and nothing is guaranteed or lasts forever. It takes hard work and a disciplined mind to practice getting better. No matter how good you think you are, you can always compete against yourself. This mindset is embodied by the legendary quarterback Tom Brady, who, when asked what his favorite Super Bowl Championship was, is known for saying, "The next one."

My teacher wasn't just egging me on; he was challenging me to challenge myself. He knew that I had more to give, and even though my two laps around my elementary school's back field was the best time of anyone's, the competition was myself, and he took this opportunity to push me to be my best. When I think about my retest, what stands out most to me is that I still think back to this event in my life and the confidence it instilled in me. It taught me that you can always improve, you can always do better, and mostly, it is up to you. It's not up to anyone else to make that decision for you to see how much further you can go. I have found in life that we all usually can go a lot further than we think. There is far more in the tank than our mind leads us to believe. Learn to doubt your own self-doubt.

Lesson: "When you feel like you've reached your limit, it is only the beginning. That is when it is time to dig deep, to find the courage to push some more." (Lebron James)

The Most Joyful Attitude from a Grocery Store Attendant

"All right, man, okay, happy blessings, God bless you, man. How is your family? Oh, your mom is good, oh, God bless her, man."

Orley was just some guy I met when I was seven years old. He worked at our local grocery store in New Jersey and was in charge of bringing carts from the stray parking spots. You could also catch Orley walking around the grocery store and saying hello to every customer, but when he said hello to you, he made you feel like you were the only person in the whole world that mattered. He was originally from Jamaica and hardly made enough money to support his family, but somehow he found a way. Orley dealt with people who left their carts all over the parking lot and who showed little respect for returning them or for the people who were tasked with returning them.

That didn't bother Orley, however. Every time my mom brought me to the grocery store, Orley was there with the biggest smile on his face to greet us as we exited the car. As a child, I never really knew who he was. But I saw how happy he made my mom and how nice he was to my sisters. He would come over to hug us, high-five us, and shake our hand, sometimes holding on to our hands for a whole minute while talking to us. No one I had ever met "held" my hands, and it is sort of a hard thing to forget as an impressionable child.

As I got older, I went to middle school, then high school, and eventually I left town to move to college. But every time I returned to that grocery store, Orley was there, ready to greet me the same way he did when I was seven. Seeing Orley was a shot of inspiration, of gratitude, and really just pure joy. He reminded me of the important things in life, like attitude and perspective. Orley understood something that many of us miss in our daily distractions of life. Orley understood that he didn't need anything else but the air in his lungs and the wind beneath his feet. He had happiness inside him; he just had to choose to let it shine. I will always associate Orley with my extended family, as he took the time to always say hello, embrace us, and share his love. He has been in my life for over thirty years now. He is a beacon of positivity and someone whom I greatly admire, and in many ways, he was the best grocery cart delivery attendant in the world.

Orley took what many would consider to be a low-paying job and turned it into one of the most fruitful jobs out there. He found a way to be rich in love and to share that love with all of his customers, even if they weren't truly "his" customers. He wore the suit every day, meaning that he showed up and acted the part. He made sure that no matter what kind of day he was having, whether sad, tired, or unhappy, you could always expect Orley to greet you with cheer and excitement. He embodies this chapter and the quote, "Be the best at what you do, no matter what you do."

I used to think that if I wasn't going to play sports in college, I wouldn't be an athlete. But in reality, I was an athlete either way. I used to think, if there was someone better than me, "Why try? Why not just let them have it, if they are better?" The idea, though, is to live within your circumstances, not your vision or dream. If you are on the JV team as a senior, show up and be the best senior JV player. Don't play down, play up. Elevate your level of play.

Many would consider the hockey player Sidney Crosby to be arguably one of the greatest to put on skates. It is well-known that "Sid the Kid" absolutely despised losing. Even if it was in a "juggle the soccer ball" team game warmup, he never wanted to be the player who dropped the ball. Even though he was likely stressed and focused on the real game in the next hour, he was fully intent on playing the little game at hand and being the best he could be at that moment. A game within a game.

There are many ways in life we can choose a path out from underneath. We can work hard, find the right connections, and even come across some luck. One might even call that serendipity, a fortuitous situation by chance. But in other ways in life, we cannot choose a path out. We have circumstances we must live by. And cannot escape. There are many pieces of our life that are out of our control. And it is in these situations we must learn to take back control with our mind, with our attitude, and how we show up.

I like Mother Teresa's question, "What is your program?" It is a profound question to ask yourself: What am I doing for others? What do I show and give to the world? What is my program? Orley's program was love, consistency, and happiness. He wasn't a blissful fool, oblivious to the fact that he had a difficult job to do. He was someone committed to a program, a program that brought discipline and awareness to happiness and his ability to choose happiness, to take back that control and use it to his advantage.

Charles Swindoll once said, "The longer I live, the more I realize the impact of attitude on life. Attitude to me is more important than facts. It is more important than the past, than education, than money, than circumstances, than failures, than successes, than what other people think or say or do. . . . The remarkable thing is we have a choice every day regarding the attitude we will embrace for that day. We cannot change our past. . . . We cannot change the fact that people will act in a certain way. We cannot change the inevitable. The only thing we can do is play on the string we have, and that is our attitude. I am convinced that life is 10 percent what happens to me and 90 percent how I react to it. And so it is with you. . . . We are in charge of our attitudes."[41]

Lesson: You can make an impression and impact even in the most trivial of jobs by being yourself. Most people are not comfortable with who they are, so they try to act like someone else or like a vision of who they think they should be. Jerry Garcia would say about his band that they weren't the best at what they did; they were the only band doing what they did.[42] Don't tame your positive attitude; be proud to show off your excitement.

Sports

"The best teams are made up of a bunch of nobodies
who love everybody and serve anybody and don't care
about becoming a somebody." (Phil Dooley)

"Success is won by those who believe in winning, and
then prepare for that moment. Many want to win, but
how many prepare?" (Herb Brooks)

Not everyone enjoys sports—I get it. But for a lot of us, sports
are a rite of passage. It is how many of us make friends, how
we measure our accomplishments, how we challenge ourselves,
and how we learn not just about ourselves but also about our
competitors and teammates. In so many ways, sports are the
ultimate platform to learn how to fail and overcome failure.
Sports have always provided me with a platform for confidence,
a way to build trust and belief in myself, and to bring out the
competitive nature that life requires. But at the end of the day,
sports are about fun. Being on a team is unlike anything else.
Playing for your teammates, stepping up in big games, working
on your craft in the offseason, showing up to practice after
practice, and finding inspiration in each new season. While
I have many championship teams I cherish from all ages, it is
truly in the non-championship teams I learned the most. It was

the difficult seasons, the mess-ups, the lack of preparation, and the wrong attitude that provided me with such crucial lessons in life.

Skiing in Mont-Tremblant

One of the very first trips my mom and dad took us on was a road trip up to Mont-Tremblant, Canada. Back then, cars did not have TVs on the back of the seats, so my parents purchased a tiny TV screen that would hang from the two passenger seats in the front. And for about eight hours, my dad drove us north toward Montreal, Canada, while the three of us siblings sat in the back watching movies on one shared twelve-inch television. Just Sarah, Emily, and me spending quality family time together.

When you are that young, you don't know that trips like this are expensive, or that it is the very first trip your parents could afford to take their family on. You just know there is going to be fried dough, movies, and fun skiing. It also was our first road trip as a family, which required a ton of planning, packing, and a last-minute Thule purchase to fit all the equipment on the roof of the car. We rode up north in Clifford, which was the name my siblings endearingly nicknamed the red-colored Tahoe, just like the big red dog.

After the first eight-hour leg, our family decided to find some rest in Montreal and pick up our trek north early the next morning. If you know my dad, when I say early, I mean pre-sunrise. Anyway, once my dad and mom got us kids in the car, we were two hours from Mont-Tremblant and a week of fried dough, movies, and carving snow up on the trails.

Pulling up to the mountain was something else. I could not have felt more transported from the tiny bubble in which I grew up, in addition to the unmistakable cold shock that chills your bones, and lungs, as soon as you step out of the car. An astounding -10 degrees Fahrenheit at the bottom of the ski mountain. We began unpacking the car, loading up our suitcases, extra boots, hats, gloves, backpacks, and any trash from the breakfast we shared in the car ride up from Montreal in the morning.

Once everything was unloaded and taken into the hotel, it was time to purchase lift tickets and give the mountain a test run. My youngest sister, Emily, was bundled up and barely recognizable, Sarah had just clipped her ski helmet tightly, and there I was, noticeably missing an important part of my gear. As I zipped up my ski coat in anticipation of readying myself to step onto the gondola, my zipper broke and shredded the entire vertical zipper path on my coat. What began as a relatively stress-free morning (remember, relatively, meaning it was still a stressful family vacation morning, just not as extremely stressful as it likely could have been) quickly turned into a moment of conflict resolution, or in other words, a hearty debate between Mom and Dad over what to do in this predicament.

"We could use safety pins," my dad suggested. An hour hadn't even gone by since we arrived for a week-long trip, nor had a single ski run taken place, but the solution had already been decided. Mom and Dad would safety-pin my jacket closed for the entire week. As mentioned, when you are that young as a kid, you hardly ever think about the consequences of spending money. But for my parents in this situation, this was their first family trip, and they were not going to let a broken jacket derail their week.

This trip was not their first display of independence, as they married very early in life and had three children before the age of 30. But this was a pivotal moment as new parents, and ski coats carried a steep premium when purchased on the mountain. Besides, they had a budget in place to stick to, and a missing zipper was not going to cost them a hotel night.

The safety pins worked well, so long as no one was judging the amount of wind chill that flew up through my coat as I skied down the mountain. Did I complain? Of course. Was I okay? Definitely. And was this child abuse? Absolutely not. When I think back on this, I maintain I would have done the same for my child. However, what remains to be discussed is the post ski après and lunch. After cruising the slopes in the morning, we would walk into town with our ski boots and crispy red faces from the wind to fill up on some soup and hot cocoa. While everyone de-layered and doffed their chairs with coats, sweatshirts, and base layers to enjoy the warmth and comfort of their soup, I was left with my coat on, as well as my sweatshirt and base layers, because the thought of unpinning and then repining safety pins was far too burdensome for my parents' predilection.

Here I am, looking like Randy from the movie *A Christmas Story* when his mother dresses him up for a walk to school in the snow, barely able to put his arms down to his side. I was a puff ball with my coat on at the table, hardly able to bring my soup spoon to my mouth from my bowl. As I learned, you are not always going to have the best ski clothes or, as will later be detailed, the best equipment for golf, or hockey for that matter. I can even remember my father spray-painting my red hockey helmet from my early childhood navy blue so that I could play for the Ice House Avalanche, a team whose colors were primarily blue. After a few games, hits, and scratches, my helmet took on several polka-dotted blue-and-red marks, much to my own chagrin and embarrassment. Not to sound too self-righteous, but I think it is great to experience a wardrobe mishap here and there; it is good for humility, and maybe it even makes a few good chapters for a book one day.

At the time, I may not have appreciated my parents' cleverness on the mountain, or my dad's resourcefulness when it came to spray-painting my helmet, but now I have complete respect and admiration for their willingness to refrain from buying me the top of the line clothing or to cosset me with new equipment anytime something broke. What they taught me through their actions is that it is about the experience, not the novelty of new gear. Yes, I do believe that if you look good, you feel good, and then you play good.

Lesson: It's not the uniform; it's the player.

Adult Golf Camp with My Non-Adult Golf Clubs

"It's not about the equipment; it's about the player." I was told this early in life. Was it a way for our parents to convey that there wasn't a need to buy the top-of-the-line sticks, gloves, or rackets every six months when the new series of performance gear was unveiled? Probably. But I always think about the movie *A Christmas Story*, with all the children looking into the glass window at all the new toys to purchase for the holidays. Or at the movie *The Sandlot*, which depicts a group of neighborhood kids hanging out all day at the baseball diamond, with torn-up jeans, scuffed-up Converse shoes, hats, and gloves. Baseball to them wasn't about having the best equipment; baseball was about the joy of the game, the competition, the spirit, and the fact that it was a common game that drew them all together along with an unapologetic love for the sport.

Growing up as a kid, this was a load of crap to me. *Of course the equipment matters*, I had reasoned as a kid. Hockey players used to play without shoulder pads, so their hits were not as effective; they skated on leather skates instead of graphite skates, which were heavier and not as agile. Gloves went up to your forearms, inhibiting the type of skillful handling of pucks that players today have no problem executing. But that wasn't the point. So let me be clear on what the point was. Go play the game. Focus on something more important. Stop worrying about something like a stick. Is it better to play hockey with a graphite stick and not a wooden stick with no curve on the blade? Of course. The idea is to rid yourself of distractions and excuses. To forget about how you look and just go play. To spend your energy on more important matters.

Some of the best players I ever played with, either in lacrosse or hockey had some of the worst equipment. Before they went on to highly successful careers in college or in the professional leagues, they had to demonstrate their skill before their team gave them all the top-of-the-line equipment. They cared far more about the team outcome than about their individual style, and it showed in their tenacity and their passion for their sport. This might seem like an obvious statement to you, but believe me, it was pervasive for me growing up, and I imagine it was for you too.

When I was in grade school, a best buddy and I attended one of the most renowned and highly respected golf schools for one week in Hilton Head, South Carolina, called The International Junior Golf Academy (IJGA). I didn't know it when I signed up, but it is home to some of the greatest golfers in their teenage years, including from places like South America and Europe. I had no idea, but I was about to be way in over my head. We flew down together and arrived a day before the camp began, which meant early mornings on the range with one-on-one coaching instructions, video reviews of our swings, and afternoon rounds on Daufuskie Island. I also didn't appreciate it at the time, but it was a dedicated school that was absolutely pumping out the next budding tour players, and my friend and I were about to be part of it all.

The first morning before sunrise, we had all eaten, packed the vans, and headed out to the course. There were about fifty players waiting for their bags to be unloaded from several U-hauls, and most were impatiently waiting around the outside of the pro-shop, eager to warm up on the driving range. The night before, I had already embarrassed myself at a mini-putt alongside some of our housemates. After a few holes, I thought to strike up some deeper conversation with one of the guys by asking him what I thought to be an unassuming question, "I take it you are pretty good at golf"? His response took me by surprise when he answered, "Yeah, ha, I am pretty good," as if to say he was extremely good, not just good. *Smooth, Kev; real smooth.* It was implied and left me feeling a bit out of my league already. But I was in for an even worse and unexpected embarrassment that morning while we were unloading golf bags.

I could feel the anticipation on the pavement that morning with all the golfers standing around, arms folded, game faces on, and not a whole lot of small talk. The players were sizing each other up and determining who was strong and who was weak, a classic adolescent exercise in survival of the fittest. I have no qualms in saying so; it is what it is. You could also sense it was going to be a steamy day out. It was not yet 8:00 a.m., but the sun was reflecting off windows and warming the backs of our necks, legs, and arms, and the air carried a crisp smell of early summer morning dew and freshly mowed grass. I remember feeling nervous to find out where I stood amongst the other golfers. After all, this wasn't my first rodeo; I had been playing a tough course back home for a few years, I took a few lessons from my grandfather's coach, I watched golf on TV, I played Tiger Woods in our video games, I and studied many golf swings through books and magazines. *Golf Digest* used to feature a player every month with a mosaic of snapshots from a player's backswing and downswing. I would hang these up on my childhood bedroom walls, dissecting the swings of Adam Scott, Ernie Els, and the myriad of other top-ranked players.

I would soon find out that not only was I one of the younger golfers at the camp, but I was also the easiest to make fun of. Each bag that was unloaded from the vans included golf bags with the best sets of irons, headcovers, towels, and custom shafts. We were young teenagers, but these were some of the nicest bags I had ever seen. I was left speechless when the kid version of my Nike golf bag was unloaded amongst all the others.

"Whose bag is this?" One of the counselors asked the entire group of golfers, as I could hear the chuckles and raillery out of the crowd. My face turned bright red, and I thought to myself, *Just play it cool and wait for the others to grab their bags first so fewer people see you walk over to your Nike bag.* My bag included kid shafts and one-quarter the number of clubs, and the bag itself was probably three times as small as the tour bags that seemed to be so popular. It was an exercise in humility, and any confidence that I might have exhibited before arriving was quickly evaporating like the dew on the grass.

While others laughed at me, I knew I had a choice to make in how I responded. Instead of proving them wrong on the course, I let their teasing get to me. I had the worst driving range performance of my life that morning. I couldn't stop thinking about how I had the worst clubs and how immature and childish everyone must think I am. As soon as I started working with the coach, though, it was all about the swing, the flexibility, the athleticism, and the player. Any anxiety I had about my clubs was quickly replaced with motivation and commitment. My coach saw that I cared, that I wanted to improve, and that even though I was likely the worst golfer at camp, he could push me to work hard and know I would be receptive to his coaching.

This became my saving grace, not only at golf camp but also in life, when the cards were stacked against me or when I felt out of place like I did not belong. I learned to look inward and remove the distractions. There will always be someone cooler than you, tougher than you, more skilled than you, more beautiful than you, smarter than you, or more popular than you. They might have nicer clothes, nicer equipment, or more experience in their arena of sport, but it is up to you whether it affects your performance. By putting yourself in situations where the talent is greater than yours, where you are uncomfortable and worried about embarrassing yourself, you develop a tolerance for temerity and a level of perseverance you can always draw from.

This goes back to fear and choosing how to respond. This also goes back to friendship and realizing that others might be better than you at something and that you are the average of the people you surround yourself with. For all these reasons, it is favorable for you to feel out of place or behind, because it will strengthen your confidence over time, even though it might initially feel like a blow to your confidence in the moment. Forget about the equipment, forget about the laughs, and just swing your swing in life. Be the player you know you can be. Remove the distractions and the questions, "Am I good enough?" or "Do

I have what it takes?" In the words of Tom Cruise, "Don't think, juot do."

Lesson: If you are the best player in the room, you are in the wrong room.

The Edge

In sports and in life, finding the edge—sometimes even the smallest of advantages—can mean the difference between winning or losing and succeeding or failing. The edge is all about finding that 1 percent difference, that one seemingly elusive piece of knowledge or that one extra push to get over the finish line. Some of life's hardest challenges and failures can be overcome by learning from your mistakes, missteps, or flops.

Playing within the rules is part of any game and is also true for life. If your boss wants you to show up at 7:00 a.m., you need to follow those rules. If your teacher says you are taking a field trip, you need to do so. Not in every game in life will we have a decision to play or not to play, but when we do have the decision to pick which game to play, it is important to pick the game that suits you best. Kobe Bryant was a Hall-of-Fame NBA player because of the work he put into his craft off the court. Of course, he went to the gym, ran sprints on the courts, practiced his jump shot, and worked within the confines of the NBA rules.[43]

However, Kobe knew he needed an extra edge to be even just 1 percent better than all of the other elite players doing the same thing. Kobe made a point of reading the referee's handbook. One of the rules he gleaned from it was that each referee has a designated slot where they are supposed to be on the floor. But if the ball is in a certain place on the court, then the two or three referees each have an area on the court. When they are in their positions, there are certain areas that are created called dead zones, and Kobe knew where these existed. Not only that, he knew how to leverage the knowledge of these existing zones. He would get away with holds, travels, and all sorts of minor violations simply because he took the time and effort to understand the referees' limitations and the rules of the game.[44]

As Laura Huang says in her book *Edge*, "Edge is about knowing how, when, and where to put in the effort and hard work. The past decade of my career has been spent studying the myth of meritocracy, but even more important, studying what can be done when you acknowledge and own the fact that risk and failure work differently for different people in a world that will never be entirely fair. I've studied what happens when you know that perception is a double-edged sword, and how you can cultivate an advantage for yourself through this awareness. And I have found that there are ways to actually have an unfair advantage—an edge—over others who seemingly already have an advantage, as well as those who don't yet know how to create their own edge. Embrace it, own it and make it yours and turn it into an advantage, craft it, hone it. Make them notice it. Be the counterintuitive presence."[45]

What I have drawn from Peter Sims's book *Little Bets* is that gaining an edge in your life, sport, or career is not about shortcuts, life hacks, or efficiency and effort (sorry, Tim Ferris and the *4-Hour Work Week*). Instead, those who excel at levels most of us dream about do so because they have a desire to constantly challenge and stretch themselves. As Peter Sims outlines in his book, Dr. Carol Dweck, a professor of social psychology at Stanford University, is one of the leading experts on why some people are more willing and able to learn from setbacks. Based until 2004 at Columbia University, Dweck has studied motivation for several decades. Sims says, "Her research has demonstrated that people tend to lean toward one of two general ways of thinking about learning and failure, though everyone exhibits both to an extent."[46]

Those favoring a fixed mindset believe that abilities and intelligence are set in stone, that we have an innate set of talents, and this mindset creates an urgency to repeatedly prove those abilities. People with this mindset perceive failures or setbacks as threatening their sense of worth or their identity. Every situation therefore gets closely examined, "Will I succeed or fail? Will I look smart or dumb? Will I be accepted or rejected?" Fixed mindsets cause people to be overly concerned with seeking validation, such as grades, titles, or social recognition. Conversely, those favoring a growth mindset believe that intelligence and abilities can be grown through effort, and they tend to view setbacks and failures as opportunities for growth.

Michael Jordan is one of Dweck's oft-used examples of someone with a growth mindset. He did not start out as a player who would obviously become one of the greatest ever in his game. Rather, he exerted enormous effort to reach that level, and even after he attained it, he continued to work extremely hard. So as an example, even as one of the top NBA players, Jordan worked to improve his 3-point range shooting. After shooting 18 percent or less during his first four seasons, Jordan ended his thirteen-year career at an average of 33 percent. He was fiercely competitive, but win or lose, he was honest with himself and constantly sought to build his capabilities. "If you try to shortcut the game, then the game will shortcut you," Jordan said. "If you put forth the effort, good things will be bestowed upon you."[47]

Meanwhile, Dweck describes John McEnroe as exemplifying someone with a fixed mindset. If he started losing a tennis match, he would blame everyone in sight for the problem, from line judges to people in the stands. Rather than making adjustments to refocus and improve his game, he became distracted and angry (and notorious for throwing temper tantrums). You can be very confident in a fixed mindset, but every time you hit a setback, every time you have to struggle, every time other talented people come around, one has to guard against that threatening information. As such, it is difficult to maintain confidence in a fixed mindset without distorting the world, such as acting defensively or blaming someone or something else for setbacks.[48]

David Goggins was another elite athlete who learned the importance of gaining an edge within the rulebook. Goggins had failed out of Navy SEAL BUD/S training several times, always getting close, but never getting past hell week. And yet, Goggins kept coming back for more. The year that he finally became a Navy SEAL, he and his classmates found the agenda the instructors put together for hell week that was accidentally left lying out on a table. One of the most difficult parts about hell week is the uncertainty. SEAL candidates are kept in the dark about what is coming next, which tests their mentality and mindset. One story tells that during the second night, the instructors take the candidates up to a sandy hill overlooking the ocean and force them to watch the sunset. During this sunset, many candidates decide to quit and ring the bell, because the instructors use scare tactics like, "Just get ready; this is going to be the worst night of your life." The SEAL candidates that fought through this mental challenge came to learn that in fact there was hot soup and tea waiting on the other side; they just needed to stick around and remain resilient in their minds.

When Goggins and his team found the agenda, they were able to know exactly what was coming next. Equipped with this advantage, they were able to outsmart the instructors and, as Goggins calls it, "steal their souls."[49] In an all-out battle or intense game like hell week, finding that edge within the rule book and within the rules of the game you are playing can be the difference. Or just like in the movie *Days of Thunder* with Tom Cruise, where the racecar drivers would brush each other on the track, saying, "Rubbing is racing." Cheating is never okay, but finding an advantage within the rules is one of the best ways to outsmart your opponent. Some top athletes call this the edge, and it is what separates the best of them.

We choose who we want to be, which leads us to choose certain actions, and those actions then reinforce our state of being, which then leads us to choose actions that more carefully reflect that state of being, on and on in an endless loop, resulting in the strengthening of the identity we have chosen. By ingraining this desire to find your edge, and to embody this state of being of looking for marginal improvements in our lives, we can create our default being with which we show up in the world. Unlike a light switch, our being is made up of little and consistent and repeated efforts. When faced with obstacles and challenges and failures, we tend to resort to our default being, and if you have years of programming the edge into your being, you will be able to battle any adversity and pick yourself up from any failures along your journey.

The edge is also about the ability to adapt, rather than remain rigid in preconceived ideas or gameplans. Using another military anecdote, the idea behind templates and plans have become obsolete amongst soldiers. As mentioned in the book *Little Bets*, Peter Sims says, "The cornerstone of counterinsurgency operations is what army strategists call developing the situation through action. Central to the process is acknowledging that mistakes will be made, like violating cultural norms or initially picking the wrong partners, because soldiers are operating in an arena of uncertainty. They must be willing to seize and retain the initiative by taking action in order to discover what to do, such as by launching frequent reconnaissance probes. In order to help soldiers become comfortable with this approach, Haskin says, 'You have to catch people making mistakes and make it so it's cool.' You have to make it undesirable to play it safe."[50]

Lesson: Growth comes when you are prepared for failure, not hiding from it.

Hockey Dad

"You only made the team because your dad is the coach."

"You only got the hardest-worker award trophy because you are the worst player on the team."

"You have the worst shot on the team; you got lucky when you scored the game-winning goal in the championship."

"You are too small to make the varsity team."

"You only play on the first line because you try hard in practice."

"You only did the most push-ups or pull-ups because you are so small."

No matter how you feel about Tom Brady or the New England Patriots, you know that his critics have always wanted to take away his successes. There is the tuck rule, the Atlanta Falcons Super Bowl comeback, the snowy field goal kick, the deflated footballs, the play call stealing, and on and on. *Tom was lucky; Tom cheated; Tom played a bad team.* As if to say the most successful quarterback in NFL history was spoon-fed his victories. But it doesn't matter to Tom; he welcomes his critics, using their taunting to fuel and motivate him to prove them wrong.

I was standing in the lobby as an eight-year-old with all of my other hockey friends, waiting for the coaches and scouts to come downstairs and post the tryout list of who made the team and who missed the cut. This is a scene I have replayed in my head for years, and a scene that I lived through almost fifteen times. Scout comes downstairs, scout paves a narrow path through a sea of bodies, scout then tapes the eight-by-eleven piece of paper on the wall with the twenty names of kids who made the team, and everyone then rushes over to either high-five their friends or walk away to let their parents know this was not their year.

"Hey, man, you know you only made the team because your dad is going to coach, right?" Admittedly, this was not the best way to meet your teammate for the first time. He was probably right, though. My dad was going to coach this year, and there were some really great players out there in tryouts, after all. *How come I deserved to be on this team? Why was I any better than the other kids? Maybe I am not as good as I thought; or worse, maybe I only made the team because my dad was coaching.*

However, this was an improvement from last year's tryout posting. At least this time I had someone criticizing me for making the team, rather than the many other years that I did not make the top team roster. One year, a highly touted player also named Kevin had made the team, and when I saw Kevin listed on the sheet of paper, I immediately ran over to my dad to tell him I made the team. His reaction was one of surprise. With almost raised eyebrows and rolled eyes, he said doubtfully to me, "Really? Are you sure that was your name?" Confidently, I ran him over to the board, and when he read the name, it did not say "Kevin Entwistle." Rather, it said someone else's name that also started with "Kevin." *Man, these tryouts suck, huh?*

While never fully inured to the defeat of not making a roster, I did learn to use the failure to fuel me. After all, whether

I made the top team or not that year, I would experience failure on any other team I played for. That is a given, in hockey and in life. During the years I did make the good teams, I learned to be scrappy. I had to defend myself and stick up for myself, which was extremely challenging for a passive kid like me. I went from daydreaming about hot chocolates in my early days on the bench to learning to take hits, deal with the bigger kids, find ways to improve my skills, and push a little harder than the rest so I knew in my mind that I really deserved to be here, and it was not just because of my dad. It became a challenge against myself: how could I prove to myself I was good enough?

During one of my seasons in elementary school, one of my teammates pulled my dad aside, who was then coaching our travel team, and asked him what he had to do to beat me out in the center position and how he could prove he was better than me and more deserving of playing on that highly coveted first line. That was a wake-up call for me, as was the time we lost so badly to Delbarton freshman year that on the way home from the rink, my dad berated me with comments about how I didn't deserve to be in my position and how people would be gunning for the center position if I did not step up my game. It was my dad's way of making sure I understood nothing was going to be given and everything would have to be earned. It was also likely his way of saying when you're on top, everyone else will be after your spot, so you better find a way to be a little better, work a little harder, and care a little more than the others.

Tom Brady always played football with a chip on his shoulder. When he was winning games by multiple touchdowns and points, he never wanted to be pulled from the game. When he was sick, he did his best to show up, and when he was tired, he seemed to find a way to dig in his heels and find a higher gear.[51] Why? Because Tom knew he was replaceable, like everyone else. He understood that if you gave someone even one extra down, they might make the most of that opportunity, and that could be it for him. That could be the last hike he ever took. It only takes one moment for someone to supplant you as the starter in life, as the go-to player. My dad had tried to instill this lesson in me many ways and many times. And I resented him for it. I turned my back to him, I talked badly about him to my siblings, and I grew reticent around him. It does not matter what level of sport anyone plays; pressure is a privilege, and this was a big lesson I had yet to learn. Luckily, through pain there is gain. And I was definitely feeling the pain and the pressure. If I could do it all over again, though, I would have allowed myself to forgive my dad early in my life. I would not have glared out the car windows after games, I would not have placed my anger on him, and I would have said, "Thank you for caring to share. Thank you for seeing what I sometimes cannot see. I hope I can be better next time and remind myself that nothing is promised and everything needs to be earned, every single day."

I still remember graduating college and watching hockey games with him every so often. He would still turn to me and say, "Did you see how tough they were on their stick? Did you see how they didn't cough up the puck in the neutral zone?" As if there was a lesson to be taught every shift of the game. I had to remind my dad in a laughing manner, "Hey, Dad, I don't need to be coached anymore on hockey; you can coach me in something else now." But he was passionate. That is who he is, and he wanted to push me, which is what good coaches do. They coach all the time.

My mom told me a story once about how she never let her friend win in tennis. Similar to Tom Brady, mom was a tenacious athlete and still has a powerful forehand. One time her friend asked, "Kathy, how come you never even let me win a game, let alone a set or a match?" And my mom's simple response was, "If I let you win one game, you might have won another one and another one. If you won a few games, you might have won a set or maybe even a match. I can't let you win." I like to give my mom a hard time about this mentality, but she is 100 percent correct. Momentum is a funny thing in life and in sports. And if you give someone an inch, they might take a yard. It is a great lesson about having a high level of competition, and I always think about that. Do not wish away the difficult portions of life; they provide the contrast needed to appreciate the joyful moments. Your critics can be your best friends. They will teach you how to dig deep and how to push yourself beyond your capabilities, and ultimately you will appreciate your wins that much more.

Lesson: When you are told you are not good enough, remember this: The brilliance of the stars would be invisible without the vast darkness of space behind them.

Humble Yourself: AAA, AA, A, B

The AAA hockey tryout sheet went up, and I did not make the team—the best team you can make. *Okay*, I said to myself, *don't sweat it*. It would have been great, but you'll have a good year on AA.

The AA tryout sheet went up, and I did not make the team—the second-best team you can make. *Wow, did I look tired? Was I not playing my best?* I thought it was a sure thing that I would at least make the AA team. *I guess it is going to be A for you this year; maybe you'll make good friends and be a star on the team.* I was scheduled to be back on the ice for tryouts, but I might as well just have fun with it, I told myself.

The A tryout sheet went up, and I did not make the team—the third-best team you can make, or said another way, the second-worst team you can make. There would be no further tryouts, and anyone who did not get picked for A would be relegated to B, the very worst team.

I was a freshman in high school at this point in my hockey career, and I had never played on a team worse than AA. Much to my own chagrin, I had never dealt with this bad of a blow in hockey. Almost fourteen years of hockey in my life, camps, practices, hundreds of games, and thousands of dollars later, and I had made the worst team. I didn't know whether to laugh or to cry.

Not often do you get a chance to prove yourself this quickly, but in our first tournament over Labor Day a few weeks later, our team had found our stride and advanced to the championship game. The opponent? It was the A team that had cut me and some of my buddies. For some reason, the tournament had allowed two separate Ice House Avalanche clubs to participate in the games, and our team was going to play the team above us. Who is to say they were better? Why not us; why can't we be the champions? Our team had a chip on our shoulders, and when I scored the game-winning goal from behind the net by flicking the puck off the goaltender's back and into the back of the net, our team knew it was time to celebrate.

Of all the big games I have played in and all the comeback stories I have participated in, I think this was the sweetest. It was pure vindication of our worth. Not only does it pay to be a winner, but it is one of the strongest wells of confidence you can draw from later in life. Winners can grow complacent, and it is only through failure that you get to really see what you are made of. It is in failing and picking yourself back up that you draw confidence and prove what you are truly made of.

We could have easily hung up the skates and thrown away the season. But instead, we swallowed our pride, dug in, and took advantage of an opportunity to prove to the coaches, to the other teams, and mostly to ourselves that we had value and that we could beat the team above us. Others had somehow missed or passed on our talent and tossed us to the side. We took matters into our own hands, rather than letting others dictate our success and failure.

Lesson: "How you do anything is how you do everything." (Tom Waits)

The Post-Game Interview

"Too many kids have been taught that the goal of high school sports is to achieve an athletic scholarship—here's the truth: the goal of high school sports is to learn how to be a better person, better teammate, better communicator, and to enjoy being a teenager . . . something you can't get back." (Coach Lisle)

I had a teammate in high school who was a phenomenal hockey player. He was big in stature, could throw his body around, and was an innate goal scorer. He was one of our most talented players, and most importantly, he was a great teammate and person to be around. Good attitude, good sense of humor, worked hard in practices—but there was one post-game interview that resulted in him being quoted in the local newspaper, and some of his linemates took offense to it. Now, this book is about my failures, not anyone else's specific moments of course corrections, but in this story, I realized my failure in making a wrong decision that ultimately led to us breaking our team's undefeated record on the last game of the season, all because we decided to take a team vote on benching him for what he said in the interview.

In a moment of frustration, this player—also one of my friends—made some off-color comments about his two linemates and how he thought he would score more goals if he was playing on the first line with players who could pass the puck better, instead of on the third line. Because of this, the captains on our team decided to have a no-confidence vote in the locker room prior to the game, as many of the players were discouraged by these remarks. No one is perfect, and many times our words get twisted in the media, but this was a good learning moment for all of us, as it relates to how we communicate with those outside the walls of a team's locker room. You cannot let your guard down and throw teammates under the bus.

Kobe Bryant once said, "When I was young, my mindset was image, image, image. I took that approach with the media. As I became more experienced, I realized, no matter what, people are going to like or not like you. So be authentic, and let them like you or not for who you actually are. I think fans and reporters came to appreciate that, and came to appreciate the real me."[52] I think if our teammate embodied more of his actual self, instead of getting caught up with the cameras, he would have taken a deep breath and found a way to avoid any confrontational questions from the interviewer. After all, he is one of the most genuine and loving teammates I have ever played with.

But as Kobe also said, "The agony of defeat is as low as the joy of winning is high. However, they're the exact same to me. I'm at the gym at the same time after losing fifty games as I am after winning a championship. It doesn't change for me."[53] And to set the record straight, though there was a necessary course correction in how our team would address the media moving forward, our team, including our teammate described in this story, was right back at it after we lost our final game of the season following a team majority vote to bench our teammate that game. It was a lesson in leadership, as the sting of defeat was not the ultimate outcome that was hoped for, but it was a decision we all had to take accountability for, including our benched teammate

Lesson: "On every team there is a core group that sets the tone for everyone else. If the tone is positive, you have half the battle won. If it is negative, you are beaten before you ever walk on the field." (Chuck Knoll)

Boston Marathon

White, cloud-shaped salt marks of sweat filled my blue-and-yellow Boston Strong hat as the constant pounding of my sneakers on the black pavement filled my feet with unbearable heat and pain. I could feel cramping in both of my legs, a sensation I had never felt in my entire life, and I was beginning to worry as I looked down at my watch displaying my average minutes per mile ticking up. Forget the infamous heartbreak hill leading up to Boston College; ever since the rolling hills began in Wellesley, Massachusetts, I started to lose a lot of energy. I was astonished at how difficult it was to move one leg in front of the other, as if I was running through water or even in slow motion. I had taken my last Gu for the day, even though I knew one more would replenish my sodium and electrolytes lost on the Boston Strong hat I was wearing. *I will puke all over the streets of Boston if I take one more Gu.*

That's it, I thought, removing my hat with a picture of an eight-year-old boy haphazardly taped on the inside of the brim. *If I am not going to finish this race, then this little boy is.* I extended my arm to a runner by my side.

"What's this?" he asked.

"I need you to make sure this little boy crosses the finish line; can you do that?" I managed to mutter, barely placing one cramping leg in front of another cramping leg. The runner could tell I was throwing in the towel, and only a few thousand steps away from the finish line.

"I can't do that, I'm sorry," he said, "but you can."

That was 2014, one year after the Boston Marathon bombing, and the very moment I came to appreciate that this race was not my race. Instead, this race was the little boy's race. The same little boy who was known for spreading peace and kindness amongst his eight-year-old classmates and for making sure even the little guy or girl had a chance at the plate during recess. *If he could step up for others, so can I,* I thought, as I crossed the finish line waving my hat in the air.

Running has always come easy to me. I was tall and skinny as a kid, and I was usually winning all the sprint races and leading my teammates when it came to endurance training. I had trained hard for this marathon when I was a junior in college, and my adrenaline had me floating on air the first twelve or so miles downhill. I was high-fiving every kid on the course screaming for the jersey I was wearing. It was the most proud and adrenaline-pumped I had ever felt. It was the culmination of my childhood fandom for Boston sports and for being part of this Boston community. It felt like a victory lap, but in a greater sense, it was for everyone else around me. I just happened to be running through the parade bearing witness to the pure joy and celebration of the strength of Boston. I couldn't help but think about the admiration I had not only for my teammates and especially those running in the race who were affected by the bombings, but also for a role model of mine, Dave McGillivray, the Boston Marathon race director. I had the opportunity to have him on my podcast, where we sat atop Warrior ice arena during a winter afternoon. Dave is the most down-to-earth person I have ever met, and his perspective from his book *Last Pick* was extremely instrumental in my own development and hardship in being a late bloomer and overcoming athletic disadvantages.

Like my own difficulties with tryouts growing up, Dave was cut from his basketball team in high school. "When the high school basketball coach cut me, self-pity could have prevented me from pursuing anything requiring physical ability. Instead, I saw it as a challenge. It was a choice. I learn from each experience, even when the results aren't as planned." Dave later goes on to recount being the last cut in tryouts, saying in his book *Last Pick*, "In a misconstrued effort to help ease the inevitable, the coach said to me, 'Dave, if you were five inches taller, you'd be my starting guard.' But the point was, I wasn't five inches taller."[54] Before he left the court, he challenged one of the centers on the team to a game of 21, which he won. Dave had something to prove to himself, and maybe even to anyone watching. He then walked off the court with his head held high, knowing full well he would never let anyone tell him that he couldn't do that which he truly knew he could do. He went straight home and put a cardboard sign over his bed that read, "Please, God, make me grow!"[55]

What I love most about Dave's story is not all the accolades he received but the internal struggle he faced daily and the choices he made to overcome any perceived handicap of his. Would he have been better off a few inches taller? Sure, but Dave took that negative emotion and anger and turned it into a positive force for good. He ran across the country in eighty consecutive days, logged over 150,000 miles for charity, was a recipient of the Jimmy Award for Dana Farber Cancer Research, runs his age in miles every year on his birthday, has written numerous children's books, completed the Hawaii Ironman triathlon, and ran seven marathons on seven continents in seven days. Among a laundry list of additional accolades, my favorite includes the fact that he is the final person to cross the finish line every Boston Marathon, usually around midnight. Dave talks a lot about his own struggles, one of which was his first Boston Marathon as a teenager, which he actually did not finish and dropped out around mile eighteen. That didn't stop him from returning the following year, but it is a great example of the course correction that Dave made, making sure that he learned from his failure and came back even more prepared for success. It was the same thought that crossed my mind as both my legs cramped. Like Mike Tyson is famous for saying, "Everyone has a plan 'till they get punched in the mouth."[56] We all will have to make course corrections along our journeys.

Running became a breeding ground of positivity and mental clarity for me. I had always been a runner growing up, usually collecting Memorial Day race medals in long-distance races in which most of my similarly aged peers were not participating. Running became an escape and challenge for myself, like when there were six inches of snow on the ground, or when the summer rain was coming down and no one else wanted to go outside.

If you ask my wife, she will tell you that it was a five-mile run through the city of Providence late on a Friday night that constituted our first date. I had been enjoying a few beers with my friends throughout the day, but I decided I didn't want to go out to the bars that night. Rather, I felt like running. Something in my gut whispered, *Go out, run free, now.* It is that same impetuous response every time, it's probably the same reason I had run thirteen miles before a club hockey game at a discount hotel out in the middle of nowhere on a cold winter day, and it's the same reason I pushed myself to run eight miles on a treadmill my freshman year in our college gym. I wanted to test my boundaries. Go a little further than I had in the past, see what I was made of. The old "why not" mentality: why not see if you can run an extra mile, or five extra miles.

I had never run past mile three on a treadmill and wanted to "just keep going," knowing full well that if nothing changes in your training, nothing changes in your life. Which is why I decided to push the boundary, even if just a little. Eight miles is not terribly impressive, especially for a self-proclaimed, if slightly exaggerated, athlete like myself. But with every extra mile on that treadmill, it felt like collecting a cookie in the cookie jar. The more cookies I collected, the more I wanted to continue, curious if I would feel more inspired on the next mile or give up.

It became this game, this dance, this curiosity in my life that separates me from who I once was and who I am becoming. It separates me from the autopilot path I might be finding myself on. In order to overcome my limiting beliefs, I needed to become conscious of them first, which usually came to my head during my runs. I learned that I was programmed to look for obstacles to overcome, and that overcoming these obstacles required a different approach than many people prescribe for you. "You're crazy; why don't you just sleep in an hour and run when the sun comes up?" *Because that's what everyone else will be doing, and I know that putting myself through a little pain now is really what I need. I know I need to wake up and practice this conscious effort of removing limiting beliefs, of pushing boundaries, of paying the rent for success every day.* Cheeky, but sincere.

As I grew older and graduated from organized sports, I began to miss the discipline of training during hockey or lacrosse season. I craved that post-workout feeling after I had poured everything out onto the field, my face red and warm, sweat still cooling off, steam floating from my shoulders, sniffles, mucus, thirst for a few bottles of Gatorade, and that feeling of accomplishment. Accomplishment is that much more rewarding when I didn't feel like showing up to practice, and yet I rolled up my sleeves and began digging in, one rep at a time. After all, your thoughts and your feelings are not exactly reality. They can deceive you and cause you to "think" you are tired, or "feel" like skipping practice.

Lesson: When you think you are exhausted, whether in sports, academics, or any passion project, you usually have a hidden reservoir to tap into. And when you are told you aren't good enough for any team, find ways to prove to yourself that you are.

Death, Fear, and Stress

"If we are ever to enjoy life, now is the time—not tomorrow, nor next year, nor in some future life after we have died . . . today should always be our most wonderful day." (Thomas Dreier)

"Everything is created twice, first in the mind and then in reality." (Robin Sharma)

We are all created with an eventual expiration. It is a deeply profound reality that we all wrestle with at different points in our life. I still remember the first time I was old enough to wrestle with the idea that one day I would no longer live on this planet. It was deeply depressing. I thought I would miss my parents, siblings, friends, and teammates. What about all my accomplishments, memories, things that I own? Do I ever come back? Is that the end of me for eternity? *I get just one shot at this?* The way we live our lives, however, shields us from grappling with our existence at this deep of a level. We have immediate gratification and distractions that pull us away from these more human and basic questions so that we never have to address such difficult questions and concerns. I try to make more time for purposeful and intentional thought on this topic. When done proactively, it can be deeply inspiring, in a way that gets me to act on things that I might not otherwise have acted on. It makes the present extraordinarily real. At the same time, such contemplation calms me down and centers me. Instead of blocking the thought or trying to push it aside, I can allow it to surface, to address it, to sit with it, and allow it to just be. It can be a real source of power and strength.

Caitriona Loughrey once shared the following sentiment: It feels like the day barely started, and it is already six in the evening. Barely survived on Monday, and it is already Friday. And the month is already over, and the year is almost over, and already forty, fifty, sixty years of our lives have passed, and we realize that we lost parents, friends, colleagues, and it is too late to go back. Despite it being a ticking clock, use this reality to enjoy the remaining time to its fullest. Keep looking for activities that fill you up and bring you joy.[57]

Finally, I encourage you to eliminate "after," as in, "I will do it after. I will say it after. I will think about it after." We leave everything for later like after is ours. What we don't understand is that afterward, the coffee gets cold. Afterward, priorities change. Afterward, the charm is broken. Afterward, health passes. Afterward, the kids grow up. Afterward, parents get old. Afterward, promises are forgotten. Afterward, the day becomes the night. Afterward, life ends. And then it is often too late. Leave nothing for after; receive the gifts all around you in your life, and do it now.[58]

Infections of the Body, Not the Mind

Later in life, I would suffer from a triple infection in my stomach, including a parasitic, bacterial, and viral infection. It started at one of my friends' bachelor parties in Vermont, and it lasted for three months following the initial debacle. I tried multiple antibiotics, many times disrupting my stomach before ever repairing it. And throughout the painful experience, I had lost my focus on controlling my attitude. I started imagining the worst and even fell into depression, almost missing the same friend's wedding in France. It scared me and left me wondering if I would ever improve. I had lost control and felt hopeless.

What I learned through the different trials in my life is that you can always find a way back when you feel lost. You can always pull from a deeper well of faith. Sometimes you feel you are facing a battle that no one else is going through or that no one understands. It can feel lonely, and the internal dialogue in your head can start to turn on you. It can cause you to question reality while stirring up false stories or beliefs. When moments like this happen, I have found that giving up my challenges, the same challenges that I think no one in life can help me with, to God. In other words, I surrender my anxiety.

I know many people who don't believe in God, and I know many people who do believe in God. I also know many people that believe in God, but it is not the same God I believe in. I am not arguing for one group over another. I am arguing that you find within yourself something or someone who can lead you out of darkness. I am urging you to consider the brilliance that you and I and all of us are here, on this planet, today and that someone or something greater than our own humanity is either a creator or, at minimum, part of our lives and existing now. What I am talking about is faith. Blind faith. Childlike faith. At any point in your life, if you feel out of control, scared, or like you are losing your grip, let go of it—all of it. Give it up to God, your God. The God who never lets you walk alone, who is always there for you.

When my gastroenterologist told me that I still had the infection, after taking two very heavy antibiotics for two months, I was devastated. The chances of beating these infections were slim, especially since there was only one other possible antibiotic that was recommended after exhausting efforts on the other two. *Would the infections become resistant to antibiotics? Am I causing future stomach issues by taking so much medicine? What if I am never the same?* These were all questions circling in my head throughout the day and night. I started praying the novena with my wife, Betta, every morning when I woke up. I let go of my fear and I turned to my faith. I prayed for ten days, with no expectation of a favorable result, but I did pray sincerely. I will be the first to tell you, I am no angel. I am even writing a book about some, not even all, of my mistakes in life. I would need an appendix the size of an encyclopedia for that and an entire afternoon to describe to a priest my wrongdoings. However, not only do I consider my many weaknesses as ailments in my own faith journey, but also, the most disastrous of all my struggles with my faith is my wavering faith itself. Like so many others, I have questioned God, I have disrespected my faith, and I have altogether lost it during moments of my life, good and bad. Heck, when the times are good, let them roll. Sure, it is nice to think God is playing a role in the background, but do I really believe that? *Perhaps I only made the hockey team because my dad is coaching? Oh boy, here we go again.* And when times are bad, God has left me stranded alone. *Where was my faith and God when I most needed them?* Some of the most religious people I know, who have studied philosophy and theology, share a very similar characteristic: their internal struggle with their own faith. And in this moment of my life, I, too, felt like my prayers were unanswered.

Despite how I felt about my faith, I still listened to the novena prayer in the song version, and the lyrics eventually started swirling in my head, flushing out the previous negative loop of thoughts. If nothing else, my prayers washed out all the negative energy fueling my central nervous system. I felt like I was able to surrender and allow someone else to take over for me. It was truly powerful and still brings unmistakable relief to me when I think back on the experience.

But what I also learned, and what I continue to improve upon, is how to control your mind. How to physically breathe positive thoughts into your mind as well as how to let go while doing so. There will be more stories on faith, stress, and overcoming challenges in the pages that follow, but I hope that if you are going through anything seemingly small or large in your life, something that is stealing your peace, hope, or happiness, remember that you can always change the way you think about something. You can biologically alter your energy by intentionally escaping your negative feedback loop in search of more fulfilling thoughts. Nothing has agency over your mind so long as you learn to understand you are not your thoughts. You are the person watching your thoughts, like a movie, and you can intentionally decipher what is true and what is false. And if that doesn't work, you can always give it up to God.

Lesson: At the end of the day, before you close your eyes at night, whatever the issue, give it up to God.

Panic Attacks

I have always struggled with a deeply emotional Achilles' heel, from childhood through adulthood, that has caused me internal depression, fear, and anxiety. Mostly though, it has stolen a lot of my inner peace, because even when I am not experiencing this dreaded sensation of panic, the insidious thoughts that set off a panic attack are always lurking in the background. I am always one stray thought away from panic overload, and after that tipping point is reached, my emotional state becomes like a weighted toy at the bottom of the pool. Trapped inside my own head and my own worries, the anxiety first starts small, feeding my mind with negative thoughts about what could happen to my family's health, or even my own, but then becoming more worrisome and impending, like the doom I fear might arrive tomorrow.

Most of my grandparents passed away before I was ten years old, all due to different medical diseases, while another family member passed away while sleeping at an early age. It is remarkable how you can remember exactly how you feel and where you were when you get the sudden and devastating news, even though you hardly ever remember anything that was said. This kind of trauma leaves a lasting mark on your memory, and it was certainly left undealt with in my own mind for many years.

While I observed more of my closest family members leaving me, I was not as attuned to the shift in my own internal behavior. Inside me, my internal fear gauge was like a bonfire with one log after another being thrown into the fire. Starting as smoke, I didn't realize how big a problem it was until it was too late to put it out.

"Mom, wake up. Can you feel my chest? It really hurts."

"Huh? What is it, Kevin? Are you okay? Here, let me take a look."

"See, you hear it, right? Something sounds odd."

"Well I can feel your heart beating fast; maybe you are working yourself up."

"I really don't like this feeling. What should we do?"

As we climbed into the car on our way to the hospital, I began to experience my first moment of competing anxieties. On one hand, I was anxious about my health. *Am I okay? Is this the end for me? Why is this happening to me?* But on the other hand, I was becoming so worried about my health that my worry was scaring me. I was worried about my worry. So when I got to the hospital and I started hearing doctors say things like, "We usually don't see anyone your age in here; I don't like to see this," my anxiety went into overdrive.

After a few hours attached to an EKG monitor in the middle of the night, the doctor came in to have a talk. "There is not much I really see going on; we have been watching the tape for a while now." Quickly, I felt the need to speak up for myself; this place was the last place I wanted to be, especially as my worry created an avalanche effect of worry, so I decided to say what I thought would give me the best chance for a jailbreak and to get all these wires off my ten-year-old body. "I actually feel a lot better; I think everything is okay with me." Shocked at my own turnaround, my mom and the doctor looked at each other suspiciously. But after taking my interest into account and weighing how to react, my mom landed on, "Okay, Kevin. I am glad you listened to your body; let's go get you home now."

This would have been a great lesson in how to better deal with anxiety, except the moment I left the hospital and stepped back out into the world, my mind played a nasty, cruel, and unforgivable trick on me. *Wait a second; that doctor said that there is not much really going on, but was there something small going on he was about to share? Did I cut him off? Is there something wrong and we just don't know about it? How can we be sure?* And just like that, I left the hospital that night, after battling an anxiety attack about my anxiety attack. It was a lot for a ten-year-old kid, so I did what any struggling child would do with questions unanswered. I spent years relying on WebMD to solve all my ailments, rarely real and almost always imaginary. It was this second layer of anxiety, the uncertainty around my health, that hatched a whole new level of stress that would bog me down in other various moments in my life.

Years later as an adult, I was back at the same hospital on a similar midnight run-in. I woke up feeling chest pains again. *Was it from my workout? Maybe I was sleeping in a position that stretched my upper body and it's probably just a pulled muscle.* Time was my greatest enemy. As each passing second went by, all I could think about was exactly that—each passing second. With each second, my pain seemed to get worse, and I began to worry I was losing time to get from my bed to the hospital. After my early days with panic attacks, I became a self-diagnosed hypochondriac, which is essentially a big, fat, scaredy cat.

Once again, I had allowed my thoughts to steal me from reality. Sure, I had some family experiences that likely led me to harboring a greater degree of concern for my own health, but I really attribute it to not having control over myself. These moments are scary, for anyone. You might not be a hypochondriac or suffer from panic attacks, but you might have another type of worry about your body, how you look, or most importantly, how you feel. In his book *Finding Ultra*, Rich Roll talks about climbing his staircase to bed at the age of forty at two in the morning, and the crippling fear he felt when he found himself out of breath, with a belly full of alcohol and sweets.[59] Fear is common, and sometimes we don't even notice our fear in the background. Or in my case, it lays dormant until I let my guard down and the fortress of resilience and positive mindfulness is sieged, leading to a big, fat, panic attack for a big, fat, scaredy cat.

Not only has health anxiety been my Achilles' heel in life, but so, too, has been the fear of seeing others depart. I am so scared to lose people. Family, friends, clients, colleagues, the stranger I met while living my routine life. I care so deeply about them, and I know how fragile life can be. In some ways, this emotional intelligence has provided me with an unparalleled perspective on life, and it has enabled me to foster many of the good traits I am advocating for in this book, like going after what you want, apologizing to others, forgiving others, and creating a life of significance, if not a life of maximum presence. But many times, this seemingly redeeming characteristic of mine, of caring deeply about those in my life, can cause me too much introspection and too much passion. In other words, I can become too obsessed with the idea of being all things to all people, you know, just in case something bad were to happen. *Ah, it's probably just my anxiety*, I think, but at times it can become a constant tradeoff in my mind between competing interests, like seeing friends or spending time with family. In moments when I catch myself feeling too obsessed, I tell myself to let go. Let go of the anxiety, as if I have any control to begin with. Let go of the expectation to be present for everybody at every moment. Find balance in your life, so you can enjoy other people without holding the fear of leaving others, even if for a short few moments. Waving goodbye to visitors and leaving guests will forever be the hardest moments for me. My sisters also diagnosed me with another -ism (how fun of them). Add it to the list, right? They call me a hyper-sensitive person (HSP), and it just means I tend to—their words, not mine—"feel the feels more." I have a deeply rooted sense of loyalty and compassion, and I feel like I need to show up for everyone all the time, sometimes forgetting to show up for myself and my own needs to let go.

When my father discovered the need for open-heart surgery, he had waited until halfway through our family vacation to let our family know. To this day, I don't know if he was more scared to go through with the surgery or to tell his kids he was having it to begin with. It became another moment in my health anxiety journey, which I have worked to overcome in my mind. The first twenty-four hours of finding out went something like this:

Over a big family dinner, my mom said, "What a great dinner this is. Does everyone have their wine and food?"

My sisters replied, "Thanks, Mom and Dad, this is such a fun family vacation. So glad we could travel to Nevis and experience this amazing destination as a family. I love you guys." They aren't twins, but they sure act like them. At least the kind that finish their sentences.

Conversation continued, and my mom leaned over her plate to start a sidebar conversation with me.

"Hey, nothing to worry about . . ."

Always a very worrying thing to say.

". . . But I think you should get your health checked out. I know you bring up that stuff sometimes. You know, just to have a baseline and so you can feel better about yourself."

I knew Mom was always great about taking care of her health. Like every pre-flight video instructed, Mom was always good about reminding us, "Put your own oxygen mask on first."

But this time felt different. Though my antennas were up, I let it slide for now.

Later the next day, as we were sipping piña coladas on the beach, Dad must've thought now was a good time to tell his kids about his impending surgery. When is a good time to drop that kind of news, anyway?

"Hey, guys, can I talk to you for a second?"

"Uh, yeah? Don't sound so ominous though, what is going on?"

He was clearly fidgeting; not often do you get to practice giving this kind of speech in front of your family.

"It's cool and all, nothing to worry about, but I wanted to share with you that I had a doctor's appointment, and it looks like I will be needing surgery."

My younger sister quickly chimed in. "What kind of surgery?"

Cat is out of the back, so cut to the chase.

"Open-heart surgery."

I don't remember anything he said after that. I just remember leaning back on my beach chair, hidden beneath my sunglasses, staring out at the ocean. *I knew it. I always knew it. See, bad things do happen to good people. Damn, this sucks.* The rest sounded like a scene from Charlie Brown. I couldn't make out a single word. All I could think about was, *Is my dad going to leave me like the others?*

The uncertainty, especially since I knew nothing about open-heart surgery except that it sounds scary as sh*t, was the most troubling. It wrecked me. And others noticed.

I cried most dinners that vacation, in the bathroom of course, but that wasn't the giveaway. It was most likely the strange tradeoff between the loud, fun-filled dinners, usually consisting of too many island cocktails and dance parties, followed by eerily quiet mornings on the beach, with ocean waves and beach plows the only mind-numbing background noise. The metal pieces on the plow caused an industrial and metallic clanking sound, similar to the gears turning in my own head. What I found later to be even more troublesome was the conversation my mom had with me in the car ride home from the hospital after the surgery.

"Kevin, I am worried about you. You are obsessing over your dad, and it is not healthy."

I probably knew that in my mind, but to hear it out loud from my mom really stung, especially since she was spot-on. It sucks getting such accurate feedback sometimes. Here I go again, my personal anxiety about my own well-being, or lack thereof, competing against my health anxiety about someone else's health. It was a negative feedback loop's dream. On and on it went. Sitting in the car as we drove along the Henry Hudson Parkway, the ping-pong back and forth battle raged in my mind.

Is my dad okay?

Shoot, you're doing it; you're caring too much.

Am I okay?

Of course you're okay; you are such a hypochondriac.

Maybe your health is okay, but your well-being isn't. You are obsessing over this.

Now your mom thinks you have a problem.

You are so pathetic! Grow up.

It was a disaster. But luckily, it was a necessary disaster, and my mom helped me out of my tailspin. Brace yourself for the cliché: we can't do it alone. It takes the careful watch and love of others. My mom didn't pull me out of the hole I was in; she jumped down and sat there with me. She told me what I needed to hear and brushed the dirt off my shoulder. Instead of walking me out herself, she gave me the necessary nudge to pick myself back up. She knew me better than I knew me. It was on me to get out of my head, not on anyone else.

Lesson: "You may not control all the events that happen to you, but you can decide not to be reduced by them." (Maya Angelou)

Let Death Be Your Compass

"You fear death because you crave life. You fear death because you think there's something to get that you have not experienced yet. Many people feel that death will take something away from them. The wise person realizes that death is constantly giving them something: death is giving meaning to your life. You're the one who throws your life away, wasting every second of it. You get in your car, drive from here to there, and you don't see anything. You're not even there. You're busy thinking about what you're going to do next. You're a month ahead of yourself or even a year. You're not living your life. So it is you who throws your life away, not death. Death actually helps you get your life back by making you pay attention to the moment. It makes you say, 'My God, I am going to lose this.' I'm going to lose my children. This could be the last time I see them. From now on I am going to pay more attention to them and to my spouse and to all my friends and loved ones. I want to get so much more out of life." (Michael A. Singer, *The Untethered* Soul)[60]

Death is a gift in that it can teach us to live every moment we are offered. It can turn seemingly big problems into small problems, and it can help you refocus your attention away from all the distractions, worries, and anxieties of life and help you live peacefully and purposefully. The way to live is to leave it all out on the table. Don't let the fear of death suffocate you or restrain you. Let death fill you up with confidence and inspiration; let death remind you of your being, right now. Much of this book is intended to help you wake up, arise from your sleepiness, and see what is happening right before you.

But death has an unbelievable promise. Even if something terrible happens, we can view it as just another experience of life. Death has made us a remarkable promise, which is that all things are temporary, passing through time and space. If you have patience and resilience, you can overcome any difficulty or challenge facing you at this moment. Nothing is permanent; everything is possible.

Steve Jobs once said, "Remembering that I'll be dead soon is the most important tool I've ever encountered to help me make the big choices in life. Because almost everything—all external expectations, all pride, all fear of embarrassment or failure—these things just fall away in the face of death, leaving only what is truly important. Remembering that you are going to die is the best way I know to avoid the trap of thinking you have something to lose. You are already naked."[61]

Jobs isn't wrong when it comes to being naked. While we all naturally seek comfort and stability in our lives, there is no doubt that at the end of the day, our days will end. But if you can harness this realization to help you better serve your purpose in this life and in this world, you can be truly unstoppable. Those willing to acquiesce and surrender to this fact will retain greater resolve, more enthusiasm, and will reap the joys and gifts of this world tenfold.

Jobs is not the only one with such motivating sentiment. Just take it from John Soforic, author of *The Wealthy Gardener,* when he said, "Here lies a man with unfulfilled potential, who chose safety and ease over discomfort, who opted for excuses over sacrifices, who waited until it was too late, and in turn denied the world the gift of his beautiful dream. Learn from a fool who chose comfort, and vow to never ignore your own inner wisdom."[62] It is easy to let time slip by and to push your goals off, but the consequences of doing so are far too disappointing. Too many of us sit on the sidelines, waiting for the coach to put us in.

When anxiety or fear or lack of motivation take over, flip the script on the narrative you might be telling yourself. Ask yourself, "Why not me? Why can't I be the one?" You can learn to retrain your brain to actually elevate yourself, to spur you into action, and to overcome any limiting beliefs that keep you on the sideline and away from the game.

Lesson: If you are living every experience fully, then death doesn't have anything to take away from you. There is nothing to take because you're already fulfilled.

A Fable on Taking Action

Three frogs are sitting on a log. One of the frogs decides that he is going to jump off. How many frogs are left?

The answer is three.

The difference is between intent and action. Simply deciding something is not the same as doing it. Your decisions won't become reality until they're backed by action.

One Thousand Miles around New Zealand with Manny

The steering wheel was shaking, and you could smell the diesel from inside the car. The windshield wipers moved in slow motion, barely clearing the torrential rain from the windshield. Watching the wipers was like watching two delicate and experienced skiers gracefully, and in a synchronized fashion, carve big, wide turns on a square blue ski trail. Not sharp turns, not tight back-and-forth carvings, but rather a smooth and ponderous back and forth, back and forth, almost with a pause between the change in direction. Hardly the utility you want out of a car embarking on a trip of over one thousand miles on the North Island of New Zealand. The car's name was Manny, and Manny was specially tuned just for us Americans. In other words, the owner of the Land Rover had just converted the car from manual to automatic for the first time, and only a mere few hours ago. *Let's hope it lasts*, I thought to myself.

My wife, Betta, and I had just arrived in paradise; however, we were welcomed with dark skies and torrential downpour. It was not the kind of rain that gets only the front of your pants wet. That rain is bad enough, but this was the kind of rain that gets both the front and the back of your pants wet, so there was absolutely no hiding from this unrelenting storm.

Twenty minutes into our one-thousand-mile adventure through the North Island, we witnessed something that would truly shake us up. Only minutes before departing, the TomTom (the GPS) started to work, and we were soon whizzing by cars on the highway with no barricade and at dangerously fast speeds given the conditions on the road. Suddenly, as if out of a movie, a truck swiped a car in passing, and both vehicles turned on their side and slid down the highway, kicking up metal parts and sparks before coming to a standstill. Here we found ourselves, in a foreign country, embarking on a two-week trip with our new pal Manny, and in an incessant storm. Here comes our first real test.

Immediately, I pulled over and jumped out of the car, ran past the three cars ahead of us, and arrived at the scene, where a father and his son were trapped in the front seat. Thank God, they were both buckled, but nonetheless they were hanging sideways. A few others and I pulled them out of the car and onto the side of the road, where glass and plastic were spilled along the entire highway for the length of a football stadium. Cars were at a complete halt and were lined up for miles. Everyone in the accident was safely rescued and eventually taken care of by the proper health-care professionals, but from that moment on, Elisabetta and I had a tough task ahead: allow this moment to distract us for the remainder of the trip, or find a way to put it behind us and move on.

This made me think of an old tale from *The Untethered Soul*: "The sparrow is not worried about tomorrow, or the troubles to come. The lily is not thinking about the seasons, the drought or the flood. The tree that is planted by the water isn't fazed by the fire. So why should I be?"[63] Elisabetta and I took a few deep breaths and continued with our trip. Though we did not completely eliminate that memory from our brains, we faced our fears and told ourselves that it was safe for us to move forward

Fear is one of the most useless emotions I have experienced in life. Yes, as a human species, we require our fight-or-flight instincts to survive, adapt, and overcome danger. The fight-or-flight instinct is important and can catalyze the proper reaction in certain situations, like boosting us full of adrenaline when we most need it. But I am not talking about our instincts in this situation. Instead, I am talking about how we give so much power to the idea of fear, especially before there is even anything to fear. We spend so much time stressed about what could happen that we lose sight of what is actually happening, which usually is totally normal, safe, and according to plan. Fear can be dangerous if left unchecked because it causes us unnecessary stress before an event occurs, or even when an event never occurs at all. It is debilitating, and it steals the present away from you. It robs your present peace by distracting you with future anxiety about potential upcoming events, most of which never transpire.

Many of us fear that we will hurt people's feelings by telling them the hard truths they might need to hear. I was reminded of this truth by June Jordan in *Some of Us Did Not Die*: "As a child I was taught that to tell the truth was often painful. As an adult I have learned that not to tell the truth is even more painful, and that the fear of telling the truth—whatever the truth may be—that fear is the most painful sensation of a moral life."[64] The fear of holding something in, of not letting out what you need to say, even if it will cause you pain, is far worse than the actual act and pain of saying that very difficult thing to someone. Of course, there are many times you should use your head and put some thought to your actions, but what this illustrates is that we should get out of our heads, master our fear, and not overanalyze all the ways things can go wrong, which will destroy us beyond anything else.

I am reminded by another anecdote from *The Art of Dreaming*, especially when I think about fear stealing your inner peace and inner present moment. Carlos Castenada writes, "If you're having a wonderful experience, the experience is coming to you via thought; if you're having a horrible experience, well, that's made of thought too. The wonderful thing about thought is that it can change in a heartbeat. And once you really begin to understand how your thoughts create your reality, you will no longer be a victim of the process. The secret is that we live in a world of thought, not circumstances. The mind works like a projector, not a camera, which is to say we experience what we think, not some kind of objective reality. Of course, just because a thought pops into our head doesn't mean it will immediately manifest in the world of form. If it did, there would be more deaths by roller coasters going off their tracks, people falling from very high places, and heads exploding due to stress than any other cause. That is because in and of themselves, thoughts have no power. It's only when you breathe life into them that they begin to seem real."[65]

What is it that makes our thoughts seem to be so powerful? It seems that the more we invest our attention in our thoughts, the more real they start to feel. As *The Art of Dreaming* suggests, when we unconsciously create more demons than angels without noticing that they flow from the same pen, we stress ourselves out and create more fear; when we purposefully orient our thoughts toward the goodness in life, we enjoy our lives more and reduce our stress. Simply even just noticing the energy of thoughts surfacing, taking form, and fading away back into nothingness will usually lead to a better quality of experience than bringing in the search-and-rescue team to control our misleading thoughts.[66]

Lesson: "If you are distressed by anything external, the pain is not due to the thing itself, but to your estimate of it, and this you have the power to revoke at any moment." (Marcus Aurelius)

Keeping Stress in Check

You and I walk around every day with preconceived notions in our own heads of how the world ought to be and how things ought to work out. You might not even realize that you organize your thoughts and your world in a nice template according to the definitions and values you place on this "system of natural order" you have created. For example:

"Someone should hold the door for me because I am holding a baby."

"During the holidays, we should give back to those less fortunate."

These notions become the playbook for your expectations. These notions will cause you to assert your will against what has already happened.

Let's say that seeing pumpkin pie stresses you out. It is unlikely to stress out many others, if any at all. In fact, a lot of people dream about enjoying pumpkin pie with a scoop of ice cream or whipped cream. So then, why does the pumpkin pie bother you? Maybe pumpkin pie reminds you of a boyfriend or girlfriend who made pumpkin pie and broke up with you around Thanksgiving. Now every time you smell pumpkin pie or see it listed in the dessert menu, your heart closes. You can't even stand to go near the darn thing because it triggers something painful inside you and causes you to resist. You see, these personal events in life leave impressions on our hearts and minds. These impressions can be caused by events of fear, disappointment, success, or in this case, stress.

These impressions left on our hearts and minds become the basis for asserting our will to either resist or cling to that very experience. The events may have happened in our childhoods (like the stories and impressions I am sharing with you in this book) or at various moments in our lives. Regardless, when they happened, they left impressions inside of us, sometimes favorable impressions of joy and happiness and other times of sadness and stress. Here is the trouble, however. Based on these past impressions that have been ironed into our minds, we begin resisting current events that are taking place here and now, creating inner tension, turmoil, struggle, and suffering. This is called stress. Think about the last time you were unprepared for something, like a test, a vacation, a birthday party, or a work assignment. The embarrassment of not feeling prepared left a mark in your heart, and either you never want to feel unprepared again, or you shirk from any responsibility or assignment that could bring back that stress again. Essentially, fight or flight. Step up or step back.

Think of how much energy is wasted resisting what has already happened. Since the event has already passed, you are actually struggling with yourself, not with the event. You are struggling with the boundaries and restrictions you have placed on yourself because of the event. In addition, contemplate how much energy is wasted resisting what might happen in the future. Since most of the things you think might never happen, you are just throwing away your energy today. You dream up all these schemes in your mind about how you will get stage fright, forget your lyrics, or trip over yourself when you see the big lights. Most of the time, we create fear in our own minds without any evidence or reasoning. If you don't learn to take control of this energy flow, it will trap you for life.

If, for example, you try resisting the energy from an event that has already occurred in life, it is like trying to stop the clouds from moving over a mountain peak. No matter what you try to do, the cloud will move right through you and continue forward. Anything you do to try to stop it could cause more disturbance, not less. If you try waving at the cloud with your fist or swarming it with your arms, only you will be left exhausted, while the cloud formation remains unchanged.

Trevor Hall sings about walking the path of surrender. Deep inner release is that path, as he sings about letting go of the stones you carry and the stress that weighs you down. Instead of resisting an event that has stressed you out, walk the path of nonresistance, the path of acceptance.

This is our predicament in life. We have experienced events that have left marks in our minds and on the energies inside of us, and for some reason, we choose to hold onto this energy by resisting the very event that has already happened. It is done and has already passed through, so let it pass through. If you don't, you will be left facing the events of the present moment, and you will not be prepared to experience them fully. You are focused on past energies and past events, rather than present energies and present events. And if left unchecked, the energies can bubble up to the point that you either implode or, contrarily, decide to just shut down to the world and the people around you. A lot of people call this "burnout."

There is no reason to get stressed out, to feel burnt out, or to shut down. If you are consciously aware of the stranglehold you place on these negative energies, you can learn to loosen your grip and let them slip on by like a passing cloud. Most importantly, though, you can take back the present moment going on in your life right this second. You can stop worrying about the past and start accepting the present.

If this is not something easy for you, don't sweat it. Pick yourself up and tell yourself you are going to get better at letting go. This is the work of a lifetime for all of us; it is the journey of opening up and learning how to relax and release energies that are harmful to ourselves. If you can, learn to focus on what is in front of you here and now. Someone once told me, "No one will think about what you said yesterday more than you will think about it." If you spend your time worried what your friend will think of you because you said something slightly out of character, or you wore something to school that might not have been your favorite outfit, you will have spent an incomparably greater amount of time replaying these events in your head than the person you are worried about who witnessed them. Let go of your past thoughts, and embrace what is in front of you. You just might feel more peace and contentment, and eventually hardly anything will ever disturb you again. So go ahead, wave at that driver flipping you off and speeding by you, and don't forget to wish them a great day.

Lesson: How you deal with your energy flow has a major effect on your life. Learn to stop resisting reality, and what used to look like stressful problems will begin to look like stepping stones to your spiritual journey.

Career

MBA vs. PSD (Poor, Smart, and Deep Desire)

A memo from Alan Greenberg: Work
To all General and Limited Partners: May 5, 1981, Bear Stearns
    There has been a lot of publicity lately about firms hiring students with MBA degrees. I think it is important that we continue a policy that has helped us prosper while growing from 700 people eight years ago to over 2,600 today.
    Our first desire is to promote from within. If somebody with an MBA degree applies for a job, we will certainly not hold it against them, but we are really looking for people with PSD* degrees. They built this firm, and there are plenty around because our competition seems to be restricting themselves to MBAs.
    If we are smart, we will end up with the future Cy Lewises, Gus Levys and Bunny Laskers. These men made their mark with a high school degree and a PSD.[67]

Like me, you might find yourself running around, looking busy and trying every possible effective life hack to increase efficiency—all the while hiding this fact from others—hoping to make them think you are like a duck in water, showing an elegant equanimity on the surface but paddling your butt off underneath the water.

When choosing a project or a path, you might be inclined to take action immediately. This can be a great quality; however, if you do not put enough thought into what deserves your attention and effort, you can end up spending your time on precious nothings with little to show later in life. Many people rarely slow down enough to notice the impact of recurring challenges that come up again and again, because they are not conscious of go-go-go behaviors until they take time to intentionally slow down and watch and observe what challenges they truly face and what next steps make the most sense. Don't get me wrong; I am not arguing for a wavering and laid-back approach to your career, but I am favoring the idea of discovery, of slowing down and breaking out of the unconscious busyness that blocks us from identifying the true purpose we want to serve.

Adam Grant shares, "Big career decisions don't come with a map, but all you need is a compass. The right next move is the one that brings you a step closer to living your core values. In an unpredictable world, you can't make a master plan. You can only gauge whether you're on a meaningful path."[68] Focus on the little steps ahead, and the big picture will figure itself out. Additionally, some of us become paralyzed by the paradox of choice, with so many careers to pursue or causes to aid, and so we have a difficult time committing and sticking to any one thing. Rather than making your life's purpose about the individual, or yourself, you could try a method adopted by Frances Perkins. Instead of organizing your life as something that begins and ends with yourself, consider removing yourself from the equation. Ask yourself not, "What do I want from life?" but rather, "What does life want from me? What are my circumstances calling me to do?" This method doesn't call us to create our lives but is a way we are summoned by life. This perspective begins not with the self but with circumstances in which you happen to be embedded. This is the perspective of the world that has existed long before you and will last long after you. You have been thrown into a specific place with specific problems and needs. All of us are part of circumstances that call out for action, whether they involve suffering, needs of family, or the opportunity to communicate some message. These circumstances give us the chance to justify our gifts. The ability to discern your calling depends on the condition of your eyes and ears, and whether they are sensitive enough to understand the assignment your life is giving you.[69]

My first corporate job out of college was at an asset management firm in their leadership training program. I always looked up to the more experienced senior leaders in management and was impressed that they arrived at the office so much earlier than others. One of the managers was reliably the loudest person in our meetings, especially the meetings held at 8:30 in the morning. I wondered to myself if I would ever be that way when I became the leader, if I would ever have that much enthusiasm and excitement one day. And it occurred to me that these leaders probably behaved the way they did because they were getting paid so much money and had overwhelming amounts of responsibility, so they had no choice but to bring their best personality to the office every day.

I am confident that these leaders I looked up to did have bad days, despite their efforts to conceal it, But it only occurred to me a few years later that it was not the money, the responsibility, the expensive suits, or the fancy offices they worked from. It wasn't the driver that chauffeured them to the office either. Instead, it was so much simpler. I later understood that it boiled down to an unmistakable choice of being. For instance, I would think to myself, "When I have that job and those responsibilities, I, too, will just naturally embody the same energy and enthusiasm for my job. I will just automatically and suddenly feel inspired enough to wake up early, get to the office, inspire others around me, and lead my team to victory." I was dead wrong.

Realizing that choice played an outsized role in my being in the office, I started going into the building early, raising my hands at meetings, and voicing my opinions as if I was already a leader. In essence, I began to act and behave like a leader, even though I did not have the title of leader or the experience (yet) of such leadership. It was a mindset shift, which allowed me to be the leader I wanted to be without requiring any outside approval. Not only did my own attitude change in the office, but it dripped into other areas of my life. Regardless of leadership styles such as being outspoken or quiet, all leaders actively choose to adhere to important values, such as treating others with care and kindness and making sure that their concerns are heard. Moreover, a leader wants the team to win, not themselves. My entire being shifted the moment I decided I was going to be a leader, because I chose to embody the qualities and behaviors of a leader. It was a game changer for my career, but it was an even more monumental shift in my life.

Lesson: You don't need to live by your circumstances. You can be the person you want to be despite your circumstances.

The Silent Killer

Nobody could cause more anxiety or fright in me than my seemingly endearing and affable boss.

Ironic?

Yes.

By mistake?

No.

"How is everything going with your program, Kevin?"

Just wait; she is going to turn up the heat on you soon enough.

"Really well; I am meeting many new people, I have been assigned a few important projects, and I am discovering what I like and don't like about each role."

Remember, Kevin, don't let your guard down; keep it at high level.

Silence.

She stared at me with a big, smiling nod. Up and down, slowly and constantly.

Should I keep going? Was that not a good answer? Is she processing what I said? Is she going to ask me another question? Wait, I am confused; whose turn is it to speak now?

I continued, possibly out of turn, "Well, everything is great, except things haven't been going so well with one of the groups. I don't think they see me as a valuable asset to their team at this point."

More silence. Now leaning forward in encouragement.

Are you kidding me? Still nothing? Just the same nods?

Now I was definitely overplaying my hand. "I think that maybe I could put more of an effort and focus on this one group so that they know I care. That way I am not spending all my time with the other groups who have already seen my good work."

It was still so quiet, you could hear my stomach growling. And honestly, at least it broke the silence.

"That is terrific, Kevin. It sounds like you are figuring out a few things."

She knew exactly what she was doing. No agenda, no interrogative interview, and no advice given. She was letting me do all the talking and steering of the conversation, and I had done the one thing I didn't want to do—let my guard down. People do funny things around silence; they feel the need to fill the air. It was a lesson for me on both sides of the fence. I knew that if or when I were in a management role one day, this would be an important skill to emulate. After all, most problems are caused by a lack of communication, and if I could help colleagues share vital information that too often they are afraid to share, we could solve a lot of problems through better communication. Secondly, it became a useful lesson that as an employee, you want to be diligent with how much information you reveal. On the one hand, I probably was too shy in revealing the difficulties I was facing. Most conversations with my boss felt more like performance reviews, so I wanted to make sure there were no dings on my resume. But while it is important to be mindful of what you are sharing, you still want to build trust and relationships by sharing some of the more difficult situations. Like with social media, a perfectionist does not get far in corporate settings.

I admit, this incredible awareness of hers sometimes still haunts me in my nightmares. She was the best listener I ever met. Her skill was silence. And it was deadly. She would often pretend not to know the specifics of a situation I was describing, just to get me to talk more. What I learned, however, was that by the time I finished talking, I had spilled the beans, come around to her side, or talked myself into agreeing with much of what she wanted to hear. *Anything to fill that dead air.*

What she knew, which I did not at the time, was that if you ask a question on a particular subject and the answer is unsatisfactory, the best response is none at all. More silence. She might have been looking for more information or for some other type of information, and she knew to ask for it by remaining silent. As you and I both know, silence is extremely uncomfortable, and most of us feel an overwhelming need to fill the dead air.

If I were to reverse the roles, I would suggest to my younger self to bite my tongue when any questions were asked. Biting my tongue would have allowed me to collect my thoughts and possibly be more careful or more judicious in what I had to say. Additionally, it could have precluded me from saying more than I needed to or should be saying to my boss. Once you are on a roll and your mouth starts moving, it is difficult to slow down the momentum—the train has left the station. Instead of being fearful of revealing a hidden secret or of saying the wrong thing, simply be mindful of what you are saying. Take an extra second to gather your thoughts, and speak at a pace that exhibits confidence and thoughtfulness instead of portraying desultory verbiage.

I was one of the worst offenders of the silence rule, but I learned to bask in it over time. Many times, your colleagues, family, or friends withhold information from you, and you might not even know it. Typically, the real answer that they want to say to you, but are either too scared to offend you or haven't felt the presence of a safe environment to share it in, lies within the second or third line of questioning. This is the "Tell me more" moment for us all to implement.

You aren't happy with this project?

Tell me more.

You're unhappy because you felt like you didn't receive credit on the project?

Tell me more.

You want the credit because you are really hoping for a promotion?

Tell me more.

If you don't receive this promotion, you are going to our competitor?

Tell me more.

Without silence, you run the risk of assumption, and you risk losing out on important tidbits from your colleagues, friends, or family. Beware of the head nod. Because the head nod means you lost them. Sure, they may agree with what you are saying by nodding their head, but if you don't give them a chance to arrive at their real answer, which is typically in their third comment after tossing up one or two lobs before the much-anticipated overhead, then they will leave your office no more committed than when they came into your office. Prying a little more, and then remaining silent and not offering your own read on their situation, not only helps you gather new information, but it also helps the other person open up and build trust with you. Silence is an opportunity to share what is on your mind. I have seen so many clients in my career get on the phone with our team or come into the office, expecting to receive an answer and prepared paperwork. As if we hold the key to all their problems. Instead, I do the opposite. I ask more questions; I remain silent. Then I think about it, but I still don't provide an answer to their challenge. I ask another question. Understanding and building trust requires silence. Many times, we are so eager to answer a question and show off our brilliance and our hard work, but when your brain switches from active listening to passive listening, you begin to lose some of the important nuances that are being told to you. You quickly become focused on cramming a solution into a problem, rather than continuing to understand the problem and the many facets that might be affecting it. Silence shows your client or your colleague that you are calm, confident, poised, and thoughtful. There is no rush to prove yourself by addressing the question head on with a solution.

Lesson: Silence is often the best form of an answer, especially until more information is gathered.

On Presentations and Communicating

I had a manager who always used to say, "Tell them what you are going to tell them, tell them, and then tell them what you told them." It is the rule of three, and it is incredibly helpful in organizing a presentation and communicating. Moreover, she used to say, "Don't tell them what to do; tell them exactly what to do." People want to be led, and communication requires specific instructions. Part of accountability is not handing the monkey off your back to someone else, but checking in, seeing if they have any questions, guiding them along the process, and remaining involved, even if at arm's length. The wrong sentiment is that of thinking, "No one can do it the way I want; I might as well just do it myself." Instead, try communicating more clearly the specifics of what you want, stay close to the project to make sure it stays on track, and watch your project success soar.

I also had a manager who could silence a room as soon as he walked in. He spoke slowly, clearly, and intentionally, as if every word had such meaning you couldn't miss it. He had many punchy sayings, but one of his most applicable was, "Make the game shorter." We often get caught up with long-term career ambitions, or deadlines in the future, or the stress of the corporate grind. Instead, he argued for breaking tasks or big projects or goals into tiny chunks. Similar to David Goggins's cookie jar mentality of collecting cookies and building a jar full of successes to build momentum and confidence, making the game smaller helps you focus on what is directly in front of you and removes the sometimes insurmountable time parameters.

Sure, we all would like to be CEO tomorrow, but first make the game smaller by focusing on achieving top-level CEO results in your current role. As John Bytheway says, "Inch by inch, life's a cinch. Yard by yard, life's hard."[70]

How can you achieve top results, no matter where you are in your career? Through what he called simple "blocking and tackling." Most jobs are simple, but not easy. In order to succeed, you will have to work hard at doing a great job at the little things. Show up each day prepared to roll up your sleeves, because consistency is what shows and will move you up. I don't love the sentiment, "Work smarter, not harder." It is true you should work smarter, but there is no replacement for hard work. Call me old-school, but there is no easy way to achieve success. It is going to require some sore muscles and playing while not "100 percent healthy."

When presenting or selling, I also recommend sharpening your message to the most important point by using the BLUF method, which stands for "bottom line up front." It is a powerful communication technique used to convey the most important info first. You can start with the main point, then provide essential supporting details, and conclude with a recap of the main point to reinforce it at the end. James Clear said, "It's not that hard on any given day, but the trick is you can't skip days. Your workouts can be reasonable and still deliver results—if you don't skip days. Your writing sessions can be short and the work will still accumulate—if you don't skip days. As long as you're working, you'll get there."[71]

Lesson: Consistency in effort is what counts.

Speak to Them Straight

"Kevin, you are next. Please make your way to the front of the room where we will all stare at you, judge you, and maybe not even pay attention to you, if you are lucky." That is what I thought my English teacher had told me, but really what she said was, "Kevin, can you please take your hood off?" I was already standing in front of my classmates when I snapped back into it. This was junior year of high school, and I was at an all-time low for confidence when it came to public speaking. *Why does my mouth always get so dry after speaking just five words, anyway? I had five bottles of water before this presentation; shouldn't I be well hydrated?* It wasn't that I forgot to remove my hood; I was actually using it as a physical prop to help me disappear, or at least as much as I could. I had braces, which admittedly is an acceptable step up from the headgear, and I was a new student transfer, so even though I grew up in town, I was amongst many new students from neighboring areas of my town, and there were many kids in class with me whom I had not met growing up.

There is always so much riding on how you are perceived in school, and it feels like no one's judgments actually portend reality. Although, for anyone sitting in the class staring up at me, they were undoubtedly equally as uncomfortable as I was, if not more. There is nothing more uncomfortable for an audience than knowing before the presentation even starts that they are going to have to suffer through a dull presentation. Oh, wait, there is. What is worse? A presentation in which the speaker is completely deflated, lacks any conviction in what he or she is saying, and is noticeably speeding up to finish sooner. But this high school moment wasn't the only time I had anxiety over public speaking.

I was enamored with mostly extroverted leaders growing up, because I recognized in most of them an innate talent to speak in a way that could rile up a crowd. They used language and emotion to help enroll others in their vision. And I was mostly drawn to this skill set because I realized a lack of that within myself. I had all sorts of leadership quotes on my bedroom walls, and I had an insatiable appetite for YouTube videos of best pregame speeches by coaches. I would even rehearse those exact same speeches in the mirror to overcome my fear and fool my brain into thinking I was a capable leader. In third grade, I showed up to my class presentation as Bobby Orr, the professional and Hall-of-Fame Boston Bruins hockey player. I remember feeling so confident to speak in front of my class because I was Bobby, the superstar defenseman who scored the Stanley-Cup-winning goal, not Kevin, the hockey player who made the worst team.

It wasn't until later in my career that I decided to make public speaking my strength. But before I did so, I had one last slipup before getting back on track. I was told I would be speaking in front of my peers, all one hundred of them, at the next sales meeting. I was rotating through a relationship management group at my firm, and we were tasked with running data and analytics on sales, revenue sources, top-performing products, and where we stood competitively amongst our peers on the street. But typically, our firm did not appoint rookies to stand up and deliver the presentation. My manager at the time told me, "Kevin, I am worried to have you speak in front of everyone. The last thing you want is for everyone to despise you." *Yeah, that would be a disaster.* "So, to make sure this doesn't happen, I would be a lot more comfortable if you could mention that you are simply acting as the mouthpiece for our group, not putting out any orders or commands, but simply speaking on behalf of the group at large." *Right, mouthpiece, got it.* What came to follow was a disastrous display of inauthenticity. I went on to tell an entire sales floor how grateful and appreciative I was to be in such an honorable position. I told them how important the work was that we were doing and that I was simply delivering the data from the higher powers that be. After all, I was so grateful for this opportunity to speak and simply fill in as the mouthpiece for the group. Had I not been so focused on my own delivery of the presentation, I would have noticed no one was paying attention, and some were even rolling their eyes or giving each other looks of raised eyebrows that if they could talk would be saying, "Can you believe this guy?"

One of the managers came flying over to me after the presentation and asked me straight up, "What the hell was that?" I couldn't tell if he was smiling at me or genuinely upset. He always did provide transparent feedback, and he liked to push me, sometimes through ridicule, because he knew I could handle it. His opinion mattered to me, because he knew who I was deep down. "Kevin, your message was borderline rude, entitled, and flat-out uncalled for. What got into you?" I was so embarrassed.

Doesn't he know that I was told to say that?

I could feel my defensive nature kicking in, my heart rate elevating, and my blood pressure pumping. But slowly, I began unclenching my jaw and loosening my facial muscles. Instead of giving into my raging desire to defend myself, I took a deep breath and said, "You know what, we need to talk about this. I am so glad you brought this up to me. Thank you for taking that risk; I appreciate the trust it shows in me." In a matter of seconds, I had turned my defensive anger into gratitude. What got me to switch from embarrassment to gratitude was the internal question, *What do I really want here?*

And what I wanted was to be an effective public speaker and leader. I had not understood that to be an effective speaker who could inspire action in others, you must be gifted at dialogue and have an ability to keep safety at the forefront of communication. What do I mean by safety? Great leaders and communicators watch for signs that people are becoming fearful. When friends, family, or colleagues move away from dialogue, such as rolling eyes or nudging one another in the audience, they begin to withhold their ideas from a conversation or a game plan, usually behind your back. But when it is safe, anyone can say anything. After all, dialogue calls for the free flow of information, and nothing blocks this more than fear. When you fear telling someone difficult feedback because of the response it might solicit, you leave that person worse off. But, when you don't fear that you are being attacked or humiliated, you can accept critical feedback instead of growing defensive. Had he not told me how unbearable that speech was, I never would have learned from my mistake.

We all need redemptive assistance from family, friends, colleagues, rules, and traditions. We all need people to tell us when we are wrong, to advise us on how to do right, and to encourage, support, arouse, cooperate, and inspire us along the way. I made a promise to myself that for every speech or presentation going forward in my life, I would start from the heart and be as authentic as possible. I would choose to be me. No mouthpieces.

Public speaking is about finding your own voice, not someone else's. It is about finding common ground with your audience, giving them reasons to trust and like you. Some of the best public speakers are not afraid to embarrass themself and actually look for ways to do so, in order to make the crowd fall in love with them. No one likes a know-it-all, but most like someone who has been in their shoes, has gone through challenges, or is humble enough to just simply say, "I don't know it all, and that is okay." There are thousands of books on public speaking techniques or classes to take, but I would surmise they all would agree with the following: the most important takeaway for anyone about to speak publicly is to forget trying to be someone else, and instead be authentic. Freeze the moment; don't get lost in the land of babble. I like to talk to the crowd as much as I can before I speak, to try to win some people over. Get to know your audience, and put yourself on their level, not above them. And believe in what you have to say. Because your thoughts become your words, and your words become your presentation. And your body will physically adjust to how you are presenting. If you believe in yourself, you will stand up straighter, speak with an engaging tone, and land your most important points. Take the first minute to use pauses, redirect the attention back to the crowd, or just suffer through any initial judgments you feel from the crowd. But after that first minute, get into the groove, and just go for it. Suddenly, your heart rate will normalize, and like a skilled diver, your breath will begin to regulate itself.

As I learned from my manager, it is not what you say, it is what they hear that matters. I had thought I was providing a clear, concise, and impactful message to the sales floor by following the script provided. Even when he confronted me at the end of the day, I argued back that I was getting the message across. He was sure to tell me I had not succeeded in that. You might have the best presentation in the world, but if your audience is not truly hearing you and following you, it doesn't matter what you said. Who cares how long you spent correcting those fine details in the slide or hanging on to every word you memorized. I was taught to give a presentation in threes: first, tell them what you are going to tell them, then tell them what you want to tell them, and then finally tell them what you already told them. Three is a magical number, and following this method removes the paradox of choice, which occurs when you provide someone with too many options, such as seven or fifteen, for example. Your brain becomes frozen by the paradox of choice, and instead of liberating someone with all the choices, they become imprisoned by them. The other coaching I have received about my many botched presentations is to read the audience. If I am losing them, it is okay to stop or pause and check in. "Hey, everyone, I can tell I am maybe drifting into an irrelevant topic; what topic would most interest you at this point?" Or something like, "I am going to let you all read about this on your own time; let's move on to the next point." If you are rushing through a presentation, like I was on the day I was wearing my hood in school, then you will miss these cues from your audience. Think about the movie *Dodgeball*, when Vince Vaughn puts the blindfold over his eyes before throwing the ball. It's a silly example, but he is attuned to his surroundings. That is how you want to be when presenting. Take your time, and be aware of your environment so you can course correct even during your presentation.

Lesson: Slow is smooth, and smooth is fast. Don't forget to be yourself, because everyone else is already taken.

~~Why I Left Gorman Slacks~~ Why Gorman Slacks Never Invited Me In

The room felt sterile, almost like an operating room, with incandescent lighting portraying a scene from the *Twilight Zone*, casting uncertainty and fear into every wobbly-knee interview candidate. I sat with my hands crossed in my legs, innocuously scanning the talent around me while taking deep, slow breaths to distract me from the pressure building up in the room.

Someone once told me that all companies hide cameras in the conference rooms during super day interviews, so that management can discreetly assess you on your interpersonal skills and how you engage with the other candidates. Whether it was true or not, like any good hypersensitive person, I was tuned into all my surroundings, and I made sure to make pleasantries with each candidate just in case. But no one wanted to converse with me; they either saw me as a threat or someone who had no chance of receiving an offer, so why waste their time with me. Instead, they pored over their resumes and pristine folders, while I hardly glanced down at my own. Like an NFL draft, with every ticking minute that goes by, you start to wonder if your number will ever get called. And if you are not careful, you get too caught up in judging those around you, putting yourself down so as to make way for the flawless resumes to stomp all over you. *Is that person's resume printed on bond paper made of fiber pulp? Oh, man, I am screwed.*

After turning any entire waiting room of candidates against me—*all I was trying to do was lighten the mood with some friendly conversation*—I was finally called into the interview room. As Alexander Hamilton might declare, the room where it happens. Either it was finally my turn to put on the Gorman Slacks ball cap and take a celebrity shot with the management team that drafted me in front of thousands of fans, or they really were watching us on camera, and they did whatever it took to remove me from distracting the other talented, and may I say, exceedingly more qualified candidates.

My hypersensitivity was kicking in as I started going through my NASA-like checklist of important matters to handle before heading into the interview.

Shoes are shining?

Check.

No wrinkles in the suit pants from crossing your legs in the conference room chairs?

Check.

Tie is pulled all the way up to the collar?

Check.

Nothing in my teeth?

Check.

Then came the incessant line of questioning myself.

Should I hold the folder in my left arm so I can shake with my right hand?

Should I ask them how they are doing first, or wait for them to start the conversation?

How much time should I spend asking about them?

I wrote down ten questions, but which one is the most appropriate to ask?

How am I going to tackle any critical reasoning questions?

Can the Empire State building hold ten billion basketballs or ten trillion?

Wait, what will the kid with the bond paper resume say? Ten billion soccer balls?

If I could fix the New York subway system, what would I change?

Crap. I don't know anything about the subway system.

Instead of living in the present momentum, I was miles ahead in the distant future. This was a huge mistake; although I am a believer in overpreparing and then going with the flow, this was an epic mental collapse of overthinking. I quickly went from cool, calm, and collected to obsessive overdrive. My old boss would say, "Just be you," and I wasn't being myself. I had lost my balance and was teetering into a full-blown Jerry Maguire who just realized he was fired—and flipper wasn't coming with me this time. While you might experience your own defensive line blitz at times in life, it is important to remember to get yourself back in line by making any necessary course corrections. In order to do so, you need a trigger that can reroute your internal chatter, similar to an audible play call in football. The quarterback reads the defense's coverage, realizes the play call is at risk, and has the presence of mind to change from the ground to the air.

Controlled internal dialogue around perception is important, however, as it doesn't take much for people to form perceptions. Moreover, it takes even less time for us to make attributions based on these perceptions. Psychologists Nalini Ambady and Robert Rosenthal found that even "thin slice" encounters that last less than fifteen seconds result in strong perceptions about character—how kind, honest, and trustworthy we believe other people are. Perceptions and attributions are made quickly. But more importantly, they tend to endure, even when people learn of evidence to the contrary. Once these attributions are made, they influence how others interact with you, how they assess the value you bring, and what rewards they think you deserve. Therefore, there's a premium on those who are skilled in coordination, negotiation, persuasion, and social perceptiveness. Not only do these types of skills have the most potential to expose us to bias, but they also give us the most opportunities to turn inherent disadvantages into an edge. They give us the chance to guide the process of how people perceive the value we bring.[72] Figuring out your own positioning and your own contexts and failures is what will give you your unique edge against all those other bond paper resumes, as well as all the Bob Sugars of the world. Remain committed in your self-belief, as opposed to spiraling out of control with that incessant line of questioning, and balance that with an awareness that perceptions will be made quickly, so show up as your most authentic, and not distracted, self.

I walked into the room not like Jake Paul on a tank before a Mixed Martial Arts cage fight but like one of those superhero characters with their hands raised above their heads in the mirror, soaking in their own power position. Same thing, right?

"Tell me about yourself." Aha, there is that question again. I wasn't kidding before; people really do ask it all the time.

Okay, I thought, *give them your rehearsed speech about how you love sports and you're a family guy and blah blah blah.* Likely my first strike, a discursive and incoherent answer with no impact and no focus. Unfortunately, I couldn't even see the bored look on the interviewer's face because I was so caught up in sharing my story from grade school through high school. Mistake one. I had already lost my interviewer by taking the bait and going into far more depth than he actually cared about. But it was mistake two that really sent me on a castaway-like raft far off to sea.

"As we wrap up the interview, what would you say are some of your weaknesses?" Well, like any self-deprecating person, I was licking my chops on this one. I thought to myself, this interview is going well—although it wasn't. Being honest and straight may admittedly be admirable, but I lacked the nuanced storytelling required if you are going to share something vulnerable. If you are going to share a weakness, or share anything that might put you in a bad light, make sure you explain what you learned and how you grew from that. Most people don't like a know-it-all, but no one likes the person who just can't seem to learn their lesson.

I answered back with my chest pumped out, "Well, one of my weaknesses is that it sometimes takes me two or three times to learn something."

"Do you think that is something you could work on though?"

"I don't know; probably. I guess it just takes me a while to learn things."

That was it. That was my big reveal. It takes repetition for me to master something. Probably something we can all relate to. And it was also something I have heard from the greats, the truly successful people in life. However, what I failed to grasp was that I needed to have a concluding point. I just served up an Andy Roddick-like serve, but now I needed to get on the other side of the tennis net and put back into play a Serena Williams-like return. Instead, I stared blankly at my interviewer, proud of my self-awareness and honesty, not unlike Ralph from *A Christmas Story* proudly submitting his seemingly flawless essay on his Red Ryder BB Gun. Unfortunately, I lacked the storytelling skills to demonstrate my self-awareness in a self-improving way or in a way that could add value to Gorman Slacks. I forgot to include that my weakness was actually a strength when used in the right way. It was like I built half the bridge and left the other half of the bridge up for interpretation, and the interviewer was not interpreting it any other way than an utter lapse in architectural design.

Morgan Housel has a great segment on this in *The Psychology of Money*, which details, "A good storyteller with a decent idea will always have more influence than someone with a great idea who hopes the facts will speak for themselves. People often wonder why so many unthoughtful people end up in government. The answer is easy: politicians do not win elections to make policies; they make policies to win elections. What's most persuasive to voters isn't whether an idea is right, but whether it narrates a story that confirms what they see and believe in the world. It's hard to overstate this: the main use of facts is their ability to give stories credibility. But the stories are always what persuade me. The best story wins. Not the best idea. Not the right answer. Just whoever tells a story that catches people's attention and gets them to nod their heads."[73] Great ideas explained poorly can go nowhere, while old or wrong ideas told compellingly can ignite a revolution.

This isn't about telling the best story to nail a job interview, and it is definitely not about fabricating the details of a resume or experience. Instead, it is about recognizing that you can start where it's less crowded, and take your time going from inexperienced to professional. You can take the time to master the basics—your own, that is, not those of everyone around you. You should be able to acknowledge, especially to your colleagues, that it takes time to get good at anything, but most importantly, that you enjoy the process of getting better and better each day. Most aspects of jobs are teachable if you are indeed coachable. But what most fail to understand, or at least communicate properly through the right storytelling, is that hiring managers want you to fall in love with the concept of learning. In my opinion, intellectual curiosity and a willingness to fail, learn, and overcome is one of the greatest indicators of long-term success.

Finally, no matter the context of your situation, the more clearly you see the reality of the world, the better equipped you are to deal with it. The less clearly we see the reality of the world, the more our minds are tricked into false narratives and misperceptions and the less we will be able to course correct and make wise decisions. You do not want to be burdened by the need to hide or shrink around the shadows of others, just because of your perceived judgments of them. You do not want to waste effort covering your tracks or maintaining disguises of who you want people to think you are, whether on paper or in reality. The more honest you can be about your strengths and weaknesses, the easier it is to continue being honest, and this will therefore help communicate your story better. By your openness, you will be dedicated to truth and living in openness, and through living in the open, you can become free from fear. Don't be like me in the conference room before my interview, wondering how I could measure up to so many more qualified and talented candidates. Be more like you, aware of your strengths and weaknesses and with a humbled confidence to demonstrate your willingness to learn and be coached, with nothing to hide and not trying to fake it until you make it. As Amy Cuddy says in her TEDx Talk, "Don't fake it until you make it; fake it until you believe it."[74]

Lesson: It is expected that you have weaknesses and failures, but learn to tell great stories about how you overcame them and what you learned from them.

My First Botched Summer Internship

"Show up, be brave, be kind, smile, and don't let anyone steal your peace." (Jim Stroker)

Whether it's your first day on the job, at school, or stepping onto a field to compete, nerves are high for anyone. The ones who can control their emotions and remain calm and composed, especially in the face of stress, will lead an overwhelmingly happier and more fulfilled life, one that embodies relentless optimism and is shielded from the opinions and negativity of others. You will definitely make mistakes, not only in your career but also with your family, your friends, and in every part of your life. But keep your head high, show up the next day, be brave, and protect your inner self-talk. Remain at peace.

Before I jump into the story, I want to preface it with a quote from Adam Grant on growth mindsets and impostor syndrome: "Impostor syndrome: 'I don't know what I'm doing. It's only a matter of time until everyone finds out.' Growth mindset: 'I don't know what I'm doing yet. It's only a matter of time until I figure it out.' The highest form of self-confidence is believing in your ability to learn."[75]

I was eighteen years old when I had my first research internship in finance. I would commute into the city, put on the suit, and "act" like I knew what I was doing (which, of course, I did not). I was eager to accept work, and when my hiring manager approached me about someone who needed help, he let me know that this person had had trouble with interns in the past; some had even cried. But with confidence and self-belief, I took the call and met with this infamous manager. We sat down and got to know each other, and then he gave me the assignment. Piece of cake: Follow his instructions, excel, and receive a full-time job offer. *They'll have me running this place in no time.* After about a week of hard work, I turned the assignment in, and he thanked me. It was out of mind, and I was moving on to the next project.

A few weeks later, I was approached at my desk by the manager, asking to see me in his office. Oh boy, the tone wasn't good, and the setting also felt uncomfortable. There is one great nugget to learn from this manager, and it is this: If you are going to give critical feedback, do it behind closed doors. There is never a time when someone should be embarrassed in front of others. Feeling apprehensive, I knocked on his door after walking the entire floor with my tail between my legs.

"Oh, you can put that notebook and pen away; you are not going to need it," the manager told me.

For the next ten minutes, he went on to berate me with criticism and animosity. He told me how lousy of a job I did and how he could not believe how poor my performance was.

"Why didn't you ask me any questions? What the hell is the matter with you?" he demanded. It was a rhetorical question, so there was no need for me to answer; I knew that much. I couldn't breathe, and my chest was tight. Here I thought I was in for my next great assignment and next mountain to tackle, and instead, I was being shoved around, finding myself in a dark valley as opposed to a bright mountaintop. It was tough love, and though I had a feeling I wasn't about to be handed a cupcake, I still felt blindsided. His face was so visibly irate, and any rapport we had built around our mutual love for guitars was immediately out the window. Afterward, I took a walk outside to collect myself, and I will never forget that aimless walk through the streets of New York City. I am surprised I didn't get hit by a yellow cab during my daze.

I am sure that manager has yet to think twice about me following that situation, but I can tell you I have thought a lot about him. It made me realize a few things. First, you shouldn't blindly accept a project, and you should schedule intermediate check-ins throughout to benchmark and make sure you are on track. Second, you should never be surprised about your performance. You and your manager should have regular updates together so you know exactly where you stand at all times. Third, a manager should not blindly hand over a project either. If you are going to delegate work as a manager, provide the proper instructions and guidance. Don't just pass the monkey. Fourth, how you give feedback is important. If you want your employees or teammates to trust you and keep their confidence, you should find a way that properly explains the missteps, the correction, and the future expectations.

The point is not to belittle someone to the point of tears. Work is very stressful for a lot of people, but you should not let their anxiety, their anger, or their deadlines excuse their negative behavior. Stand up and protect yourself, accept that you will make mistakes, come up with a solution to make sure it won't happen again, and then get back on the wagon and raise your hand for the next assignment. For too long, I let this experience haunt me. I lost my swagger and my desire to take on new projects. But I realized that I was carrying the weight of someone else's opinion far too heavily. This one project did and does not define me. I needed a short memory so I could move on, but instead, I kept replaying this conversation in my head.

Quincy Jones shares some insight about fear after failure and why it is important to dust yourself off and move on: "Cherish your mistakes. Get back up no matter how many times you get knocked down. There are some people who face defeat and retreat, who become cautious and afraid, who deal with fear instead of passion and that isn't right. I know it seems complex, but it's relatively simple; let go and let God. You can't get an A if you're afraid of getting an F. Growth comes from mistakes. Cherish them, so you can learn from them. Your mistakes are your greatest gift."[76]

I had a coach, Jim Stroker, who would say, "Show up, be brave, be kind, smile, and don't let anyone steal your peace." I wish I had remembered this sentiment, because although I had some things to work on, it would have been a great tool and mindset with which to equip myself when I received the beatdown from my boss. One of my failures was the fact that I turtled after this confrontation, that I stopped raising my hand for my assignments.

In a YouTube video, President Barack Obama had advice for similar situations that went as follows: "Just learn how to get stuff done."[77] What he means is that he has seen at every level people who are very good at describing problems, people who are very sophisticated in explaining why something went wrong or why something can't get fixed. "What I am always looking for is no matter how small the problem or how big the problem is, someone says, 'Let me take care of it.' If you project an attitude of 'I can handle it and I can do it,' whoever is running that organization will notice. You don't have to always be so impatient; the best way to get attention, no matter what is assigned to you, is just nailing and killing it; people will notice and think to themselves, 'That's somebody who can get something done.' "[78] While I did eventually get over the scar tissue from such an embarrassing moment, I wish I had taken this advice sooner and that I had immediately asked for my next assignment, instead of shying away from that manager. Just having an attitude to get things done would have shielded me from the desire to run away from my problems.

Lesson: You decide your value. You have to pat yourself on the back and pick yourself up, because most of the time, no one is coming to save you.

Family Business

There is typically a divide between the generation above and the generation below. Who owes what, who deserves what, who earned what, who created what, who continues to grow what. When I first joined my family business, I knew the answers to all of these. Mom did. Mom is the super woman. Mom is the client-centric type, who works all day and night, executes and gets it done, all while making sure to keep up with her family, her social life, and everything else going on. She entered her business when there were very few females involved, and she grew her business after many years of serving her community.

What I had failed to see over the years is the nuance in her famous saying, "If you are not growing, you are dying." There was always a way to improve the client service model, or the business strategy, or the way we worked as a team. But what I realized after many missteps, wrong decisions, and lessons learned was that the quote was missing something. It wasn't just about growing; it was about willingly changing and poking holes in our already established and well-functioning operating model.

Like many businesses in the heat of COVID-19, our team faced operating challenges. We lost three of the last pitch-offs, had no face-to-face contact with clients (an important part of our business), and the phones incessantly rang with client concerns about impending recessions. Hardly the right foot to begin on, especially given the fact we had just started at a new firm. Suddenly it sank in; no one was coming to save us. Though

I was inexperienced in crisis management, the following two years brought a rapidly changing and uncertain environment, as I began stepping out of the shadow of my senior partner and taking responsibility for leading our team out of the darkness.

Over the next two years, belief was forged through a listening tour, as each teammate shared their concerns and vision for the future. We reopened communication lines, and together we pivoted the strategic vision of the business by rebranding and refocusing our service model. While I learned that change is never linear and is a messy one-step-forward and two-step-back process, I also realized this: managing a mature company is not just a constant process of breaking out of archaic structures and policies. You must also be consciously, actively, and aggressively punching holes in the company's conventional wisdom while improving upon inefficiencies.[79] This is a concept Mark McCormack mentions in his book *What They Don't Teach You at Harvard Business School*, and it can be applied to many other businesses.

I had failed at many things, such as understanding the importance of communication in leading a team or how caring for a team in a crisis is just as important as caring for your clients. Gabriel Landeskog, a Colorado Avalanche hockey captain, is on record in a post-game interview, saying, "Sometimes being a leader is not about the rah-rah speech but just looking out for your team." I couldn't agree more, especially looking back on moments when I was trying to be the rah-rah guy but was forgetting to look out for others. But one thing we as a group came out swinging on was change. We took our founding partners' words of wisdom and tweaked it to have an innovative lens to it. We were not only accepting the change under way from COVID-19, but we were actively looking for ways to restructure the normalcy or standard operating procedures of our team. Never waste a good crisis, they say, and we dug our heels in to change on our own terms. Upton Sinclair once said, "It is difficult to get a man to understand something, when his salary [or his job] depends on his not understanding it."[80] Our team rose from the turmoil of COVID-19 and all the saga around these "unprecedented times," and other pandemic-riddled headlines that the media was pushing, and found a way to think outside the box. We were able to step away from our industry's "normal" way of looking at things and to throw rocks at glass windows to start rebuilding with more efficient ways to operate. The idea is to not get bogged down with the way things have always been done but to actively seek out new ways to do them. Rarely are such large events cast upon an entire economy to warrant the wholesale changes sometimes required, but even in the day-to-day operations, there are ways to tweak and add on to the old playbook, to dust off chapters, incorporate new authors, and redesign the cover. Just because your industry has always done it one way and pays you to do it that way does not mean there is not a better way.

Engineer Wei Dai said, "Once you achieve high status, a part of your mind makes you lose interest in the thing that you achieved high status with in the first place. You might feel obligated to maintain an appearance of interest, and defend your position from time to time, but you no longer feel a burning need to know the truth. One solution . . . is to periodically start over.

Once you've achieved recognition in some area, and no longer have as much interest in it as you used to, go into a different community focused on a different topic, and start over from a low-status (or at least not very high status) position."[81]

It's about humbling yourself enough to learn, even when you're at the top of your game. It's about knowing the moment you get comfortable being an executive is the moment you begin to fail. Pitbull once said, "It's about realizing that if you want to continue being Mufasa, at the same time you have to keep being Simba."[82]

Greener Grass

"Kevin, without a doubt we are all so happy to hear about your great news, but there was a much better way to go about sharing that you are leaving our company." For fifteen minutes, my boss had built me up, told me how great my job performance was, and how she was so happy for me that I was moving on to a new company and position. But right as my guard was down, she hit me with the facts. She did not appreciate how I had arrived at my decision and the way I chose to address my departure with key leaders at the firm, including herself. I could feel my stomach turn upside down as she just stared at me following her abrupt about-face. She was no longer smiling. The room was silent, her comment like a cement truck weighing me down in my seat and causing all kinds of noise in my head. I stared back blanky at her, unsure of how to react. My emotions quickly turned from embarrassment to slight defensiveness. *Oh, I see what she is doing now. She is sticking it to me and making her point. And now she is just filling the room with deafening silence.*

Of about twenty exit interviews with senior leaders, this was the least likely to blow up on me, but nevertheless it did. Leaving a company on good terms is never an easy task, no matter how much gravitas you have built amongst your peers and managers. It is undoubtedly a breakup, so even though the company may be happy for you, in a way, you are telling them that you think there is something better out there and you don't want to waste a second longer in this less-than-optimal environment. Other thoughts that come to mind: You don't respect me, pay me enough, listen to my opinions, promote me, or have a product I believe in selling or building; you lack the values or vision I want to align with at this point. But as the band the Eagles might suggest, there is no way to hide those "Lyin' Eyes." Instead of blatantly calling me out, she discreetly called me in, feeling betrayed, and enough so to leave a sting on the way out of her office. I had unintentionally waited to tell her my news and told other key leaders first. And she was the one who gave me my shot, hired me, and trained me. She also hated the quote, "It's not personal, it's business," and instead felt, "If it isn't personal, we can't even begin to do business." This act of betrayal was personal. And I had personally handled it incorrectly in her eyes.

While it's not always the case, as life and business are extremely situational, most of the time it is better to be forthcoming and to trust in your ability to have difficult conversations in order to negotiate for what you really want. As I found out after leaving Boston for the greener grass of San Francisco, I didn't actually know at the time what I really wanted. I just knew that I wanted an adventure, and I assumed that my company would not accept this dream of mine. This was pre-COVID-19, when proximity to the office was critical for high performance as an employee. I was in a leadership training program, with all the support, sponsorship, and mentorship I could possibly desire, with a hundred new friends and colleagues, living in the city I loved and always dreamt of moving to when I was a kid. I was well paid, promoted within two years, and given many opportunities to travel the country on business trips. Mostly, though, I built a lot of trust with my manager and key senior leaders. So why did I feel I had to hide from them all when I began considering a pivot and a new route in life? Why did I suddenly withdraw from my reservoir of support? Possibly because I had lost belief in myself. Maybe because I believed I wasn't good enough that my company might support my desire to move. Possibly because I wasn't actually practicing the transparency and trust that I had become known for, and it was really just a front. Or what I really think happened: I hit an upper-ceiling problem when I was promoted into an analyst role that a colleague of mine far more deserved and desired than me. Now on an island and feeling increasingly isolated, it was fight-or-flight mode. Here I was back at hockey tryouts again, feeling undeserving of a valuable position.

I chose flight without even bringing up any of my concerns to my manager, and from that decision forward, I began withdrawing inward from all the support and mentorship I truly had but chose not to value. I started dreaming of greener pastures at other companies, where people would "obviously" never put me in such a bad position (not even close to being true), and I became so narrowly focused in my decision that the only thing I cared about was getting out. In other words, I had taken my recent promotion personally. There were five of us in my rotational leadership program, and while my manager promoted me to the job I dreamt of, an analyst on the investment strategy team, it was clearly the wrong fit. My new manager and my colleague in the program were the perfect fit, and they were both shocked and disappointed when instead of the knight in shining armor, it was Kevin who showed up. I was never able to shake that belief, and it slowly rotted away inside of me. To illustrate my point, imagine the number-one draft pick being traded for a fifth-round player. It sounds brutally honest, and it was. That was exactly what I had felt in my heart, and from that moment, I knew I wouldn't last.

Regardless if I stayed at this company for just a few more years or the rest of my career, I would likely have saved a lot of wasted time researching, interviewing, and traveling to find new career opportunities if I had trusted in my value and skill set to bring this up to my manager. I lacked self-confidence, even though this promotion was a direct result of many key leaders at the firm writing recommendation letters and stepping up on my behalf. I lacked the maturity to bring up a difficult conversation to my manager; after all, all of my meetings were mostly pats on the back and keep-up-the-great-work summaries. Quitting, I thought, was better than showing even a slight bit of weakness. I would come to find that the grass is not greener on the other side of the fence.

There were red flags everywhere; I just chose to ignore them. First there was the departing analyst, who said, "Whatever you do, do not take this job." Or the interview that my hiring manager never showed up for. There was the helpless desperation coming from the hiring manager when she finally did show up six hours later after calling me back into the office. Or the other departing analyst who pulled me aside in the hallway and said, "I don't know if you already heard, but believe me, you really do not want to work here." *Nonsense, they are probably lazy and don't work hard enough; I am the person for the job.* There is a

YouTube video of a gorilla walking through a crowded room of people playing basketball, but most viewers miss the gorilla altogether because they were told at the beginning of the video to watch the basketball. I was clearly watching the basketball and missed the gorilla.

I had moved across the country from Boston to San Francisco, despite the many red flags, to begin my job as analyst for a top-producing advisor. I was tasked with creating investment proposals, updating balance sheets, and reviewing our investment lineup. On paper, it seemed great. All the clout and prestige I had been hoping for. But in reality, it was the last place on earth I felt I should be. And the truth was that I realized this mistake the very first day on the job. I walked into the office to find a bunch of fires going on with clients, and no one paid me even the slightest attention until midafternoon, which, by the way, in San Francisco midafternoon is usually closing time for east coast firms and their west coast counterparts. I had sat at my desk for nearly eight hours before anyone even greeted me with, "Welcome to the team." It was scary knowing I made the wrong decision. And it would become a pride-swallowing, gut-punching next nine months.

Although I did not see eye to eye with my team, I knew I could still learn and grow along the way. I learned the importance of managing up and properly communicating expectations to a boss. I also learned a key lesson on quitting. In my mind, there are two types of quitting, the first of which involves my decision to leave my first company. It was rooted in a narrow-minded decision to move on without contemplating alternative options.

In the TV show *Suits*, Harvey Specter asks Mike Ross, "What do you do when someone puts a gun to your head? You do what they say or they shoot you, right? Wrong! You take the gun, you pull out an even bigger gun, you call their bluff, or you do one of another 146 things."[83] I had not only quit my job, but I had also lost my ability to reason and think about the bigger picture. I grew myopic in my intent to leave so I could prove to others and myself that I was capable of finding that greener grass. The other type of quitting is more along the lines of failing fast, which can be a much more admirable course correction. Failing fast is an entrepreneurial ideal that entails cutting the rope on something when there is no feasible runway, either because there is no market for a product or because something has changed and severed any existing market. In this case, when I left my second company within nine months, this was an admirable course correction in that I failed fast and moved on quickly.

These are not dramatic stories of hardship at work but rather relatable moments we all go through each day. We all make the decision to stay or leave, to hunker down or sail off into the sunset. I look back on some of my key decisions in life where I made a change, and while I was not better off from all these quitting or course-correction moments, I will say a majority of them brought me closer to where I wanted to be. I went to a private high school my freshman and sophomore year, only to move back to my local public high school for my junior and senior years. I quit saxophone, piano, and percussion before I finally stuck with guitar. I worked at a warehouse for four weeks one summer before I decided I wanted to work outside and became a lifeguard and a caddie. Many people believe there is a sunk cost the longer they commit t... ...ing. How can I quit now? I have given so much time, ...nd investment into this endeavor, and it will have all bee... ...ste of time if I cut the cord and pivot now. Right? Wrong. ...se corrections are exactly that: identifying the journey you ha... been on and leveraging those experiences in your current life. Not everything is a stepping stone, adding one derivative to the next, but there is no shame in growing where you are planted, learning valuable skills, and eventually taking those lessons to other areas of your life. Change is not a lack of commitment or a lack of loyalty. Hiding the fact that you are looking for growth and are in need of change is disloyal. And that is what I did with my first company, I hid the fact that I wasn't growing and that I felt betrayed. Change is not a resume burner. And mostly, change is an important ingredient if you want to build your resilience to keep up with the evolving world. I encourage you to decide whether you are quitting because you are running away instead of addressing your challenges, or if you are making a change because the runway no longer exists and you need to cut the cord now rather than later.

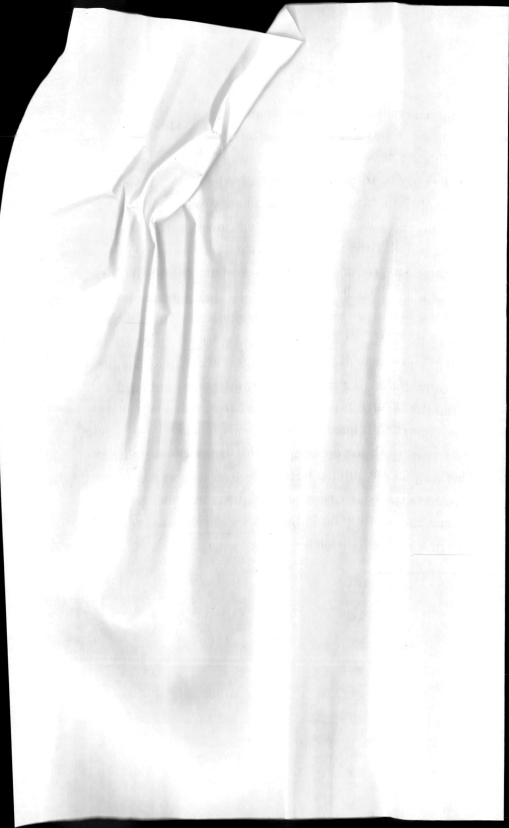

Dreaming, Play, and Childlike Wonder

"Don't give up on your dreams, or your dreams will
give up on you." (John Wooden)

Choosing a worthy cause to fight for and chase in life is important, because without passion and purpose, you might find yourself flailing in the wind, never feeling tied to a community or even left wondering what impact you are making on others. There is nothing more important than choosing a dream and, equally as important, nurturing a dream. We must learn to take care of our dreams, to grow them and breathe life into them over time. And as we garner new experiences and meet new people, our dreams will surely change and evolve. The older you get, the more important it becomes to continue dreaming. Most of us age and become more cynical, having seen too many failures, experienced too many disappointments, and witnessed too many people give up hope themselves. We even start to ridicule those who carry their dreams, "Why don't you just relax and kick your feet up like everyone else? Aren't you tired of running around? Don't you think it is a little unrealistic?" If you don't take time to dream about what you want, you might become like the American executive who, in an old anecdote, arrives on a beach on a beautiful island.

The executive strolls down to the beach and notices a fisherman rowing into shore. His boat is chock full of fish, and the executive asks him what he's doing.

The fisherman replies, "I've been fishing because I love it. And now I'm going to have a barbecue on the beach with my friends. I'll play guitar and sing and hang out on the beach, and then in the evening I will dine with my wife under the stars."

"That's crazy," says the executive. "You've caught so many fish! I can invest in you, and we'll sell the fish and make a ton of money!"

"Why would I want to do that?" says the fisherman.

"Well, in a few months, we could invest the profits and buy a bigger boat and make even more money," says the executive.

"Why would I want to do that?" says the fisherman.

"Well, in a few years, we could invest the profits and open a factory on the beach and process our own fish and make even more money," says the executive.

"Why would I want to do that?" says the fisherman.

"Well, with all the profits from that, you could eventually retire early. And then you could go fishing just because you love it. And then you could have a barbecue on the beach with your friends. And you could play guitar and sing and hang out on the beach. And then in the evening dine with your wife under the stars."[84]

Play is one of those fundamental values, an intrinsically good activity in and of itself. Unstructured play engenders creativity. Kids are constantly playing and are some of the best at finding joy in the simply brilliant moments that pass us by, whether it's recreationally outdoors or on the fields of different sports. Kids are not worried about a mortgage or a job or their health. Kids play because it feels good, because it is fun and exciting and brings out their best self and best personality, with no inhibitions.

I noticed I had become so narrow in my thinking of success and what a fulfilling life looked like that I had subconsciously started to fear becoming "average," or "regular," or "not enough." Many people, whether inadvertently or directly, taught me that success followed a narrow, conformist, and linear path only, with no depth or roundness. Fear infiltrated my mind with this nagging idea that I somehow would get left behind, be revealed as an impostor or someone who was all talk and no action. Instead of focusing on performing the way I thought would be most natural and comfortable, in my job or in my life as a husband, I had become hyper-focused on performing how I thought others would want me to perform, and thus, I lost a lot of my natural ability. Fearing that if I was not getting better, I would be getting worse, I lost a sense of balance in my life. I felt I always had to be performing for my family, my friends, and my clients.

I had to ask myself, "Where is the space in life where I do not feel like I am performing something?"

Culturally, we are constantly bombarded with what performance looks like, forcing us to ask ourselves "Am I wearing the right thing, am I connecting in the right way, is my profile adequate on social media?" In the most nuanced and yet simple ways, we have almost commoditized ourselves so much we don't know how not to perform, and there is not enough psychological space left at the end of day to not be performing, which is an enormous drain on our mental health. How then do you learn to take your mask off and show up as you? How do you find deep authenticity if you have a fear of rejection, abandonment, or unworthiness? Try taking conscious action to face your fear by letting go of the chains holding you back, of wanting and needing to have everyone's approval, and learn not to place so much importance on the trivial matters of life. You will have a lot more fun in life, and you will lower your stress considerably.

Don't just believe me; take it from Jim Carrey, who said in a YouTube interview, "I think everybody should get rich and famous and everything they ever dreamed of so they can see that that's not the answer."[85] If you think of your future self, living in that beautiful new house, you imagine jumping in the pool overlooking Hollywood's hills or watching a movie in your movie theater, everything feeling great. What's easy to forget is that people who have all of these "things" get the flu, have psoriasis, have lawsuits slapped on them, argue with their spouses and strain relationships with their kids, are suffocated with insecurity and frustrated with politicians, which at any given moment can rob them of any joy that comes from their material success. Future fortunes are imagined in a vacuum, but reality is always lived with the good and bad taken together, competing for attention.

A Voicemail and a Dream Come True

"I don't believe in guilty pleasures. If you f***ing like
something, like it." (Dave Grohl)[86]

Hardly ever is anything as bad as it seems, just like things
are hardly ever as good as they seem. While this may be a really
good leadership sentiment that can help you remain calm and
balanced, it is not the best personal sentiment. When my life
was going well, I grew fearful of what was waiting for me around
the corner. *This is too good; I must protect myself from the trouble
that lies ahead.* These types of thoughts robbed me from my
present joy. I would act cool and temper my excitement, so as to
make sure that the inevitable swing of the pendulum would not
hit me in the head unknowingly. *I had been burned too many
times before. I will not let my optimism get the best of me again.*

"Hi, Kevin, this is Joe from a top New England Small College
Athletic Conference (NESCAC) school. We saw your last game,
and we were really impressed." My ears began to perk up as I
listened to this nearly two-minute voicemail from a college
scout. I had always thought my dream to play college hockey
was possible, but hearing it directly from a coach's mouth was an
adrenaline-filled excitement I had hardly expected to feel in my
life. "So listen, Kevin, we think you have a great offensive mind,
good neutral zone play, make smart decisions, crisp passes, and
have superior puck protection. We would like to have you on
campus, meet the team, and see what kind of opportunity we

can offer you." I was currently touring the campus of Holy Cross when I received this voicemail, and my dad was a few hundred feet away. I couldn't wait to tell him the news. Dreams like this were not something we talked a lot about together. *Better keep things in check and not get ahead of ourselves* was our unwritten code. After all, life can be devastatingly disappointing. *Why would we want to dream something so grand only to let ourselves down? There was that time I thought I made the hockey team, but that was just a different Kevin, after all.*

Ultimately, the world treats you more or less the way you expect to be treated. I had never expected a phone call from a college scout, and maybe that is why I wasn't that let down when I realized that this voicemail was not from a scout but from some of my teammates playing a prank on me. It was a pride-swallowing moment, especially when I had to go back to my dad to tell him that I was not, in fact, being recruited. *Damn, I was so excited when I told him. I really got my hopes up; he must think I am an idiot.* I could have let this moment saddle me with embarrassment; I could have even quit the team. Just because you are on a team does not mean everyone will act like "brothers" or "sisters." This would become an important lesson in dreaming for me, which is to guard the mind against the negative influence around us and to be more concerned with my character rather than my reputation. Character is who you really are, while reputation is merely what others think, and clearly, others thought I was not good enough at my sport or was too stupid to believe I even had a chance to realize my dream.

Whatever we say, we are always talking about ourselves. By this I mean that others will judge you for your dreams, and if they don't think they are capable of reaching those dreams themselves, they will make sure you don't believe in yourself either. Ignore them. Instead, choose to follow your dream. By doing so, you will begin choosing certain actions that reinforce the state of being you dream of, which will then lead you to choose actions that more fully underscore that state of being, and so on. This will culminate in the strengthening of your being the person you always dreamed about. The consistency of doing these activities that reflect the desired state of being helps reinforce that state of being to greater and greater degrees, making them more and more the actual state of being with which you show up in the world. It is the strongest feedback loop to reach your dreams, and it simply requires ignoring everyone else's negativity, disguised in practicality, statistics, and love. It is not love if someone tells you to aim lower. As David Grohl states earlier, if you want to accomplish something, don't water it down; dream it and go for it. Forget about fifty-fifty chances. "Maybe I will; maybe I won't" is a losing proposition. The only winning proposition is 100 percent. Remember that one?

Mark Groves said this about self-worth and dreaming: "To love is easy. To be loved requires the belief that we are worthy of it. And the only way to feel worthy is to allow yourself to be."[87]

Lesson: We can coexist with others without giving them the keys to the door of our dreams.

Dreaming Is Not for the Faint of Heart

Dreaming requires imagination, time, dedication, and belief. But mostly, dreaming requires your blind faith and full attention, because if you are dreaming big enough, you are never going to be sure how you will accomplish your dreams, and you will never fully understand the path to success. You should first decide on your dream, and only then can you nurture it. People in life will want to take your dreams away from you, especially people who love you. They might not want you to be disappointed, or they might not want you to realize the possibility that you are just average. But you must be careful not to let others' opinions and guidance weigh too heavily on your pursuit of your dreams. Guard them with your life, and even when it seems silly, trust in the pursuit of your dreams.

As a young child, I had unequivocal faith throughout my elementary and middle school days. I would pray on my knees every night before bed and felt connected to a higher being, like someone else was behind the driver seat and had the directions to my next stop. I just believed that I was protected and that I was safe and capable of achieving success because I was being watched over. I believed despite a thousand reasons in life not to believe.

But because I slowly started to question my belief, because I was lured away and persuaded that my blind faith was immature, I began to lose my belief all together. *This is silly; an adolescent or adult getting down on their knees and asking for help or thanking some fictitious God? I am too old for this.* As my faith slipped away due to the combination of shedding my childlike wonder and becoming an adolescent shell, my lost focus started translating to other areas of my life. I lazily began to apply this non-belief to other parts of my life, like tests, sports, and friendships, for that matter. It doesn't happen all at once. But slowly, over time, your non-belief becomes pernicious and permanent. Like a balloon that slowly deflates over the course of many days, for example. This is no way to live your life, however. Life is meant for the dreamers and the believers. Life is so much sweeter with belief. If you have a goal or a dream, don't let anyone steal that from you. Don't let the excitement of being cool rob you of your non-cool ideas, visions, hopes, dreams, and passions.

While visualization techniques serve a purpose, a dream without extreme dedication and accountability will never come true. Maybe you can rely on your sheer talent to accomplish a dream or two, but I would argue that dream was not big enough. In order to achieve dreams, life-changing dreams, dedication and preparation are critical. Those who fail to prepare for their dreams should be prepared to fail. Dreams are not goals; they are not check marks on a resume or an endpoint. Dreams are continuous, flowing, and full of joy. A dream can instill hope and provide purpose and drive in your life. A dream is a chase. So make sure the chase is worthwhile.

Lesson: "We should be dreaming. We grew up as kids having dreams, but now we're too sophisticated as adults, as a nation. We stopped dreaming. We should always have dreams." (Herb Brooks)

Play Is ~~Only~~ for Kids

"Fire, fire, fire!" my uncle yelled from the front lawn of our beachfront summer home. I was pretending to sleep on the couch in the living room, when I would suddenly awaken to the sound of the front porch bell that my family was ringing back and forth. *Ding, ding, ding, ding, ding.* I would immediately spring up from the couch and out of my "dreams" so I could fight this imaginary fire.

I was wearing my 101 Dalmatian pajamas; after all, the live-action movie was a huge hit in the nineties, and they were anything but the pink bunny footie pajamas Ralphie wore in *A Christmas Story.* Rubbing my eyes to wipe away the "sleepy dreams," I then ran over to the staircase by the front door. Quickly, I jumped into my shiny black coat and yellow striped fireman outfit, which was glossy, prominent, and undeniably the outfit of choice for all five-year-old rescue heroes.

The jacket fit like a glove, and while it was supposed to stop at the waist, it ran down to my knees. I then grabbed the plastic fireman helmet, with the sticker emblem of the ladder number on the front, and slid into my rubber boots and out the door. My family was in the front yard, watching me as I dove into action, sometimes literally diving off the porch and onto the grass. I would reach for the hose in the bushes and spray down the front and side-yard grass, bushes, and shutters to the house.

My family would shout, "Over there, the fire is popping up again!" and "Quick, now it's flaming over here!" I would swing the hose over to the right side of the house, gripping the hose with both hands in a side stance, squatting down to make sure I had a good athletic stance and angle to hit the "flames" head on. After a few moments, I would then swing the hose back to the left side of the house, where the flowers and bushes were drying up and needed some more water. Not a bad effort on my parents' part to have me do my part around the house!

After a few arduous swings of the hose, I had put out the "fire" and completed the job. The yard was watered, the flowers and bushes taken care of, and my family had found a new way to channel five-year-old Kevin's never-ending energy in the mornings. The look on my face said it all. I went from sleep to action to intense focus and concentration on the mission at hand. But it did not end here. After the fire was put out, I would return the hose to the garden, walk back inside, lay out my fireman outfit by the staircase, with the black-and-yellow striped shiny coat hanging on the railing, my boots laid out perfectly in proper order, and only then would I get back onto the couch in my 101 Dalmatian footie pajamas and "fall back asleep." Moments later, I would hear my family yelling from the front yard again, and the fire bell would ring from the front porch once more, back and forth, back and forth, to reawaken me from my slumber and spur me back into action.

There was the rubbing of the eyes, the mad dash to the staircase, the equipment placed over my pajamas and the unbalanced and shaky sprint of a five-year-old in boots too big for his own feet through the front door and out to the bushes once again, grabbing the hose with two hands and putting out the fire that had reignited.

I cherished these moments as a child. Youthful innocence is one of the greatest gifts in life. You might have heard the saying, "Youth is wasted on the young." I was unaware of the challenges of the world at the time; I was unscathed by the sinister outlook many of us develop as we age, the incorrigible belief system and traps we fall into and the negative media we all face. It was in these moments as a child that my imagination was on full display. There was no wondering if I was a good fireman or not, or whether I was the best fireman or the worst fireman in my firehouse. All I knew as a five-year-old kid was that I *was* a fireman. That was who I was being. Someone who cared for others and wanted to protect society and keep everyone safe. I simply wanted to put out fires, and that simply made me a fireman.

Whether you think you can or cannot, you are right. Who you tell yourself you are being is who you are. Sometimes we adults think we need to have something to be someone. First, we need the degree before we can get the job and be a business person. Or first we need money before we can make an impact on a charitable organization. Or first we need the approval of others before we can approve of others. The truth is that you alone get to decide who you are, and who you are requires an imagination and a belief that you are intrinsically who you say you are. Is the best fireman the best because his unit rewards him with a medal, or is the best fireman the best because he knows he or she shows up to work every day proud to wear the uniform and protect their community? While a medal is honorable and those awarded them are certainly deserving, I would argue that all firefighters can be the best firefighters simply by choosing to honor that by behaving as the best firefighter would.

The older you get, the younger you want to be. As I write this, I can report that a few years back I had an epiphany. My sisters kept telling me I was the golden child—though I didn't feel like it—and then they started calling me their older brother, despite one of them being the older sister. Because I had started to surpass them in all of life's check boxes. On paper things can seem great, but without the presence to appreciate all of your gifts, all you can think about is what comes next. I had everything I wanted and more, so why didn't I feel like the golden child?

With accomplishments come responsibility, expectation, and shockingly, boredom, believe it or not. I began to tolerate my life, as in to say, "Sure, this is all great stuff, but is this it? Is this everything in life? I seemingly have it all; what more could I want?" Was I ungrateful? Of course not. Was I complacent? Perhaps, although I have always had an obsession with my wife and a work-hard mentality or self-improvement attitude. So, what was it? Why was I simply tolerating my life?

I realized I had lost one of the most important facets of life: playfulness. I forgot how to play. I left behind the front yard fire rescues and traded it in for a desk. Believe it or not, as a kid, I used to pretend to work with my younger sister, Emily. We would set up desks at home, and I even purchased a fake beeper from Walgreens. We would take notes, have calculators and pens at the ready, and would just pretend to work. It was simple and creative. There was no productivity from it. Nothing in return we received. We didn't make money, we didn't advance our careers, and we didn't compete with others in the office. We were simply playing.

It is my hope for you, and for me, to capture more play in our lives. It is okay to read a book that does not instruct you on something, like a fiction book, for example. It is okay to sit on the beach and ponder the ocean, ponder life, or ponder nothing. Sometimes, doing nothing is doing something. We all have to turn the engine off sometimes, perhaps lessen our deep and intense introspection at times. We all have to let go of being an adult at times and take a time-out. Being an adult comes with a perception. How are we being perceived? We always want to put our best foot forward, but sometimes we need to not put any feet forward. In fact, sometimes adults should stop being who people expect them to be and stop acting like how they think they are supposed to act. Being an adult is a gift, don't get me wrong. As an adult, you gain freedom, expression, and experience. However, too many adults take life too seriously simply because they are adults. They think it comes with the territory and that they have a job to always put on that they are successful and well-mannered.

Play is one of the greatest joys in life. There is no sense of responsibility. No sense of advancement or productivity. It is a simple way to enjoy life. To embrace the beautiful rhythms of life. Play is something we all are drawn to naturally. There is no order, no structure, and no rules to necessarily follow. You make them up as you go; you let your creativity take you outside the walls of "in bounds" to the outer edges and beyond in your imagination. To me, play is drawing outside the lines. Play is about creating and exploring and expressing with pure intent and no restraint. But it is you, and no one else, who must decide whether or not to foster more play in your life.

Lee Ann Womack sings in her famous song *I Hope You Dance*, "When you get the choice to sit it out or dance, I hope you dance." I hope you dance when given the choice. Dance in playfulness, laughter, and love. Dance your way through life, as my wife tells me. Don't take yourself too seriously. Maybe even make a fool of yourself; that is fine. Learn to laugh at yourself; it makes you more relatable, and it helps you forgive and enjoy yourself more. Don't act reserved for the sake of appearing more mature, older, or responsible. Don't hide your desire to play. Get out there, be weird, be different, stick out, don't fall in line. And mostly, rid yourself of any preconception that as you get older, the less you play. We are all children at heart and should stay that way. Play is incredibly healthy and something we all must do.

Light Watkins shares some impactful sentiment on acting your age: "The advice shouldn't be to act your age. It should be to act your spirit. Your age may try to prohibit you from dancing like that, or starting over, or starting something new. But your spirit would never do such a thing. If something feels aligned, your spirit wants you to go for it, whether you're 15 or 85. Acting your age makes you fit in more, while acting your spirit will indeed cause you to stand out—in a bad way to people who act their age, but in an inspiring way to those who act their spirit. Try acting your spirit from time to time, and you can see for yourself which path makes you feel more alive."[88]

During most summers at the beach, not only would I dress up as a rescue hero, but I would also play in the ocean with my uncle. I used to be terrified of jellyfish in the August months—later in life that fear actually did materialize, when I was stung by a Portuguese man o' war that washed up on the beach of Bermuda, but I digress—and I would make up every excuse as to why I would not swim in the ocean like the hundreds of other kids enjoying their days. I was in my head, and I could not find a way to get out. Well, like the "fire" calls my family would make at the beach house, my uncle found a way to bring play into my life on the beach too.

My uncle would let me wrestle him in the shallow waters of low tide in the afternoons. He was much larger than a five-year-old, obviously, but he was also very big and muscular as a human. He was a baseball player in college and had arms bigger than my waist. He would pick me up and run me down to the ocean and toss me in a few waves. I would get so mad at him, and I learned to turn this madness into a "screw it" mentality. Once I was in the water and had touched hundreds of jellyfish, I would say to myself, "screw it." In conquering my fear, I could finally open my eyes to the idea of play. I would grit my teeth, throw up my fists, and jump on top of my uncle.

He would lie in the shallow water and take every possible beating from me. I would jump on his back, and he would roll me over into the wave. I would grab his forearm, and he would lift me out of the water, as I dangled from his bicep. I would rub his face into the sand and oncoming waves, and he would fire back by throwing me into more waves. I will always remember these moments because it took getting out of my own way, getting out of my own head, to realize how much fun life can be. It is simply a decision, like the lyrics I mentioned above, to sit it out or dance. I hope you dance too, and swim in the ocean, even when there are jellyfish, even when you are scared to dance, even when you are not sure what others will think of you. Because when you get out of your way and jump right in, you, too, will find joy and happiness in the act of play.

Lesson: "Do it badly; do it slowly; do it fearfully; do it any way you have to, but do it." (Steve Chandler)

The Fort > The Mansion

"I can't keep the roof from falling down," my friend yelled across the room.

"Try adding a few of those textbooks over there," I yelled back, as I had both my hands holding the other corner of the sheets to the bedroom dresser.

"Okay, let me see if that works," said my friend, as he nudged a few precarious books onto the shelf, where the other corner of the sheet would hang.

It was a labyrinth of architectural mishaps, but it was our fort. Bedroom sheets hung from every corner in the room and were held down or tied down by different heavy objects that were only inches from toppling over onto the ground. I even remember the concern of my friend's mom that halfway through the night the entire thing would come tumbling down on us.

Building forts is a rite of passage for kids. It is all about creativity, ingenuity, and building. Forts are a way to transform your world, to create a house within a house, and to design something that was not there before. But the best part about forts is that they are not permanent. The point of a fort is not to enjoy it next year; the point of a fort is to enjoy it now. A fort only requires the essentials, such as a roof, some flashlights, and probably some candy or soda. But that is all it takes to enjoy a fort. You have your friends, your shelter, and the endless conversations your imagination evinces.

Bringing creativity and imagination to your life as you get older will help remind you of the days of fort building. It will ground you and make you more present. A fort is meant to be enjoyed in the moment. There is nothing to hoard, to save for, to protect, or to worry about, and there is definitely no manual or instructions on how to build a fort. You must use the resources at your disposal. The materials might include sheets, cardboard boxes, chairs, dressers, and sleeping bags, but there is nothing shiny, lavish, or tawdry about a fort. It is well written and preached in life that we should remain in the moment and not wish our time away. Too many times, I myself look forward to the changing of the season or the next big purchase I am going to make. But fort building is a good reminder that you don't need to compare your homes to others, and you don't even need to worry about what car is in your driveway or how many bedrooms your fort holds.

A fort provides for your necessities, and most importantly, it provides for your fun. You can make it whatever you want, and if you can dream it, you can build it. Find ways in your life to be creative, and look for the all-too-serious areas in your life, where comparison and anxiety may be coming from. Supplement those parts of your life with play and creativity, and you will find happiness in your fort, whether it is your house, your apartment, your childhood bedroom, or the fort you build with your friends in the backyard. Don't take life too seriously; instead, build a fort when life gets too complex or too stressful.

Lesson: Don't lose sight of your childlike spirit.

Playing Grease and Acting

I was in fourth grade, and our school was putting on the play *Little Shop of Horrors*. I wanted the lead role so badly, but instead, my friend one grade above got the role. And I was relegated to Carmen the Cactus, which was actually a fictitious role, a role with one, maybe two lines at most. My costume entailed lots of green fabric over my chest, back, and arms, with hundreds of toothpicks sticking out, and green-and-black face paint. My stage instructions were to hold my arms out to my sides for a few minutes at a time and sing and dance as a background singer, not in the front of the stage, but off to the side. *Man, what am I even doing this for?* I thought to myself. This is a dumb role and a waste of my time.

It wasn't until fifth grade that I landed the lead role of Danny Zuko in *Grease*, a play that pits the Greasers against their cross-town rivals in a race to build the fastest car on thunder road. Rather than one or two lines, I had over two hundred lines I had to memorize, as well as song lyrics and dance moves that we practiced almost daily after school for a few months. One of the lines I had to remember was, "Rama lama lama, kaddinga kaddinga dong, shoobock, shawanana dippity dip da do." Try that a few times in a row, or just look up online the hand jive scene from the movie.

What I learned from this experience was that you are not always going to get the lead role, especially not right away. But you can still play a role on the team or in the play. While I didn't want to be a cactus, it was still important for the success of the play to have one on stage. And without the supporting roles in *Grease*, all of us Greasers would have no play to put on.

Lesson: Everyone plays a role on a team, no matter how seemingly insignificant.

Pride, Humility, and Victim Mentality

When you acknowledge and accept your weaknesses, you start to see the contours of the playing field. Knowing your weaknesses and your basic goods helps you figure out where you can create an edge. But knowing your weakness is not about slumping your shoulders in defeat; instead, it is about harnessing that weakness for good. Victim's blame externalizes fault, but those with pride pick themselves back up. As a hyper-sensitive person, I am constantly aware of my surroundings, constantly judging myself for how others perceive me and my identity. Therefore, when I don't see something perfect in myself, I tend to hide that piece of me from the world. The point is, you don't want to harp on your weaknesses; you just want to be aware of them. If you let yourself harp on your weaknesses, you will drag yourself into a negative feedback loop that will preclude you from achieving even the most fundamental accomplishments in life, like friendship, love, and career success, as examples. This is *your* life, so take pride in what you set out to accomplish, be proud of who you are and what God gave you, and mostly strive to have a humble confidence about yourself. Being proud requires a choice of your own, not an outside acknowledgement like an award or the support and impression of a friend. Pride is completely self-curated, and it must be watched carefully to keep it from becoming distracted by a victim's mentality of endless comparison and inadequacy. Instead, lead a life of abundance and gratitude. If nothing else, it is a lot more fun.

.

Auditory Processing Disorder Is Not Actually a Disorder

"It's as if I pointed at that doorknob and asked you if you could name what I was pointing at. You would look at me and say simply, that is a door. But I would point harder and closer at the doorknob, looking for a more specific answer, and you would still say, oh, that is a door." (Mom)

Until I decided to write this book, I had not researched much about auditory processing disorder. In fact, when my parents were faced with deciding how to address this challenge of mine as a young kid, there were very few options, as this was a new discovery, and many coaching and training facilities were nascent and unproven. These were brand-new tactics and strategies for children with auditory processing disorder, many of which incorporated computers and software programs in learning centers. For those born before 2000, computers were not like the sleek laptops we now all own. These were heavy, large blocks with dark screens and unimpressive graphics.

What is the best part of school for any kid? It is not the long hours in class, the tests that teachers force you to take, the projects that are assigned, or the homework required. The best part is the conclusion of the school year: summer. Summer means freedom. Freedom from your teachers, your homework, and the discipline of sitting in a classroom chair for more than fifteen minutes, especially as a restless child. Summer was usually great for me, except when I was in first grade. Instead of pools, beaches, and running around the neighborhood with my friends, I was planted in a different kind of classroom, one with computers, cold rooms, and spinning chairs that would leave my little first-grader feet dangling in the air, a reminder that even this place was nothing like my regular classes and regular school setting. I had a mop haircut back in the day, thanks to my parents, and I would have to put these big, poofy, goofy headsets over my head, obviously before Beats headphones became a trendy look.

I would practice actively listening for different sounds and raising my hand when I heard them. I would practice matching pictures to words on the computer screen. I would practice waking up early each summer morning so my mom could drive me to class, with a cold Eggo waffle to enjoy in the car ride over to summer school. I don't remember learning anything I could apply to my daily life, as this was more of a rewiring of my brain connectors. I know that doctors told my parents it worked, and that I was "all better," after initially scaring my parents by saying, "We don't know if this kid will ever get into college, let alone pass high school." But even after combatting my auditory processing disorder, I had difficulties in the classroom. In a second-grade spelling bee, I spelled the word *jar* as Y-A-R, after I conflated it with the pronunciation of one of my favorite hockey players to this date, Jaromir Jagr, pronounced, "Yaro-meer Yah-ger." I also spelled the word *center* as C-E-N-T-R-E, thanks to some of my NHL player trading cards I had collected over the years. Or maybe it was my favorite hockey player Petr Sykora, who shared the same birthday as mine, who left the *E* out of the American spelling, P-E-T-E-R. Oh well; that spelling bee trophy is probably collecting dust somewhere in someone's old bedroom.

I know that I still had to work very hard in school, extra hard compared to my classmates, to master the curriculum. I know I stayed after school late to meet with my teachers, and I know that in this journey of mastery, I developed a secret weapon called flipping the script. James Clear has something to say about this mindset: "People usually judge you based on where you are currently, not what you could become eventually. Don't let one comment stop you from trying; file it away to use it as fuel; focus on getting better. Someone else's analysis of your current position doesn't tell you anything about your current potential."[89]

It was only after all this practice that I learned to flip the script. To throw out the playbook and create my own playbook and principles. I embraced my individuality wholeheartedly. After many failures, like almost flunking out of third-grade math, I found a hidden reservoir of high performance deep down inside that just required a mentality shift.

Undoubtedly, I made lots of mistakes and errors through grade school, especially when it came to spelling. Most people would never know this about me, but Emily, my sister three years younger than me, learned how to spell her name and count to one hundred before I did. The school would pull me from my first-grade class once a week to meet with a specialist to write my name out over and over again. Grinning now, I tell others this was my way of practicing my autograph, of reminding myself who I was.

In her book *Grit*, Angela Duckworth tells the story about a McKinsey report titled *War for Talent*, which became a best-selling book. The basic argument was that companies in the modern economy rise and fall depending on their ability to attract and retain "A Players." What do they mean by *talent*? Answering their own question: "In the most general sense, *talent* is the sum of a person's abilities—his or her intrinsic gifts, skills, knowledge, experience, intelligence, judgment, attitude, character and drive. It also includes his or her ability to learn and grow."[90]

The real breakthrough moment occurs when you switch from telling yourself, "This is all I can do," to asking, "Who knows what else I can do?" At that moment, you start wondering, "Who am I?" Am I a learning-disabled kid with no real future, or maybe something else? You subconsciously assign titles to yourself, such as *slow learner, wannabe athlete,* or *annoying brother,* and you then subconsciously fulfill these titles through your actions. Slow learner? Well, then, why expect an A on your report card? Maybe you should just cruise through class, since mediocrity is your thing. Wannabe athlete? No sense working too hard in the off season to make that team you always dreamed of. Annoying brother? Let's keep making fun of your younger sister. Sometimes it's not even the labels you assign yourself but the labels you take on from the opinions of others. The moment you reevaluate who you really are, not who you or others might think you are, you begin to shed a constraining layer of laziness. If you don't examine your thoughts, they will soon become low-grade, low-frequency, and permanently damaging. This is where the prestige of the struggle comes into play, or as Ryan Holliday writes about in his book *The Obstacle Is the Way*, how you can turn your trials into triumphs. So then, is it better to be naturally talented or to be talentless but willing to work hard in your disciplines?

Those who struggle may actually have it better than those who naturally pick up on things. There is a benefit to having to practice over and over again rather than learning something in one fell swoop. So the questions follow:

Do the precocious learn the lesson of doing something repeatedly, like those do who are naturally talentless?

Do they discover that the capacity to do something repeatedly, to struggle, to have patience, can be mastered, but not overnight?

Those struggling early on may actually learn an extremely valuable lesson compared to those who easily pick up a skill or talent. If you are someone who does not instinctively and effortlessly learn new skills, there is good news. By having to sharpen your pencil or stay late after practice, you can begin building confidence in your stamina—you can learn to go over something repeatedly, no matter how difficult it is. It can become an advantage, an edge of sorts. John Irving, a great storyteller of American literature, observed, "Rewriting is what I do best as a writer. I spend more time revising a novel or screenplay than I take to write the first draft. It's become an advantage." Irving has observed of his inability to read and spell as fluently as others: "In writing and in life it doesn't hurt anybody to have to go slowly. It doesn't hurt anyone as a writer to have to go over something over and over again."[91]

Furthermore, Will Smith wrote this on talent, effort, and skill in his book *Will*, "I've never really viewed myself as particularly talented. Where I excel is ridiculous, sickening work ethic." When asked to explain his ascendancy to the entertainment elite, Will said, "The only thing that I see that is distinctly different about me is: I'm not afraid to die on a treadmill. I will not be outworked, period. You might have more talent than me, you might be smarter than me, you might be sexier than me. You might be all of these things. You got it on me in nine categories. But if we get on the treadmill together, there's two things. You're getting off first, or I'm going to die, it's really that simple."[92]

When I met my cousin for the first time at a family reunion in Boston, we discovered we both shared the same last name: Entwistle.

"How do you spell it?" he asked.

"E-N-T-W-I-S-T-L-E," I said, confidently.

Matt's jaw dropped to the floor. "Hey, that is how I spell it!" he declared.

If you don't think I hear that story retold at family dinner tables every few years, you are mistaken. And yet, there is something to cherish about this. There is something so damn authentic about having awareness of your true self and true nature. So authentic about an unadulterated and embarrassing experience. It is usually the embarrassing situations in our life that make us so relatable, so likable.

We as humans are a collection of individual profound moments. These moments, so mundane at surface level, represent the greatest abundance in our lives. The best part is that moments like these are unexpected treasures in our lives, differentiating us, helping us to stand out, and providing comic relief in our rigid and busy lives. The small stuff is the good stuff. To borrow a quote from Robin Williams in the movie *Good Will Hunting*, "Those little moments, oof, that is where the good stuff is."[93]

What I have come to understand about myself later in life is that I once used these failures subconsciously as a crutch, an excuse, a limitation. I used it as a ceiling, something to keep me from going after something so seemingly unachievable (especially for someone with auditory processing disorder). To prove my point, I told you at the beginning of this chapter that I didn't even know much about this challenge I had to overcome, only that it existed for me at one time in my life. So why then would I assume or apply this challenge to other parts of my life without even knowing the circumstances? It is a short-cut my brain took to keep me from going after things I thought were impossible.

Lesson: "Until you value yourself, you won't value your time. Until you value your time, you will not do anything with it." (M. Scott Peck)

Take Pride in Your Baseball Cards

When I was ten years old, my friends and I collected professional sports cards. For us kids, sports cards were a currency and a social status. For example, if you owned Mark Maguire's rookie baseball card, and your friend wanted to trade you for it, you would demand from them either a handful of some of their best players, or a card that was equally as important.

To build a collection of these cards, however, you first had to make some money so you could go to the store and buy a new pack. In the summers, my friends and I would wash cars in the neighborhood. We would charge anywhere from $10 to $20, depending on the type of work needed and the time it took to clean them. And in the winters, we would shovel driveways. We could earn $20 a driveway, which went a long way as a kid. After the five of us shoveled five driveways or cleaned five cars, we had accomplished about $100 in sales, leaving $20 for each one of us to put toward our pack of cards.

With that amount of money, we could buy a deli sandwich, a slushie, and a few packs of cards. We would make a dash over to the card store, and because we were all under five feet in stature, we all had a direct view into the clear glass containers holding some of the most prominent cards. The cards on display were usually more expensive and, in my sophomoric state of mind, seemed unattainable. In hindsight, that was a false narrative I subconsciously created. Of course, I could have shoveled more driveways or cleaned more cars, but even though I was wrong in thinking I couldn't find a way to afford those specialty cards, I realize now that more is not necessarily better or what is right for me. In fact, my friends and I felt twenty dollars was just perfect. And that right there is a lesson I try to revisit to this day. Know your target, know what you want, and know when you have reached it. The unrelenting chase of something is not admirable if you have the wrong reasons for the chase.

When we returned home, we would all gather around and start ripping open our tightly wrapped packs of cards, careful to go through each player one at a time in order to fully analyze their batting stance, stats, team, and (truthfully) admire their in-game photo on the front of the card. Like anything else wrapped up as a present, there is always the promise of something spectacular, or in our case, someone spectacular waiting to be unwrapped. My one friend would always exhale in great joy and excitement over the players that he unwrapped. As he saw it, he was now one proud owner of some of the best players in the league.

Oh, man, now it was my time. I'll rip open my package, which by the way was so tightly and perfectly wrapped it would give you one of the most pleasing sensations: the smell of fresh cards and possibility. Boy, can sports cards turn anyone into a helpless romantic. Well, here's the thing: I would tear through my cards without recognizing most of the names and never fully appreciating the underlying talent within each player. My excitement quickly grew to disappointment as I flipped through my cards, hoping to share the same cards as my friends, who seemed so happy with their own cards.

If you couldn't initially see the disappointment on my face, then all you had to do was wait a few more cards to shuffle through before it became unequivocal. Card one, still smiling, but I don't recognize him, okay, move on. Card two, also unsure of this player, smile slightly fades. Cards three, four, five, and suddenly my smile flattened. Cards six, seven, eight, and suddenly the redness in my cheeks began to illuminate the frown on my face. Who the hell were these players anyway?

By the way, I hadn't even checked the back of these cards for their stats, batting average, home runs, fielding ability, seasons played, or even arguably the most important achievement, championships won. I had quickly judged these cards at face value, based solely on my first impression of not knowing them, and judging them because these were not the same cards that my elated friends owned.

The lesson I learned later on was that your reaction is your choice. Unfortunately, I did not know how to take pride in my own cards. My one friend had the "best" players, and I had the "worst." Says who? Says me, because my level of enthusiasm did not even come close to matching my friends' enthusiasm. How did I get stuck with such bad players? Why was this pack of cards so bad?

Thankfully, I had family around to teach me a valuable lesson. They would go back through each card with me and explain how every player brought something valuable to their team, like their on-base percentage or runs batted in. My family reinforced in me that teams are made up of different players, styles, and types. Just because my players were different from my friends' players did not intrinsically make them worse or undesirable. In fact, because of the difference in their style of play, they likely helped their team's overall performance because they brought their own skill set to the team. As I listened to them slowly build up my confidence, one player at a time, it dawned on me that I had a good pack of cards and players, and I was not a complete failure like I had originally thought.

I now look across many areas of my life and intentionally seek out places where I am comparing myself to others or underappreciating my own cards. My enthusiasm is my choice, and my pride is a function of the confidence I have in myself. Better said, the way I perceive a situation is my choice and should not be contingent on outside opinion or perspective. I am not saying that simply choosing to remain positive, grateful, or proud miraculously changes my reality, because I am not arguing for unwarranted belief. Being honest about a situation can help us course correct while there is still time. What I am arguing for is a certain level of confidence and pride that I should carry with my players. They are my players, they were opened in my pack, and they are good enough for me.

You have a choice in life. You can be excited and proud, or you can compare your situation to others and feel weak. And I promise you, if you choose to be proud and excited, life brings more possibilities than you could ever have imagined. Whether it is the school you attend, the position in sports you play, the team you play on, the friend group you find yourself in, the family you are part of, the home you live in, the clothing you wear, or the equipment you can afford, be proud. Especially when you do not have the chance to choose your cards or the circumstances of your life, you have the chance to choose your response. You can be humble and proud; the two are not in opposition. Confidence is not arrogant; it lets others know that you respect yourself, and just as importantly, it lets you know you respect yourself. We can always reach for greater heights, compare ourselves to others, or focus on what we don't have in life. However, it's an exhausting way to live life. Try to appreciate your life journey for what it is, and don't forget that your identity is not tied to what you have or don't have, what you've accomplished or not accomplished. Your identity is tied directly to how you present yourself with the confidence, pride, and gratefulness for the many parts of your life that make you different from all the others and the many parts that make you, well, you.

The best card or player in the deck is easy to identify, but what we don't know as much about are the players with extreme possibility who have not yet proven themselves. In other words, we don't have an intuitive understanding of how to navigate the nuanced nature of the disadvantages we all will face at some point in time and how to build the capacity to cultivate the skills and tools that will allow us to take control and create a new starting position for ourselves. Most of us will not be granted the best card in the deck, so create circumstances in which grit and attitude help you reap the benefits, rewards, and successes. Robert Louis Stevenson once said, "Life is not a matter of holding good cards but of playing a poor hand well." Your inner belief and pride become your edge.

You are dealt the hand that you are dealt, but you get to be the one to play it. There is nothing inauthentic in being dealt a hand and then deciding that you're not going to let others tell you it's a weak hand. Replace these beliefs with new ones that every successful person—regardless of their starting position or the disadvantages they face—begins with: the future can be better than the present, and I have the power to make it so.

Lesson: You don't always get to pick your cards, and yet you should still hold them in the highest regard. They are your cards, and you should not compare your cards to those of your friends.

Headgear and Jay Leno References

It was 10:00 p.m. on a school night, and I was at my childhood home in the second-floor bathroom, staring into the mirror with tears dripping down my face as my eyes locked onto the metal wire wrapping around my head. Was I really going to have to wear this for the foreseeable future?

If you don't know what headgear is, it's essentially a metal wire that wraps around the back of your head, connecting its circular shape around the front of your head in alignment with your mouth. It's a halo, if you push the halo from above your head down to your mouth. As if the idea of headgear wasn't bad enough, it turned out that my orthodontist was prescribing reverse headgear. Instead of wrapping around my face, reverse headgear would connect from my forehead to my chin in a vertical fashion. There is a pad that presses against the middle of the forehead, a bar that moves down the nose line, and it finishes with a perpendicular cross at the bottom of the contraption, protruding out a couple inches from the face. Every kid's dream.

Before bed each night, I would connect two separate rubber bands to both the metal clips between my teeth and the cross, thus forcing a pulling tension on my upper teeth so that I wouldn't have such a bad underbite. It was a nightmare and extremely embarrassing and humbling. Imagine Halloween for a child, only every night was a reminder of Halloween as you stare at your hardly recognizable face in the mirror.

I grew up thinking there were a lot of things wrong with me. It wasn't the constant ridicule I received from others about my skinny legs but the internal chatter in my own mind that something was wrong with me. Or it was that first day when I started noticing more and more moles on my body, feeling helpless in my efforts to make them stop growing. Most kids deal with puberty the same way—the kids who grow up quicker are usually cooler. Comparing shoe sizes with friends, or playing basketball games with skins versus shirts—these were always opportunities for me to beat myself up even more. But believe me, it doesn't stop there in life. If you don't reign in your own mental chatter, that voice inside your head, you will always have a mindset of inadequacy. What I had failed to comprehend at the time was that inversion is the antidote to self-doubt. Confidence and peace of mind often occur when we flip the script and invert or upend or turn something upside down. By taking ownership of our weaknesses, even if only perceived, we can identify and remove obstacles to success. I had to embrace it as one of my assets, just like someone else would embrace their strong quantitative skills or their communication skills. Every failure was not about dropping out; rather, it was about clearing the way to continue doing. When we own our constraints, magical things can happen. Indeed, when we leverage difficulties and use them as tools to propel us toward success, we start to carve out our edge.

According to the National Association of Independent Schools, many people think of the brain as a mystery. They don't know much about intelligence and how it works. When they do think about what intelligence is, many people believe that a person is born either smart, average, or dumb and that he or she stays that way for life. But new research shows that the brain is like a muscle; it changes and gets stronger when you use it. When you learn new things, these tiny connections in the brain actually multiply and get stronger. The more you challenge your mind to learn, the more your brain cells grow. Then things that you once found very hard or even impossible, like speaking a foreign language or doing algebra, seem to become easy. The result is a stronger, smarter brain. A Harvard Medical School article explains, "Your brain has the ability to learn and grow as you age—a process called brain plasticity—but for it to do so, you have to train it on a regular basis." The article continues quoting Dr. John Morris, "Practice makes permanent, and that goes for brain function, too. 'You can't improve memory if you don't work at it,' says Dr. Morris. 'The more time you devote to engaging your brain, the more it benefits.' "[94]

Figuring out your own positioning and your own contexts and failures is what will give you your unique edge and will help you identify your limiting beliefs, ultimately aiding in your own course corrections to help you understand who you really are, not who you perceive yourself to be due to flaws or weaknesses. At my present age, I have learned to intentionally control my own narrative, intentionally creating a perception that I have failed, I have practiced, I have learned, I have struggled, and that ultimately I am okay with failure because I have my eyes set on goals that require all of these trials and struggles. I don't show up as a perfectionist or know-it-all. I show up as a constant learner, with intellectual curiosity and a willingness to try something new, to sharpen my edge, or in other words, to fail. People underestimate me because of it, and I use that to my full advantage.

Where there is smoke, there is fire, and so reverse headgear was not my first experiment with uncomfortable orthodontic equipment. The expander, which I was forced to wear permanently in my mouth, unlike a retainer that could be removed at any time, was similarly a challenging test of my mental fortitude. I had it placed in my mouth on my birthday, so how could I forget? Most kids brought donuts in for their birthday for their classmates and celebrated in school, but I was at the orthodontist, the furthest place from friends and donuts. Because I had a swallow reflex, I had a very difficult time eating anything tough to chew, like most proteins such as steak.

For the three years I wore the expander, I did not eat very well. In fact, my diet lacked many nutritional components and led me to reaching for sugar-filled and easily swallowed Go-Gurts and Capri Suns.

My grandparents religiously rented a summer house every year in Spring Lake, New Jersey, which had a lake in town but was known for its gorgeous two-mile sandy beach, boardwalk, and some of the best homemade ice cream. Spring Lake, the same place I grew up dreaming of putting out fires and saving the community with my heroic efforts, reminds me of many great memories but is also riddled with moments of discomfort and painful challenges.

One summer, while vacationing with my extended family in Spring Lake, I decided to broker a deal between my orthodontist and my parents, in a dashing attempt at diplomacy, fashioning my negotiation like a real-life foreign affairs exchange between two nations, prevaricating with olive branches and specious promises. This ploy was my way to compromise and make my doctor and my parents feel better about the whole situation. Maybe even this could be the summer we removed the expander from my mouth and I could actually have a shot at meeting a girl at the beach. I wasn't skimboarding the waves of the Jersey Shore for nothing, nor was my shark tooth necklace a means to scare girls away; quite the contrary. Especially since my parents wouldn't allow me to bleach my hair blonde like some of my other California dreamin' friends.

I had massaged all parties and successfully brought my parents and my orthodontist to the table. Now was the time to strike while the iron was hot. Everyone had their guard down, so I brought up the remaining timeline for wearing the expander. Admittedly, as much as I believe I brokered the conversation, my father's intimidating Boston accent and mannerisms likely did the trick. Don't believe me? Spend five minutes with him and you'll see what I am talking about. Or just look up the *Saturday Night Live* skit in which Affleck plays the construction worker in a Dunkin commercial (or any Affleck performance, for that matter). Fortunately, my dad successfully bent my doctor's ear who cut the remaining time drastically to a couple months. His only stipulation was that we remain extremely focused on making sure to "expand" my teeth every day.

For sixty days, we would use this tiny, Cheerios-sized, metal key with a rope to turn my expander tighter, thus expanding my teeth further apart. A few years beforehand, when the expander was first placed in my mouth permanently, my mom went to turn the key by reaching her hand into my mouth, which required me to open my mouth wide. As she locked the key into the expander, she went to remove the key, but in a moment of panic, she let go and left the key hanging in the expander. Now that the key was stuck, I was helplessly forced to keep my mouth wide open, with every few passing seconds gagging on the key.

My dad came running down the stairs to yank it out, which really required a delicate touch rather than a strongman's grip— ironic for this macho-man of a father I described earlier. If you know my parents, who have been married over thirty years as of this book, you probably can envision what came next.

"Kath, what the heck is going on?" Except he didn't say heck.

"We have to do something; we can't just leave the key in there."

"Ah, ah, ah," I managed to get out, with my mouth still wide open, catching midnight flies.

"I don't know! It is stuck; what should we do?" Mom was clearly struck by panic. She is great in nine out of ten scenarios in life, but not the panic-stricken scenario. After some more arguing, Dad finally unlocked the key, and I was breathing normally again. Crisis averted.

Safe to say this was a scarring moment in my life, so for me to agree a few years later that we would try this routine again was undoubtedly a compromise. By definition, a compromise is when both parties sacrifice something desirable, and I felt l was giving the farm up, but at least there was an end in sight. Here we are in Spring Lake, every morning going through this painful dance between child and parent. It was an exercise in trust and required mental preparation before every time we turned the key. Dad and I would walk into the bathroom, take a few deep breaths, play a pump-up song to inspire us, and then, like a fine surgeon, Dad would gracefully lock in the key and then remove it from the expander, applying pressure to my teeth but at least mechanically pulling the challenge off. It felt like a miracle every time he performed the maneuver.

On a positive note, my family made me pancakes for breakfast, lunch, and dinner that summer, as an award for overcoming my fear. It never got easier, but at least I learned to stand up to my fears and trust the process. It reminds me of my experience with auditory processing disorder. After a summer of correcting the auditory pathways in my brain, I was awarded with my first-ever toddler-size Jeep. It was a battery-charged, double-seated, yellow-and-red Jeep from Toys "R" Us, and it was the only thing I wanted as a kid. I was obsessed with cars, and besides playing with them in the dark hours of the morning as a child and riding on them at Jenkinson's boardwalk, I wanted one of my own to cruise around the dead-end street on which I grew up. I don't think there is a lesson to be learned about incentivizing or bribing children with gifts and food so that they overcome their fears, but I know there was a lesson for me in choosing how to deal with difficult situations in life, and to show up no matter how you feel.

The reality is that we love seeing raw truth and openness in other people, but we are afraid to let them see it in us. We're afraid and anxious that our true self isn't enough—that what we have to offer isn't enough without the bells and whistles, without editing, and without impressing. Our regular self, or living-room self, is messy.

In her novel *Daring Greatly*, Brené Brown explains that we all have both light and dark inside us. As Brown says, "What matters is the part we choose to act on. That's who we really are. We all have shame. We all have good and bad, dark and light inside us. But if we don't come to terms with our shame, our struggles, we start believing that there's something wrong with us—that we are bad, flawed, not good enough, and even worse, we start acting on those beliefs. If we want to be fully engaged, to be connected, we have to be vulnerable."[95] In order to be vulnerable and to connect with others more fully, we have to develop resilience to shame and be willing to share our flaws with others.

Vulnerability is about your willingness to engage with your weaknesses and your failures. The more you are able to exemplify the courage to accept your vulnerabilities, the more successful you will be in finding deeper connection, not just with others but also with yourself. When you spend your life waiting until the perfect moment before you set out for something, you will likely sacrifice golden opportunities or key relationships, pass up your time, and turn back on your true gifts. For me, my skinny legs, headgear, auditory processing disorder, and freckles became my edge. I still feel imperfect, vulnerable, and afraid sometimes, but that doesn't change the fact that I use these fears as reminders to be more brave. In a podcast interview on *How I Built This*,

Guy Raz's guest, Sarah Blakely, paraphrases this about owning your weaknesses: "I was going door-to-door selling my product, and sometimes I would immediately ask to come in for a glass of water before anything else. This was usually surprise number one. I would then tell them an embarrassing story about myself, something like how I tripped over the last doorway I sold to, because it always made me more likable."[96] Sarah used her clumsy weakness as a gracious and good-humored strength. I have found in life that most people will cheer you on all the way to the top, and being an underdog is always a good storyline. But as soon as you reach the top, most will try to tear you down. Don't be scared to slip up, make a mistake, or expose your weakness. The more relatable and likable you are, the more successful you could become.

Lesson: Problems are created in the mind. "Choose not to be harmed and you won't feel harmed. Don't feel and harmed and you haven't been." (Marcus Aurelius)

Friends

Friends might disappoint you and might leave you, but they will usually return to you.

Friends are one of the greatest joys in life to cherish and love. They tell you when you have salad in your teeth, they stay up after midnight watching movies with you, and they sit next to you during lunch when having a friend is more important than having the answers to your math test next period. Truly, what reason is there to celebrate anything in life if not with your friends by your side? In order to develop our friendships, we all need to nurture our friendships, spend time nourishing them, and paying attention to them. Some friends come and go and others stick around for a lifetime, but ultimately they are not beholden to your every wish and desire. You cannot control your friends; you can only support them through their own journey in life, however windy and bumpy that might be.

It is important that you show up for your friends, gain their trust, tell them how you feel, and bring your authentic self to the relationship. What someone else thinks of you is none of your business, but that does not mean that you can't extend your hand first and speak honestly from the heart. A friend should always know where they stand in your relationship. If you can't speak straight to your friend, you will never fully earn their trust.

I encourage you to always celebrate and honor your friends. When they do well, tell them you are proud of them, show them you are proud of them, but mostly, be proud of them. At times, your friends will need space to try new things and meet new people. Support these stages of their lives. Allow your friends to grow, and don't hold them prisoner to your own friendship. The best friendships are like rubber bands: the further you stretch them, the faster and harder the two ends snap back together.

One of my favorite sentiments in life comes from a movie called *Green Street Hooligans*, which details the great fortune of deep-rooted friendship. One of the members of a European football fan club says, "My favorite part of friendship is not knowing that you have my back, but that I get to have yours."[97] Like our being and attitude, we have a choice to decide who we want to show up as, and who we want to show up for. Do we want to be an incredible friend and embody all the support, love, and camaraderie that comes with it, and who do we want to do this for? Because while you have many friends that will pass through your life, there are only so many that will become part of your circle and your most important core group.

I had a friend who used to say, "I'd rather eat chocolate cake with my friend than veggies alone." It stuck with me because it offers a choice. Choose to be happy or choose to be miserable— the amount of work is the same. Maybe it is my obsession with self-improvement, which likely needs course correction at times, but as long as I can remember I have been fascinated with finding happiness. Almost eighty years ago, a Harvard Study of Adult Development set out to unravel the secrets of human happiness and well-being. They included over one thousand participants, and upon summarizing their hypothesis and results, they received over forty-two million views on their TED Talk. Among the original recruits of men were eventual President John F. Kennedy and longtime *Washington* Post editor Ben Bradlee (women weren't in the study because the College was still all male). Scientists wanted to find out how early-life experiences affect health and aging over time. Some participants went on to become successful businessmen, doctors, and lawyers, and others ended up as schizophrenics or alcoholics, but not on inevitable tracks. Over the years, researchers have studied the participants' health trajectories and their broader lives, including their triumphs and failures in careers and marriage, and the findings have produced startling lessons. The director of the study, Robert Waldinger, who is a psychiatrist at Massachusetts General Hospital and a professor of psychiatry at Harvard Medical School, said this: "The surprising finding is that our relationships and how happy we are in our relationships has a powerful influence on our health. . . . Taking care of your body is important, but tending to your relationships is a form of self-care too. That, I think, is the revelation."[98] Close relationships, more than money or fame, are what keep people happy throughout their lives, the study revealed. Those ties protect you from life's discontents, help to delay mental and physical decline, and are better predictors of long and happy lives than social class, IQ, or even genes. That finding proved true across the board among both the Harvard men and the inner-city participants. Waldinger reveals, "Loneliness kills. . . . It's as powerful as smoking or alcoholism. . . . It's easy to get isolated, to get caught up in work and not remembering, 'Oh, I haven't seen these friends in a long time. . . . So I try to pay more attention to my relationships than I used to."[99]

Relationships are a two-way street, however. It is important that you are also open to receiving and not just giving. You will exhaust all of your relationships if you are not open to receiving back support and love. In the book *The Go-Giver*, Bob Burg and John Mann write, "All the giving in the world won't bring success, won't create the results you want, unless you also make yourself willing and able to receive in like measure. Because if you don't let yourself receive, you're refusing the gifts of others— and you shut down the flow. Because human beings are born with appetite, nothing is more naturally geared toward being receptive than a baby, and if the secret of staying young, vibrant, and vital throughout life is to hang on to those most precious characteristics we all have as children but which get drummed out of us—like having big dreams, being curious, and believing in yourself—then one of those characteristics is being open to receiving, being hungry to receive, being ravenous to receive!"[100]

Don't Shrink Yourself So Others Feel More Comfortable Around You

We choose who we want to be, which leads us to choose certain actions, and those actions then reinforce our state of being, which then leads us to choose actions that more fully reflect that state of being, on and on in an endless feedback loop, resulting in a strengthening of the state of being that we have chosen. The consistency of scheduling (and then doing) activities that reflect the desired state of being (i.e., loving, being grateful, and so on) helps to reinforce that state of being to greater and greater degrees, making it more and more the default being with which we show up in the world.

Showing up in the world as a good friend requires charisma, or the ability to draw people to you. People enjoy being around people who enjoy life, and people enjoy people who are easy to read and authentic about themselves. There is a level of discomfort friends might feel when they don't know how you will respond to something. To help friends understand your values, your motivations, and what matters to you, share yourself. Be open and transparent about who you are, where you have been, and what you think. While we cannot completely block pride, insecurity, moodiness, perfectionism, and cynicism, we can be aware of the effect they have on our ability to nurture our friendships.

In sharing yourself, you will be exposing yourself. Not everything about you will be agreeable to your friends. But I have learned that you can shine your own light, be the light for others, and design a life around your own inner brilliance, regardless of the external treatment you receive from people and the world. Just because certain friends might not shine as bright as you doesn't mean that you need to dim your light. Show up as your unapologetic self, and you will receive respect for your consistency, if nothing else.

One trap to beware of is not to associate too closely with those who find the negative in everything. You know who they are—the complainers, the gossipers, the grousers, and the embellishers, who love a good rumor and have no problem with ruffled feathers. Misery loves company, so they say, so avoid getting too close to those who are constantly miserable; they will try to bring you down with them.

In John Maxwell's *The 21 Indispensable Qualities of a Leader*, he states that commitment and attitude are what separate the doers from the dreamers. He says there are four types of people:

1. Cop-outs: People who have no goals and do not commit.

2. Holdouts: People who don't know if they can reach their goals, so they're afraid to commit.

3. Dropouts: People who start toward a goal but quit when the going gets tough.

4. All-outs: People who set goals, commit to them, and pay the price to reach them.

Because of the lower frequency of negative energy, I encourage you to be aware of it. Negativity is pernicious; it slowly eats away at you, and it can even ossify and become a permanent mindset that will limit your life to such a great degree that it could completely remove the beauty of life and the hopes, dreams, and wonderful sensations it can bring you.[101]

"Why even try? You know the management team will never promote you, Kevin, right?"

"Can you believe that professor or coach or boss or friend? Can you believe they really did that to us? They must not care about you and me."

Careful, because when you hear people talk like that, they usually get a jolt of adrenaline and confidence the more they can convince you to agree with them, submit, and acquiesce. If they can't chase their own goals, they will keep you from chasing yours.

To stay above the fray, you will need to actively shape yourself for good. Practice just like a musician practices their music or a Buddhist constantly prays. Practice in order to believe in the good, to see the good, and to be the good. Just because you remind yourself once to be positive or because you wrote it on a sticky note and put it on your steering wheel or bathroom mirror doesn't mean it is cemented permanently in your mind. It is very easy to be negative, but when a focused attempt to deflect negativity becomes inveterate in your daily routine, you can truly elevate yourself and those around you tenfold.

While it is important to not let others affect you, it is possibly more important not to dim your light around others so that they can feel better about themselves. Let others find ways to deal with your greatness and your positivity. If it bothers them, then move on. Your greatness will reach them when they are ready and open to it.

Lesson: "The Sun doesn't ask for permission to Shine, he just does. He doesn't seek approval for his light, for he knows he is the light." (Naked Treaties)[102]

You Can Pick Your Friends; You Can Pick Your Nose

"Despite what some people say, you don't have to follow the crowd. You don't have to want the same things as everyone else or go down the path that everyone else is taking. If you feel as if something is not for you, then you shouldn't feel obligated to do it. Whether that's school, marriage, kids, careers, relationships, anything. You are allowed to follow your own path and do things on your own time." (Free Souls)[103]

My dad once said, "You can pick your friends and you can pick your nose, but you can't pick your friend's nose." In my own translation, my dad was teaching me that you do get to pick your friends, but you don't get to pick what they think or what they do. You can pick your nose, but you can't pick their nose for them. I love this saying because it speaks to the truest type of friendship: an unabashed and unbridled friendship that can withstand differing opinions and perspectives.

You'll always be young in someone's eyes and old in someone else's eyes, talented to one friend and terrible to another. The world is never going to agree on a definition of what you are, so you might as well ignore that stuff, be whatever you want to be for yourself, and be whatever kind of friend you find to be most natural and kind.

And just like you shouldn't have to believe the same beliefs as your friend or hold the same opinion, you should also consider that your own perspective might not be entirely compatible with your friends. As the Sufi saying goes, "Don't cut the person to fit the cloth," meaning that you shouldn't try to fit your friend into your own clothes. Instead, allow them to fit their clothes to their own physique. In the same way, you shouldn't impose your own beliefs on them. You should learn to view the differences in your friends, whether that refers to looks, tastes, habits, or views, with open eyes and ears. In *The Untethered Soul,* Michael A. Singer states, "When you walk through a beautiful botanical garden, you feel open and light. You feel love. You see beauty. You don't judge the shape and placement of every leaf. The leaves are of all sizes and shapes and they face every which way. That's what makes them beautiful. What if you felt that way about people? What if they didn't all have to dress the same, believe the same, or behave the same? What if they were like the flowers, and however they happened to seem beautiful to you?"[104] This quote perfectly captures the beauty of being different and standing out. Choose your friends wisely, because it is better to have a tight circle of true friends than a hundred fake friends, especially friends who all look the same, sound the same, and think the same.

Be around people who you want to be like, and consider the fact that your friends can be better than you at sports, school, or anything else that might seem important to you, and that is okay. You can always be a friend to someone, but when choosing your friends, there are things you might want to look for in their character, such as motivation, curiosity, and loyalty. Not everyone will fit that bill, and we all need different friends in our lives, but your closest friends will have the greatest impact on your life, so make sure you protect your inner circle. I like to call this the "no-jerk policy." This thought was put best by a college roommate during the first week of school: "Hey, Kev, I am trying to meet as many people as possible. It is like a tryout; you want to find the good ones amongst a sea of okay ones." Luckily, this tryout, unlike some of my hockey tryouts earlier in life, was successful. And that mate with the above quote is still one of my best friends and will be forever.

Ultimately, beyond the sayings and quotes, and at the risk of offering too many trite remarks, I hope you stick by your friends, stand up for them, and pick them up when they are down. We will all be down on our luck at some point in our lives, and your friends will be the ones to pick you up. Nobody gets out of this life unscathed, and it is your friends who you want dusting you off and getting you back on track. Learn to forgive your friends, learn to ask for forgiveness from your friends, and be magnanimous when your friends succeed, even if their success comes at a cost to you. Celebrating your friends is not only good for them, but it is also good for your own soul.

Lesson: Your worth is not defined by what you achieve or acquire. It's a question of who you become and how you contribute to others. Similarly, don't be impressed by your friends' money, followers, degrees, and titles. Be impressed by kindness, integrity, humility, and generosity.

Stick Up for Those Weaker than You

When it comes to friends, not only will they disappoint you at times, but you will also certainly disappoint them too. For that reason, it is important that you learn also to forgive yourself. Forgiving yourself does not mean letting yourself off the hook. You still need to apologize and own up to your mistakes. But forgiving yourself allows you to move forward and be better next time. Forgiving yourself is healthy and required. I know I have forgiven myself for these stories and moments in my life, but that does not mean I don't remember to be better than I was when faced with similar situations in my current life.

One of the most important values I could ask my children to embody is to stick up for those weaker than them, whether friends or foes. There comes a time when we all need help, we all need extra love, or we all need just one friend. It is one of the most important responsibilities of our lives. When a friend needs you, be there, no strings attached. And maybe even more so when someone who is not your friend needs a friend—be their friend. Period. Just because they don't play the same sport as you or dress like you or talk like you, when they need a friend, that is your time to be better, to take the higher road, to make sure they feel seen and heard. Each of us holds the power to change someone's life by the simple love we decide to show, especially in the ordinary, everyday loving gestures. It does not have to be a heroic attempt of any kind. A simple friendly smile and wave or telling your friends to knock it off when they crack jokes goes a very long way. And if nothing else, a paid-for ice cream cone usually does the trick.

It is not our job to save every lonely individual, but remember, it also takes very little effort to acknowledge someone or share a conversation with them. You never know what that conversation will do for someone. The juice is worth the squeeze. So be a friend to those who need your love more than they need anything else. After all, laughter is the same in all languages.

Lesson: "Strong people stand up for themselves, but stronger people stand up for others." (Suzy Kassem)

~~Bullying~~ Kindness Is Cool

We were hiding in the bushes on the way home from elementary school, and we knew that he would be right behind us. We waited until he came down the street to start our unrelenting chant, yelling out like cowards from our inconspicuous positions. Who cared whether we had been seen or not? We had just made fun of a neighbor of ours who could have used our friendship instead of our teasing. It was possibly even worse than that time I made fun of that commercial telephone salesperson in front of my mom. Upon second thought, this felt even worse, since I knew the kid and went to school with him every day.

What caused us to feel like we needed to make fun of him? Was it being in a group with our friends and wanting to earn one another's trust, have them think we were cool? Or worse, did we feel we needed to push others down in order to raise ourselves up? It is sad to think about how people bully one another. Even just standing there in the group, I felt ashamed and embarrassed, guilty by association. If I could go back and talk to myself, I would put my hand on my own shoulder and say, "Choose kindness." They might seem like the easiest instructions to follow, but sometimes they are the hardest instructions to follow. After all, no one wants to be left out, and everyone wants to make sure they have an impeccable reputation amongst all their friends and classmates. As adolescents, we topple the other so we can raise ourselves up, but at what expense? It is at the highest cost, putting yourself first at the expense of someone else, and there is no glory in the popularity or friendship that you gain because of such tactless efforts.

Choosing kindness should be non-negotiable. Showing kindness is not a position of weakness; it is indeed a position of strength. Only those who are strong feel comfortable in their own skin and do not feel they need to bully others.

The coolest kid at school will always be the kid who stands up for those who are weaker. And if you don't feel like the coolest kid and don't want to stand up to bullies, then at least do not be a bully yourself. As kids, we are constantly benchmarking and measuring ourselves against others. It is part of growing up and figuring out where we stand amongst the others, and with kids growing at different times, having different interests, and learning to meet new friends, there are a lot of opportunities for us all to show off our bullying skills. If you think bullying only exists in movies, books, or cautionary tales from parents, you are mistaken. Bullying is more prevalent now than at any other time, and the easy solution is to choose kindness. I like the motto "choose kindness" because it is just two words, requires no energy, and is easy to remember. And incidentally, it has a remarkably positive impact on others, quite possibly changing the entire way they feel about themselves. We are all going through our own struggles and challenges, no doubt, even the bullies, so it is important to remember we do not know exactly what anyone is going through at any time, not just in childhood. Parents, too, have a whole mess of issues they are trying to navigate, so choosing kindness evens the playing field. If nothing else, it is a simple gesture and acknowledgement to another that you understand they are going through life's ups and downs, even if you don't know exactly what they are going through. We are all going through highs and lows in life, so don't be that one reason someone despises going to school, or walking home from school, for that matter. Choose kindness, for them and for yourself. You will never regret lifting others, but you will always regret hurting others.

There was a time my mother asked me to reach out to another boy in my class because he was getting bullied. "Just invite him over to play with you," she requested.

But I looked at her with a blank stare and responded, "But Mom, I am just a kid. It is not up to me to make sure that everyone is okay."

Character, or who we are when others are not looking, or even when they are obviously looking, is built not only through dramatic moments in life but also through the everyday moments. Remember those individual, profound moments I had alluded to? I think these moments play out every day in our lives. The catch is that you have to look inside before you can look outside.

"Mom, I have other things I need to be doing. I can't just carry this kid's cross; I have my own problems." I sure did have my own problems, starting with lack of self-respect.

Whether dealing with your closest friends or strangers, your allies or your enemies, or even just to the one kid whom no other kids (or adults for that matter) want to hang out with, the way you present yourself to others is really a reflection of your own internal struggles. If you want to make and keep great friends, then you must understand yourself and, importantly, respect yourself. Have you ever walked in a room and been immediately drawn to one person? They were either holding court or had some sort of undeniable charisma? People with character like this may sometimes be outgoing and other times be more reserved, but one thing these charismatic people have in common is self-respect. As David Brooks explains, "Self-respect is not the same as self-confidence or self-esteem. Self-respect is not based on IQ or any of the mental or physical gifts that help get you into a competitive college. It is not comparative. It is not earned by being better than other people at something. It is earned by being better than you used to be, by being dependable in times of testing, straight in times of temptation."[105] Not only was I not reliable to someone else, but I was also tempted into putting myself above them because in reality, I didn't want other friends to see me hanging out with our classmate who was being made fun of. I thought that being associated with him would lower the opinions others had about me. It was a self-centered viewpoint with limited self-respect.

If I could share a piece of hard-earned wisdom with this other boy, it would be that whatever is happening around you, such as bullying or exclusion, don't take it personally. Nothing other people do is because of you; it is because of themselves. There is a lack of self-respect or a self-consciousness about them that they are sheltering and do not want to expose. Not everyone is going to want to be your friend or extend an olive branch, so it is best to not take it personally. Kobe Bryant says, "People are too concerned with being #1, your fans are your fans, and to them you are #1. Don't worry about everyone else and what they think."[106] I have learned that in order to love someone else, anyone else for that matter, I must first know myself. We are adaptable humans, so we don't have to give in to our identities. But I have spent time struggling with my internal challenges, such as pride, competitiveness, and desire to be liked, and this has helped me course correct and reflect a more pure and wholehearted friendship I am willing to offer others.

In some ways, understanding yourself is really about letting go. Yung Pueblo says, "Letting go doesn't mean forgetting; it means we stop carrying the energy of the past into the present."[107] You don't have to be nice to everyone; if someone doesn't deserve your time or your love, then it is best to ignore them before they drain your energy. But whether we choose to or not, we will always find ourselves, either on the playground or out at parties or functions later in adulthood, shining our light toward others. And if we are comfortable with ourselves, and we recognize and have accepted our own weaknesses, we will be less likely to hurt others. David Brooks goes on to conclude, "The self-effacing person is soothing and gracious, while the self-promoting person is fragile and jarring. Humility is freedom from the need to prove you are superior all the time. Humility is infused with lovely emotions like admiration, companionship, and gratitude."[108]

Lesson: We cannot truly love others until we truly love ourselves.

Ditching Your Friends Will Lead to You Getting Ditched

When others are running away, it is best to be the one running forward.

"On the count of three, let's all bolt toward town and run away from our friend."

"Yeah, let's ditch him so we can go hang out without him."

We were all on the same page: we did not want to hang out with our one friend, and instead, were going to run away and ditch him. At least this time we weren't hiding in the bushes taunting someone, which is probably the lowest form of bullying. This time, we had the nerve to run away from his face. Still, it is a very low form of friendship.

Why do friend groups have to be so divisive? Why do we solo someone out, like we are all on the acclaimed television show *Survivor*, on which someone gets voted off the island and survival of the fittest is celebrated. Sure, friends are supposed to tease one another, call out one another's flaws, and sometimes find other ways to reconcile their quandaries with one another. But deciding as a group to run away from someone has longer-lasting implications than simply messing around might suggest. In fact, if someone is ditching you, I would ditch them right back. They are not worth your time and energy.

Again, if I could go back and put my hand on my own shoulder in a solicitous manner, I would say, "Hey, Kevin, instead of running away from your one friend whom everyone has decided to run away from, why don't you run away from the group and put your arm around this friend, who probably could use you more than you know." We usually are trying to impress the larger group of friends or the most popular friend in our group. Instead, don't. In fact, try this: Don't impress them. Do the opposite. Be the hero when others want to be the villain.

It is not anyone's fault, but the human condition is innately burdened by our existence. I do believe even the nicest people in this world have this fault, though it might not always appear that way at face value. So don't beat yourself up if you have bullied someone or were thinking about it. It is natural; we have competitive and natural forces at play. Hunt or be hunted, some might say. What I am illustrating here is that if you can recognize these moments in your life when someone is being neglected, or you can recognize when you subtly cut your one friend or family member out of a conversation or invitation, then you can at least be aware and find solutions for being a better friend in the future.

Ultimately, the lowest form of friendship is banding together against one person. The highest form of friendship is elevating yourself above these childish games by focusing on the person who is subjected to such bullying. Turn your attention inward and, rather than seeing someone for their weakness and faults, find that one reason to see them for something greater than their faults. I promise that you will feel like a hero if you can learn to stand up in a group setting and learn to defeat the bullies. Oh, and don't worry. You will have plenty of opportunities in life to practice this and improve, especially if you haven't been the best friend in a while.

One question you can ask yourself is this: When you look at someone, can you find yourself in them? If you can answer yes to this question of inclusivity, you should have no problem finding a way to treat someone with love.

Lesson: Bullies don't walk around schoolyards pushing kids over like they do in movies. Bullies are usually found in the quiet corners where groups team up together. If you can learn to recognize when these situations are occurring, you will have an easier time choosing kindness and removing yourself from the toxic environment.

Inspiration and Faith

As paraphrased in Scott Peck's *The Road Less Traveled*, "As human beings grow in discipline and love and life experience, their understanding of the world and their place in it naturally grows apace. Conversely, as people fail to grow in discipline, love, and life experience, so does their understanding fail to grow. Consequently, among the members of the human race there exists an extraordinary variability in the breadth and sophistication of our understanding of what life is all about. This understanding is our religion. Since everyone has some understanding—some worldview, no matter how limited or primitive or inaccurate—everyone has a religion. We suffer from a tendency to define religion too narrowly. We tend to think that religion must include a belief in God or some ritualistic practice or membership in a worshiping group. We are likely to say of someone who does not attend church or believe in a superior being that they are not religious."[109]

The fact of the matter is that everyone has an explicit or implicit set of ideas and beliefs as to the essential nature of the world. Do you envision the universe as basically chaotic and without meaning so that it is only sensible to grab whatever little pleasure you can whenever it is available? Do you see the world as a dog-eat-dog place where ruthlessness is essential for survival? Or do you see it as a nurturing sort of place, in which something good will always turn up and in which you do not need to worry much about the future? Or a place that owes you a living no matter how you conduct your life? Or a universe of rigid law in which you will be struck down and cast away if you step even slightly out of line? Find out your religion as soon as you can, as your worldview is typically an essential part of your problems, and a course correction in your worldview is necessary for a cure.

Traveling the World with Your Friends

An itinerant group of recent grads, my two friends and I did not study abroad, so after graduating from college, the plan was to fly into Paris, France. We spent a month living out of our oversized backpacks, with a few showers in between, some hostels, some Airbnbs, and mostly the wherewithal to spend four weeks together. What could possibly go wrong?

We took trains and planes from Paris to Amsterdam, Berlin, Prague, Rome, Florence, Barcelona, and back to Paris. It felt like we climbed every spiraling staircase of every church in Europe, visited every college watering hole, and logged over twenty thousand steps each day—which is a lot when half the day is spent nursing a pint. While we had organized a few flights and overnight stays, a majority of our trip remained unplanned. We felt that a desultory approach to backpacking would give more credibility to our vagabond desires. I even picked up Louis L'Amour's novel *Education of a Wandering Man* in hopes of finding inspiration on the road. Usually I would suggest the motto, "Overprepare, and then go with the flow," but in this case, we were underprepared and overflowing! The plan was: there was no plan.

While I could share many stories about our evenings spent enjoying blueberry steaks in Florence or an eight-course meal straight from the sea in Barcelona, that is not my intention for this book. Instead, I wanted to use this story for two reasons. The first is that learning stuff is less important than learning about oneself. Exploration and travel are not just whimsical niceties;

they are an integral component to life's sampling process. Secondly, those who are constantly seeking something are never fully present where they are, never fully finding comfort and identity in their home. Rather, they find themselves deprived on the never-ending and circuitous road to fulfillment.

In the following few pages, I summarize one of the most profound depictions of a heart always on the run, of a person always looking for something they don't have and someplace they don't live. I would encourage everyone to travel as much as they can, to see the world, to experience different cultures, and to never grow comfortable staying home and watching movies every night. However, I think it is crucial to understand the difference between running away and running toward. I would argue that most of us run away and that instead, we should course correct and run toward. Your thought patterns, the narratives you repeat to yourself, the limitations you place on yourself, and the person you are being and showing up as cannot be shed simply by finding a new home.

Lois Greiman states in her book *Heart on the Run,* "It might be youth, it might be inferiority complex or the boredom of small-town claustrophobia or the hungers of ancestors whose aspirations have sunk into your bones, pushing you to go. It might be loneliness, or it might be the search for a mother or father or even just yourself. It might be greed or curiosity. It might be liberation or escape. There might be a million other reasons, *but we all leave.* You can leave without a bus ticket of course, and you can depart in your heart and take an existential journey to anywhere but the here that's stifling you."[110] I found this passage extremely relatable.

My friends and I left home because we were looking for something, and we were inspired by the potential to find it. Find something. Find someone. We left because we yearned for something else, something more than what we were experiencing. We left searching for some piece of us that was missing or latent. Or was it that we hit the road to leave ourselves behind and recreate who we are and who we want to be? We hit the road in the hopes of finding what we were looking for—or at least adequately distracting ourselves from the hungers and absences that fomented our departure to begin with.

And, oh, how the road does not disappoint. The road offers an infinite ribbon of sights and sounds, and the flashing signs and signals promise exactly what you're looking for: happiness, contentment, purpose, and joy. Perhaps the road has a bizarre way of underscoring to us what looks like a destination in the distance, and yet it only portends another destination beyond it upon reaching it. Just when you think friendship or wealth or family or influence or wisdom or passion was your ultimate destination, you spend some time there for a while, and suddenly the place starts to dim. You no longer feel that fire in your belly when you first arrive.

What once captured your fascination and enthralled you— even if for only a moment—doesn't do it for you anymore. It might have even seemed like it was your reason to live, but in a mercurial fashion, it begins to wane in significance, like falling out of love with it. Of course, you won't admit it to yourself for a long while, especially since you are a proud and committed person. After all, you sent out all those celebratory announcements to your friends about your new home and new journey. Essentially, you told everyone you had arrived, and you believed it yourself. But at some time in your journey, you will be forced to face the music and become honest with yourself about the disappointment you feel. Eventually, that disappointment will fade into frustration, and you won't be able to hide it from others, let alone yourself. Fortunately, right when your awareness heightens to this reality, you begin to understand the promise of a new destination down the road. And so, the journey restarts itself. The wheels on the bus go round and round, and the exhaustion of the road returns.

We try to convince ourselves that the road is life, making restlessness, peace, and uprootedness home. "You going to get somewhere, or just going?" The answer, most of the time, is "Just going." Do we tell ourselves we are just going in order to guard against the disappointment of never arriving? Do we call the road home to avoid the pain of never being welcomed? Do we assume that this is how life should be, always struggling, always looking, never fully feeling at home? In some senses, the road is a crutch and an excuse. It helps us deal with failure, with uncertainty, and with holes in our lives.

You, the good person that you are, wake up one morning and realize that even the person with less wealth, less family, less power, and less success is enjoying their life more than you, and you start to ask yourself some questions, like, "What the hell am I doing here?" And "Who am I?" And even, "Whose am I?"

It's possible that you start to question whether your family would even take you back. By some indescribable grace, you are guided on your way back home. And as you begin playing these conversations in your head, you start rehearsing the litany of reasons for your return and why things didn't pan out as you had intended, because undoubtedly, this was out of your control, or so you think. And right when you start feeling sick about the whole thing, of having to throw up the white flag and dragging yourself back home, you see your family running toward you, gathering you in their arms, while you hide your face in their embrace so as not to show your weakness. Your family later tells you, "We walked to the end of the driveway every single day, waiting for you to come back home."

Understanding yourself is a matter of plotting your misguided steps while searching for love in all the wrong places. It is like a choreographed dance to the wrong song. The range of our geographical wandering is paralleled by the range of our soul-searching inward wandering. Your own spirit and heart can be an unexplored place of wandering, and this lack of homeness with yourself can be the cause that propels you to run away from home. How can we find what we are searching for if we don't know what to search for in the first place?

If we never fully arrive, growing bored of each place that promised to be the end of the road, it's because the environment of our own spiritual life is a forest of insatiable desires, always reaching for the next thing once we receive the first desire. We think leaving home will help us find what we want, only to find out later that it does the opposite and leaves us asking more questions than when we began. The truth is that you will never find what you set out to look for, because it already exists within. Whether you decide to backpack Europe, South America, Asia, or even America, for that matter, whether with your friends or not, you, too, can be searching for a new home without ever even stepping foot outside your home. What I am speaking to is the desire to escape here by looking there, or by looking outward. Instead, look inward.

In life, our restlessness comes from the way we assign happiness to the end goal rather than to the journey in arriving at that goal. To us, the accomplishment is the place to land, not the act of accomplishing in the first place. It is like the Bruce Springsteen song lyrics: "Everybody's got a hungry heart." The heart's hunger is infinite, which is perhaps the reason that anything finite in our lives leads to less than an extraordinary experience. Try as we may, we can never be fully satisfied with anything that is created on earth, because there is always something missing, something else to look forward to once we reach the destination.

What then? What do we do if we have come to the conclusion that no place offers unadulterated happiness and so lose inspiration and decide to give up on the quest altogether? What if the road is long and dangerous, and we grow sick and tired of highway rest stops and hotel beds and the excitement and the pleasures of this quest turn staid?

It's not just a matter of finally settling down or coming to the end of the road once and for all. It's a matter of coming to this concluding reality, that we find rest because we are found, and we make it home because someone comes to get us. As you will read further along in the faith chapters, regardless of your religion, belief, or even non-belief, we are all children of some higher power, whether you think of it scientifically, metaphysically, divinely, or whether don't give much thought to it at all. The story of the runaway child, or the prodigal child, remains the purest lesson we can all learn and apply in our own lives.

While we still have a long way to go and will never reach perfection, we are not alone in this world and do not have to face the journey on the road alone. We can let go of the exhaustion, the chase, and the constant search, knowing that we have been found. God, or some higher energy, is not folding his or her arms judgmentally as you quietly sneak up the stairs into the safety of your bedroom, with each tiptoe leaving a footprint of guilt on the hardwood floors. No, your God is the one running toward you, arms wide open and smiling from ear to ear. But it is up to you to rest from the road, to turn toward something greater than your underlying pursuit.

We cannot free ourselves from our unhappy wandering. We need someone or something else to say to us, "Take the step forward; I will carry you. I will carry you to the end, and even at the end, I will carry you some more. I am here with you." An authentic, happy life, as St. Augustine suggests, can be reached by "Setting one's joy on God."

The soul's hunger for peace is a longing for a kind of rest from anxiety and frantic pursuits—it is to rest in God. You will never feel fully rested, not by a good night's sleep or a new adventure to chase. Rest is achieved, true rest from anxiety, when you realize you no longer need to perform because you are loved regardless of your performance. You discover peace because you are loved no matter what. Period. There is nothing for you to prove or demonstrate. When thinking about how you want to spend your time in this life, how much stress you want to carry, and how much soul-searching you want to do all the while, ask yourself some important questions before committing your life to the road.

I will conclude my journey in seeking peace with this quote attributed Gautama Buddha: "Peace comes from within. Do not seek it without. It can be argued that peace and happiness comes from the subjective internalized perspective of realizing things could be worse and being grateful they aren't. The alternative view that peace and happiness comes from the objective external perspective of having more and better things than at present, while important for growth, can be a never-ending source of jealousy, dissatisfaction, and disappointment. A balance of the two, where people are grateful for what they have while striving for more, seems the best blended perspective."[111] Remember what I said at the beginning of this book: a good life is lived by asking good questions. Make sure to consider the why before your journeys and endeavors. Understand truly what you are searching for, because in many ways, there is nothing to be found that you cannot discover right here and now. Take comfort in knowing you can rest and still be enough. You can rest and still accomplish great feats. Look nowhere else but inward for the answers you crave so deeply.

Lesson: "Our hearts are restless until they rest in Him." (St. Augustine)

Faith Is Not about Rules or Principles

"Your relationship with God is the same as your relationship with the sun. If you hid from the sun for years and then chose to come out of your darkness, the sun would still be shining as if you had never left. You don't need to apologize. You just pick your head up and look at the sun. It's the same way when you decide to turn toward God. You just do it. If instead you feel guilt and shame interfering, that's just your ego blocking the Divine Force. You can't offend God, as its very nature is light, love, compassion, protection, and giving, and you can't make it stop loving you. It's just like the sun. You can't make the sun stop shining on you, you can only choose not to look at it. The moment you look, you'll see it is there. This is how you know something about God. You become one with Him. Ultimately, the only way to know about God is by letting your being merge into God's Being, and then seeing what happens to you." *The Untethered Soul*[112]

Much of the following excerpts are my own paraphrases and interpretations from the book *The Untethered Soul*. This book changed my life in many ways, and is meant to be about love rather than about your God versus my God. In fact, you can replace the word *God* with *love* if you prefer, but I encourage you to read this chapter not from the lens of rules and principles but as a no-strings-attached outlook on life that will completely change your life too. These next few chapters are entirely about you and will provide you with new ways to think about the world and the people in it.

This is universal consciousness, and the qualities of the beings who have attained this deep state are similar in every religion. To sincerely experience this reality, think about if you decided to feel an overwhelming love for all beings on earth, for every plant or flower, for every animal or pet, and for all nature's beautiful settings. Imagine if all the children of the world seemed like your own children, and you viewed every person you came across like the beautiful flower they were, with their own design, shape, pigments, and expression. As you apply this to all things in your life, you start to notice a phenomenal transformation in that you are no longer judging anyone or anything.

As you drift back into Spirit, you will see that those are the eyes that look out upon this world. It can be exhausting to have your shield up, constantly and subconsciously judging others, protecting your own image, and restraining your love and support for all the beautiful miracles around you. It is much easier to view the world with love, with a heart that shines down upon everything and everyone. Through that perspective, the most judged of creatures looks beautiful, and that's the part that no one understands or fully appreciates. Some might suggest that a higher being looks down on the earth with disappointment and dismay. However, the saint sees that a higher being goes into ecstasy when looking down upon our earth, under all conditions, and at all times of the day. Ecstasy is the only thing known to this higher being. Nature is eternal and conscious bliss. No matter what you or I have done to "mess this up," you're not going to be the one thing that ruins it. No failure is great enough to empty the cup of ecstasy.[113]

You might be reading this and thinking to yourself, "This is all nice, Kevin. But it's not that easy to just love everyone and everything. It's not that easy to let go of all my judgments and show love to anyone, especially those undeserving of my love." But the miraculous beauty is that you and I can experience this ecstasy with no payment or transaction in return for such ecstasy. It is a free gift, if we are willing to receive it.

And when you begin to feel this joy and let go of the constant judgment, that's when your faith will grow tenfold, because you will have come to understand the nature of faith and love. You look at everyone like your own, and your love is commensurate with that feeling. Upon this realization, nobody will upset or disappoint you, and nothing will create a problem. Besides when you let your love finally shine through for others, your natural state of being will get higher and higher, and you will feel love shining back at you. If you try reading and learning about faith, you will run into a slew of books and podcasts that contradict one another, not to mention the multiple interpretations from just one author's interpretation. Someone will publish one book, and another person will receive a degree proving that thesis incorrect. Knowing and growing faith comes from actual experience.[114]

Will Smith had a major fear of the ocean that took years for him to overcome. I am so impressed by his ability to overcome this fear through his experience of his own faith and surrender. In his book *Will*, Smith says, "I settled into the acceptance of my powerlessness, which strangely liberated me. 'Surrender' had always been a negative word for me—it meant losing or failing or giving up. But my burgeoning relationship with the ocean was exposing that my sense of control was actually an illusion. Surrender transformed from a weakness word to an infinite power concept. I had had a bias toward action—and I began to realize that their opposites were equally as powerful—inaction, receptiveness, acceptance, non-resistance, being. Stopping was equally as powerful as going; resting was equally as powerful as straining and silence was equally as powerful as talking. Letting go was equally as powerful as grasping. 'Surrender' to me no longer meant defeat, it was now an equally powerful tool of manifestation. Losing could be equal to winning in terms of my growth and development. I began to understand a perplexing phrase that Gigi used to use, 'Let go and let God', that had always seemed wrong to me. It felt like absolving yourself of your responsibilities, like something that people say when they're too lazy to do what's necessary to build the life they want. But all of a sudden, it took on new and magical meaning. There is an energy that's at work while you're asleep—the energy that fires the sun, that moves the ocean, that beats your heart. You don't have to do everything; in fact, most of the things that get done, you don't have anything to do with them. Actually, it's a great thing you were asleep, because if you'd been awake, you would probably have messed it up. And then a new wording of Gigi's axiom came into my mind, it's not just 'let go and let God', but 'let go and let God work'. The surfer and the ocean are a team. The mountain and the climber are partners, not adversaries. The Great River is going to do 99% of the work—your 1% is to study it, to understand it, respect its power and creatively dance within its currents and its laws."[115]

Lesson: Act when the universe is open, and rest when she is closed.

We have so many belief systems, differing views of faith, and various concepts, but the issue is that they all have been created by people. Ultimately, our ideas about faith conform to the various views and religions from which they are derived. To reiterate, this chapter is not about religion or secular belief systems. Fortunately, there is an intrinsic nature within us all that connects us to a higher power, whatever the power is that you choose to believe in. There is something in our being that goes beyond our personal self, and you have the choice to consciously identify with this part of your being rather than identifying with your career, your body, or your achievements. When you choose to look inward to the natural being that already exists within you, a natural transformation begins to take place within you, and your life will never be the same. Your love and faith will be boundless, and you will have the confidence to soar to new heights.

As Scott Peck details in *The Road Less Traveled*, "To develop a religion, or world view that is realistic, that is to say, conforms to the reality of the cosmos and our role in it, as best we can know that reality, we must constantly revise and extend our understanding to include new knowledge of the larger world." He continues, "We must constantly enlarge our frame of reference. We are dealing here with the issues of map making. The process of expansion of knowledge is a major theme in our lives; in order to show love to someone we must expand ourselves, and in order to learn something new we are required to give up the old self and a death of outworn knowledge. To develop a broader vision we must be willing to forsake, to kill, our narrower vision. In the short run it is much more comfortable not to do this, to stay where we are, to keep using the same map, to avoid suffering the death of cherished notions. The road of spiritual growth, however, lies in the opposite direction. There is no such thing as a good hand-me-down religion. To be vital, to be the best of which we are capable, our religion must be a wholly personal one, forged entirely through the fire of our own questioning. When it comes to questions of meaning, purpose and death, secondhand information will not do. I cannot survive on a secondhand faith in a secondhand God. There has to be a personal word, a unique confrontation, if I am to come alive. The path to holiness lies through questioning everything."[116]

Lesson: "The key to giving is being open to receiving." (*The Go-Giver*)

Love

Kristen Corley says, "I think the key to staying in love is staying grateful. When you have something and someone good, don't go looking for something better. Learn to appreciate what you have. Learn that the best relationships are the ones where you don't give up on each other. We are living in a generation where it's easy to move on and give up when things get hard. Don't do that. Cherish what you have, be that story that says—we made it all the way, and that's because we never gave up on each other, or walked away from the love we found. We made it all the way because we reminded ourselves, every single day, just how lucky we really were."[117]

In many ways, love is a two-way street. But before you can give your love away, you must first be able to retain it. You must show yourself love before you can love another person. If you can't stop judging yourself, you will be unable to stop judging others, no matter how much good you see in them. Love is not only a two-way street, but it is also a lifelong building process, constantly requiring nurturing and attention. You don't just choose love one day; rather, you must work on that love each and every day. How can we make sure that others help us nurture that love? Well, we can build love when we allow our most vulnerable and powerful selves to be deeply seen and known, and when we honor the spiritual connection that grows from that offering with trust, respect, kindness, and affection. That is why love is a two-way street, because we have to be willing to show our own vulnerabilities while simultaneously accepting someone else's vulnerabilities. We can only love others as much as we love ourselves.

In other words, when we love one another, we face our sh*t. We face our limitations and failures. We show others where we are not strong. We put it all on the table for others to see how bad at communicating we might be, and we have to be willing to feel the sense of unworthiness. But when you turn toward love, instead of running away from showing affection, whether to a friend or someone you admire, you are turning toward another person who sees your light and wants to love you for that light. You see, loving is easy, but remaining open to being loved requires the understanding that you are indeed worthy of their love. But how do you feel worthy of love, especially when your automatic response might be to duck from the love of others? It is simple: allow yourself to be loved by consciously deciding you are worthy. How you love can actually define you. Forget about the missions of life to solve diseases, travel space, or sell the next greatest business for billions. Instead, focus on others. How you use your gifts to help others defines you. Your gifts are part of your purpose. Even if you say you don't know what you want out of life or what your mission is, you can still have purpose by starting with your center, or your heart. Start with helping others. Our world needs love more than renewable energy or trade agreements.

Rainstorms of Love

My wife warned me several times before pregnancy that this could happen, but like many important pieces of wisdom she shares with me, I shook it off as hearsay and an unlikely event to occur. If you have seen Seth Meyers' Netflix special *Lobby Baby*, you know that Seth's wife gave birth to their second child in the lobby of their New York City apartment building—riveting stand-up material. Seth goes on to describe the utter shame he felt upon his wife giving birth and "lion-kinging" her baby in front of strangers without any help from her husband, who, as he described in his monologue, was the scared dude looking on from the corner.[118] While I laugh at his skit and understand the feeling of shame he felt, I had no such experience. Instead, I found myself doubled over in complete admiration for my wife after bearing witness to the miracle she performed. I was less focused on my own incompetencies and more enamored by her own stratospheric strengths.

First the nurses shuffle into your room, with their voices calm and delicate, as if they had rehearsed it in medical school like a two-minute *Saturday Night Live* audition. They tell you that you are doing such a great job and that things are progressing nicely. *How lovely and wonderful; everything is going according to plan.* Then they come back into the room, your room, where your underwear is on the floor and your suitcase is showing off that self-improvement book that has every other page bunny-eared for reference. The nurses pretend not to notice the mental mess the husband must be in, let alone the underwear lying out—they must have been taught to pretend not to notice while auditioning at medical school—while you sit there contemplating the fact that your wife made you pack half of your closet in suitcases that you received for your wedding. But instead of using them for vacations to the Mediterranean, like the wedding envelope promised, you are instead using them for packing oversized overnight bags for the hospital, where the service is actually better than any five-star Mediterranean resort but the sun-kissed tans are traded in for sweat and tears. *I don't think the staff scoffed at the six suitcases we brought in, did they?* The nurses start probing around your wife, the same wife you promised to protect, love, and defend on your wedding day, and you begin to wonder if you'd feel more comfortable watching them probe around your suitcase—you know, the one with the stinky underwear—rather than your sweet and loving wife. It starts to get personal, and like any good teammate on the sidelines of a nail-biter game, you start buying into the game plan with unrelenting fist bumps and words of encouragement, mostly starting and ending with expletives.

Then the nurses come back in, letting you know that the baby isn't happy and neither is mom—yet still in their assuring voices. *Is this also what they learned in medical school, that a baby in distress means a baby isn't happy? This isn't a preschool; what does that mean?* They keep you waiting, while your wife has tubes running through her nose, wet wash clothes on her forehead, and a vomit bucket next to her bedside. *Is anyone going to do anything?* I feel helpless as I continued to "try" and console my wife with backrubs and Bon Iver playing on Spotify. Then they come piling back in, only this time they are like a pit team in NASCAR, making all sorts of adjustments to the bed, the cords connecting from every which side of the bed, like an unused and tangled Nintendo-64 set of controllers at your parents' house. One doctor is pulling her arm one way, another doctor is pulling her leg the other way. Suddenly, their calm and melodic voices were no longer in medical school character. They were unrecognizable, like an entirely new crew of nurses and doctors had shown up, like a substitute teacher with a worried look of timidity, unsure of the impending response of the students. More computers begin beeping in the room—*I hate beeping hospital computers*—adding to the cacophony of sounds that had our hospital room feeling more like a high school pep rally than a Bon Iver concert only a few minutes ago. Cue the red alert, because the medical terminology was now being thrown around, with terms, procedures, and possible risks all so hard to understand and comprehend. *What happened to the baby that is not happy? Can we go back to words I understand?*

"Don't worry, the best surgeon is in today."

So we have a cocky doctor on our hands; great.

"We are going to use the maximum amount of numbing, because it is better than having to add while we are in the operating room."

Fantastic, my wife is going to look even more like a bag of Jell-O. Didn't you give her enough drugs already? She doesn't look like a bag of Jell-O, Kevin. C'mon, pick it up.

"Dad is going to need some sugar so he doesn't pass out in the operating room. Dad, would you like apple juice?"

Who is Dad? Oh, wait, that is me. Finally, someone remembered the coward in the corner needed some love too.

Everything was changing so quickly, but luckily I learned so much about the importance of changing on a dime in hockey. My dad would scold me after hockey games about my love for taking big wide "rink turns," as he called them. Kind of like this lazy, whistle-blowing, Sunday open-ice session for all recreational skaters, instead of the fierce and quick "stop and go" pivots needed in a fast-paced hockey game. I guess now it might be clearer to you as to why I never made the AAA teams back in the day. But in this situation, when my wife needed me most, I actually found a way to stop and go rather than taking my usual roundabout way of arriving at the solution to a problem. Proud to say no rink turns were made that day, coach.

Immediately, I began tidying up the room, repacking all of the suitcases, loose underwear, and self-help books that I really wish I had finished before this procedure. I got dressed into my own blue surgeon gown, equipped with a standard hospital hair cap. Except it was not the cool kind that triathletes wear but more like those worn by your proverbial kindergarten cafeteria server. Last time I wore one of these, my friend had just bitten through my head with his braces in sixth grade at a sledding hill, and after arriving at the hospital in an ambulance, the doctor required me to wear a hair cap for a week to school. Luckily I already had friends, and most of them only made a few jokes. I then placed the scrubs over my shoes, and at a moment's notice, I watched as my wife was wheeled out of the room for her emergency C-section—you know, that possible event that she had warned me about several times leading up to her due date. I was crushed. At least when we checked into the hospital I could sleep by her side, talk to her over the arm of the hospital chair I slept on, and make her laugh when she was tired of the blubbering lyrics of Bon Iver. Sometimes you just need some heavy metal to reset the mood, or a stand-up comedy act from your cowardly husband. The same husband who otherwise would still be pretending to text his wife's family while sneaking in some chicken noodle soup before his malnourished wife could notice, the same wife who wasn't permitted to eat anything until giving birth. My wife was carrying our son in her belly, and I was carrying a load of pathetic shame as I tried to eat away my inadequacy. No amount of eating at any steakhouse in New York City could have removed even a sliver of inadequacy that factually existed when comparing my wife's bravery to my lack thereof.

I sat outside the operating room, staring at the eight-foot white door with that tiny little window into the room taped over. For all I knew, Oppenheimer himself could have been developing the next atomic bomb there. There were hazard signs along the wall, and there was not a single hospital doctor, nurse, or other staff member in the hall besides myself and my thoughts. The feeling was similar to the time I walked into the Naval Academy interview with the fifteen decorated veterans. Uncertainty crept back in my mind, similar to the time I had to walk down the hall and open that big wooden door, behind which all of these highly intimidating and impressive veterans would grill me for the next hour on my capacity to serve in the United States Navy. I was feeling tired, the adrenaline rush of the emergency wave had passed, and my stomach was growling. *Oh sh*t, I remembered, anxiety now pouring over me. No one brought me apple juice.*

"Okay, Dad, we are ready for you."

I got up from my chair and walked toward the same door I had been staring at for fifteen minutes.

"Okay, let's rock and roll."

"Please be very careful; we just spent twenty minutes setting up the room. There are buckets, machines, and cords everywhere, and don't touch anything, as it is all sterilized."

My mind thought back to the Fun House at the Jenkinson boardwalk down at the Jersey Shore. It was a nightmare walking through those rooms, particularly the operating room with a mad scientist throwing up green bile into a bucket. Likely a misnomer, that Fun House. *Oh, God, I am back in the Fun House; not again.*

"Betta, Betta, can you see me? I am here." I managed to eke out a somewhat-convincing "It's going to be okay" tone of voice. Heck, I might have even fooled myself, the notorious hypochondriac.

Her eyes were bloodshot, but she grabbed and squeezed my hand. We were behind a big blue curtain, and there were at least eight people talking to one another on the other side of the curtain, playing real-life *Operation*, the twenty-dollar board game you can buy from Amazon. These events happen every day, but they don't happen in your everyday life. I couldn't think about this, though; my wife needed me. If not to love, defend, and protect, then at least to be by her side. She was physically shaking, even though she couldn't feel anything, I was told. It was like she had fallen into a pond during the winter, with her teeth chattering and her body jerking every so often. She was scared, and so was I. As I was promised before I entered the operating room—by the way, at this stage they no longer call it a delivery room, which is another change when they stop using the comforting and delicate language in the early hours of delivery—the surgeon told me the baby would be delivered within two minutes of sitting down beside my wife.

"Okay, Betta, you are going to feel some pushing and pulling. Dad, why don't you stand so you can get a photo."

My legs may not have gotten me a Division 1 hockey scholarship, but they better get me out of this chair and on my feet now. As I stood, I witnessed the most incredible moment of my life, as I watched my son take his first breath into this world, the same world I described in the first chapter that spins around in circles in a galaxy full of matter, with enough gas and water to sustain human life. Don't believe in miracles? Go watch a baby being delivered, or Herb Brooks and his 1980 U.S. hockey team. The most beautiful sight I could ever see, like meeting God, or learning that humanity is saved. It was utterly and phenomenally overwhelming, and brought me right back down to my seat afterward. But it wasn't the beauty that brought me to my knees, but rather the unexpected meconium that caught the surgeons by surprise. And once again, the tone of the voices in the room changed, just like it did earlier in the day. Suddenly, they were talking faster and moving quicker. In a moment's notice, my baby was born, and at the same time, we were not out of the woods. *What was happening? Is this normal? Why isn't anyone talking to us?* I was completely freaked out. But at the same time, I was called around to the front of the room to help cut the umbilical cord. As I walked around the table, the one with triple the amount of cords and tubes as the delivery room had had a few hours ago before we departed for the operating room, I caught a quick glance of the operating table. And like a kid accidentally witnessing a horror movie on TV, I immediately turned in the other direction, mind racing from what I had just seen. *Did I just see what I think I saw?*

After all of the stress testing and measuring of the baby, I was asked by one of the nurses to let mom be and to find my way to the recovery room with the baby and another nurse. *But what about my wife? Is she going to be okay?* I was disoriented, still in shock from seeing the birth of my son, but even more so in shock from how unprepared I was for this moment. I had ten months to get ready, and no excuse not to be prepared. *How could I not be ready?* Maybe it was the lack of apple juice in my blood, but I was looking more concerned than any substitute teacher I had ever come across in grade school. I later pieced together the fact that during all the chaos of the NASCAR pit change, when the nurses switched from "baby is unhappy" to "I am so sorry, but we are going right to the operating room," I never heard, or it was never explained to me, that Mom would be in the operating room for some time after delivery. Here I was thinking that something terribly wrong was occurring with my wife, who, as far as I was told, ran a fever and was experiencing blood pressure issues. *Something has to be wrong, right?*

I sat in the recovery room with my new baby and a nurse who was not my wife. It was nothing like how we planned. He looked extremely upset; after working so hard to find the way out, he was equally frustrated with the way things changed on a dime. I wanted so badly to share that beautiful moment with his mom, for her and me to smile at each other, hug our newborn, and breathe a big, fat sigh of relief, together, all three of us. Instead, Betta and I were robbed of that fairy-tale fantasy. But what I received that day was a blessing in disguise. While I had never experienced such a high level of concern for my wife, I was even more so moved by the adoration I had for my wife. I had always loved her sweetness, silliness, motherliness, and athleticism, but watching her deliver our baby was the crowning moment of our relationship. It was like we were at level 99, and the bonus round for level 100 was fought on top of Bowser's Castle. We had lost our moment of anticipated sheer joy as a family, but it will be replaced forever by thousands of new moments together, thanks to my wife's resilience and bravery. Princess Peach had truly defeated Bowser, once and for all.

My wife gave me the greatest lesson of all, that nothing is more important than family. For a hypersensitive person like myself, it should not surprise you that this event was monumental for me. But it surprised me. After our family came to visit us at the hospital, I had a few minutes to run home and take a shower. But when I let the water pour over my face and over my eyelids, I began sobbing for almost fifteen minutes. It was a complete release of emotions. It was my body breathing that sigh of relief that I never experienced with my family like I had hoped for. It was a shedding of my cowardice and a renewal of my love for my family. With each passing teardrop mixing in with the beads of water running down my face, I grew more and more sure of myself. I was going to step up and make sure our family grew stronger from this. That our son and my wife would develop the closest bond possible, despite their twenty-four-hour fight they had to put up together. What doesn't kill you makes you stronger, and I couldn't have been more proud of the resilience of our family that day. It made a father out of a hypochondriac, and I will be eternally grateful to both of them for that.

Snowstorms of Love

One of the best snowstorms to hit Providence had arrived, and it was only a few days from Christmas break. Lugging a fake Christmas tree across campus with my two roommates was the easy part, though. My wife's friends had given us the access key to their dorm room so we could sneak in and place the tree inside the room and set the scene up right. All week I had been working on creating the ornaments for the tree. When I was no more than six years old, Mom and I used to create snowflakes out of paper. We would fold them up and start cutting into the edges, zigzagging our way through the rigid pieces. Finally, when we were done cutting, we would open up the papers, and our very own homemade snowflakes would litter the dining room table and floor.

I took this "skill" I learned as a child and applied it to the ornaments I would make for her Christmas tree. I created these snowflakes, but instead of leaving them empty and white, I printed out pictures of all the activities I wanted to do with her in the next year. There were pictures of paddle tennis courts, ice skating, surfing, hiking trails, and almost everything else you can think of. There were at least twenty ornaments, and I thought that if she was willing to go on one adventure, she'd probably be willing to go on twenty. It was also my way of hedging a date. If she said no to dinner at an Italian restaurant, maybe she would say yes to snowshoeing in the Rockies. For the record, she is Italian and would never turn down an Italian restaurant, and in fact, we later went on to hear "Scenes from an

Italian Restaurant" by Billy Joel on Valentine's Day at Madison Square Garden, an experience you must see for yourself.

As the storm continued and the roommates were out to dinner, leaving the apartment empty, the three of us placed the ornaments on the tree, turned on some music in the background, and hid a few of the presents under the tree. We even strung some tacky lights around the fake tree from Savers Lot, a dollar store just a few neighborhoods away, to really show this thing off.

This was going to be a Christmas tree with a cherry on top, and an experience she would never forget, I thought to myself. We received a text from one of her friends, "We are on the way back and a few minutes away." Quickly, I dashed into the back staircase where no one could see me and listened to the arrival of her friend group returning from dinner. I then heard some laughs and conversations right outside, and I knew it was her and her friends. They walked up to the door, and as they stepped through the doorway, the room grew silent. I smirked and thought that I had to go see this for myself. There was some confusion at first, but as everyone was in on this except for Elisabetta, she then came to realize that this was entirely for her. She was a bit unsure of how to respond, looking toward her friends for some reassurance and support.

"Thanks, everyone; this is so nice," she blurted out.

That was when her one friend responded, "Betta, we didn't do this."

I walked in and threw my hands up in the air, and that is when she realized who was behind all of this.

It was one of my favorite surprises, partly because of all the support and help I received from my friends, but really because it was the first time and last time that I would ever have to surprise anyone in that way ever again. I knew right then that we were going to eventually need a bigger tree, with more ornaments and activities and, yes, probably more presents too. Even though the ornaments were made from paper and printed-out pictures, Betta still shined brighter than any Christmas bulb or ornament that could have been hanging on the tree that night. With the winter storm whirling in the background outside the windows and the dim lights of the room, it had all the trappings of a holiday postcard, etched in time, but forever in my heart.

Love is the one superpower we all share; it's just that not all of us have learned to tap into it. We all have our own challenges and parts of life to deal with. We need to keep up, be successful, prove our worth, and battle adversity. But when you learn to embrace love, to love your brother and sister, to show compassion not just toward those you have intimate feelings for but also to everyday strangers, then you will see your life truly change for the better.

Lesson: "People don't care how much you know until they know how much you care." (Theodore Roosevelt)

Love Is Mostly Silliness

Life can be very tough for your neighbors, and you never fully know what they are going through. To me, showing love is like being a safe harbor for someone. Life is hard and beats you down, but if you can be someone's safe harbor, you will be rewarded with trust and love in return.

Part of showing people how much you care is in the way you transform your inner love into outer action. My dad facetiously reminded us every year on our birthday that for his own birthday, he received only a handshake and a smile from his dad. No presents, no big celebrations. While my dad fostered a more reserved and modest outlook when it came to public shows of affection, my mother is always looking for an excuse to celebrate something, essentially being the polar opposite. After all, as mentioned in the introduction, life is full of profound individual moments. Take time to mark these moments, to cherish them, and to bring joy to them. Don't hide behind love; embrace love and show love. The days of needing to act tough, reserved, and modest have passed, and I know this because even my dad enjoys a good birthday now. For twenty-five years of my life, he never liked his birthday gifts and never wanted our family to throw parties for him. Now, he gushes over his gifts, loves to raise a toast, and throws a good dance party.

When it comes to love in your marriage, the intimate, unparalleled, and unconditional love, I found these few things to be extraordinarily useful. At a few weddings over the years, I have come across this aphorism: "To the newly pronounced husband and wife, my one piece of advice is this: never go to bed mad at each other." Pithy, to the point, and mostly true. But I would argue we should take this one step further. I might suggest to never go to bed mad at each other, but if you must, then at least touch toes at the end of the bed under the covers to let each other know, "Hey, yeah, I am mad at you, but I know we will work this out somehow, and when I put all this aside, I love you and I am always here for you." This is the kind of love you want. When someone cares for your soul and your spirit, when they push and challenge you and make you a better person, only then will you know you have found the one. Thanks to Chris Pratt for the brilliant idea he hatched on touching toes before bed.

My wife is constantly making games out of the simplest daily routines, and we make it a daily habit to dance in the kitchen. I am not a good cook, and I really don't like to cook either, but we find a way to have fun in the kitchen and to keep things interesting. We like to dance around like lunatics, sometimes waving around pots and pans and sometimes chasing each other around in our slippery socks on the hardwood floors. Some of the best moments are the silliest ones, with pasta hanging from our earlobes and sticking out our nose. Wes Angelozzi says, "Go and love someone exactly as they are. And then watch how quickly they transform into the greatest, truest version of themselves. When one feels seen and appreciated in their own essence, one is instantly empowered."[119]

There are times, however, when you need to put the pasta and silliness away and focus on realigning, or as I like to say, course correcting. You can't control the other person, and you can't fit them into the box of what you want your husband or wife to be. You should encourage them to be themselves. To be fully them. There are times when you should say sorry first, and every time, you should both be willing to go not just 50 percent each toward one another. Rather, you both should be willing to go 60 percent of the way, adding that extra 10 percent of selfless love voluntarily. Or as I recently heard in a father-of-the-bride speech, there are no sacrifices, only decisions. And a decision to love is a great priority to decide on.

Society encourages us to seek out accomplishments, recognition, and fame, but unfortunately these are dead ends. Fame and fortune favor the individual, not the collective, and that is coming from a capitalist-minded individual (me)! Of course, you should passionately pursue endeavors in your life, reach for the stars, and go after what it is you want, whether a career, a partner, a family, or that HBS degree that always seems to elude me. You can't win or gain happiness or love from others. Additionally, you can't win or gain more love once you have received love. Love is unconditional and not dependent on what you do. Ask any celebrity where their greatest joy comes from; ask Taylor Swift or Bruce Springsteen or Tom Brady, and it is not likely their happiness comes from their previous accomplishments or how their fan base feels about them. Sure, it is important to them, but it is not what drives their happiness, because their happiness is driven by themselves or their choice to choose happiness.

There are no relationships, careers, or houses that can fill a hole of unhappiness. There is nothing you can reap from the material world that will create inner peace (obviously, we have heard this before). What you might not have heard before is that inner peace and happiness come from our own output. It is not something you get from other things or people but something you cultivate yourself. In the end, it will not matter how much you were loved by others because of your accomplishments, but it will matter how well you loved others. Allowing the best within you to serve and unleash the best within others is how you can cultivate your own happiness. It is through this form of giving, of giving love away, that you will receive love. Everyone is struggling; everyone is having a hard time. Life can be excruciatingly brutal, and most hearts are starving for love. So love them; give to them; serve, protect, and nourish them. That is the secret to happiness.

In *The Artist's Way*, Julia Cameron says this about happiness and presence: "Success or failure, the truth of a life really has little to do with its quality. The quality of life is in proportion, always to the capacity for delight. The capacity for delight is the gift of paying attention."[120] In other words, Cameron is arguing that your ability to delight someone, pay attention to them, show up for them, and be there for them is a much higher compounder of happiness then, say, focusing on your own achievements only. When it comes to showing affection or love, whether romantically or in the way of friendship, we might say we are scared by failure, but what frightens us more is the possibility of success. Cameron says, "Take a small step in the direction of a dream, or in love, and watch the synchronous doors fly open.

Seeing, after all, is believing. Remember the maxim, leap and the net will appear."[121] With love, you don't have to wait; you can choose to love before receiving love back.

Cameron goes on to share a story about a Scottish Himalayan expedition, quoting W. H. Murray, who tells us his explorer's experience: "Until one is committed, there is hesitancy, the chance to draw back, always ineffectiveness. Concerning all acts of initiative (or creation) there is one elementary truth, the ignorance of which kills countless ideas and splendid plans: the moment one definitely commits oneself, then Providence moves too. All sorts of things occur to help one that would otherwise never have occurred. A whole stream of events issues from the decision, raising in one's favor all manner of incidents and meetings and material assistance which no man would have believed would have come his way."[122]

Bringing play into your love life is far more rewarding because it is fun and low pressure. I like to say that those who have the most fun usually win. They are more excited, passionate, have their guard down, and are open to opportunity. In other words, they are less self-conscious and are the types of people you and I usually find ourselves wanting to spend more time around. *Wow, how fun is Kevin? He always seems to have a good time with what he is working on or who he is around, he never seems to be complaining, and he shows up for others and chooses to have a good attitude.*

Lesson: Don't ever go to sleep mad at someone; just touch their toes with yours to let them know you love them.

Conclusion

"Tiny deviations from the optimal course are
amplified by distance and time. A small miss now
creates a very large miss later. This highlights the need
for real-time course corrections and adjustments."
(Sahil Bloom)

The longer I live, the more I realize the impact of attitude on life. I could argue that perhaps attitude is more important than the facts to a story, and it is more important to the past in which these stories live. We hardly have control over where we grow up, into what family we are born, or the IQ that we are born with. But our attitude is like the North Star. When stargazing, you can follow all the distractions and noises, you can pay attention to all your failures and moments of weakness and doubt, or you can focus on that one shining star that can guide you to living a life of significance. We cannot change our past, but we can learn from it, acknowledge it, and learn to live a more informed and self-reflective life. We can shed ourselves of the many wrong turns and dead ends we have faced and rely on our attitude to get back up that tenth time after being knocked down nine times.

Whether you are ten, fifteen, twenty, thirty, fifty, eighty, or ninety, you must base your future on a different view of yourself. But how can you gain this view? By reminding yourself that the center of our lives is not in ourselves. You cannot be perfect. No matter how many degrees, trophies, medals, or promotions you receive (even participatory), there will always be someone better and more accomplished. Even if you are exceptional at something, it is unlikely you will be exceptional at everything. Is the perfect parent also the perfect worker? Is the perfect athlete also the perfect politician? So how then do we create the future view of ourselves, if we are riddled with failures and course corrections throughout our life? You do so by finding the heroism in your struggle.

There is something heroic about a person who struggles with themselves, strained on the rack of conscience, suffering torments, yet staying alive and growing stronger, sacrificing worldly success for the sake of inner victory. The purpose of the struggle of failure, suffering, weakness, and shortcomings is not to win, because that is not possible. It is to get better at waging it. It doesn't matter if you work at a hedge fund or a charity serving the poor. There are heroes and schmucks in both worlds. The most important thing is whether you are willing to engage in this struggle of inner confrontation.

The stories in this book are wide ranging, with different experiences of mine following many different course corrections. Some moments demonstrate the idea of intense introspection, while others might argue not to be so introspective. Some moments portray me when I was very hard on myself, and in other moments I was very accepting of myself. Some moments I am taking control of my life, while other moments I am surrendering my life to grace. Should you stay in your suffering or move on from it as soon as possible? Should you keep a journal to maximize self-awareness, or does that just lead to paralyzing self-consciousness and self-indulgence? Should you be humble or self-expressive? Should you take control of your own life or surrender it to grace? Either way, there's a lot of room for each person to chart a unique path. But all of these moments of mine show a deep vulnerability while undertaking an effort to course correct that vulnerability. You can be redeemed by your weakness if you are willing to course correct and rise to new heights of self-respect.

While this book is meant to be instructive and to help you design your life and learn to accept, face, and overcome your own weaknesses and struggles, I do love this sentiment from Bruce Springsteen about how we can use writing and creative expression to better understand our life: "First, you write for yourself . . . always, to make sense of experience and the world around you. It's one of the ways I stay sane. Our stories, our books, our films are how we cope with the random trauma-inducing chaos of life as it plays."[123] He later goes on to say in his book *Born to Run*, "You lay claim to your stories; you honor, with your hard work and the best of your talent, their inspirations, and you fight to tell them well from a sense of indebtedness and thankfulness. The ambiguities, the contradictions, the complexities of your choices are always with you in your writing as they are in your life. You learn to live with them. You trust your need to have a dialogue about what you deem important."[124]

After reading through some of my many missteps and course corrections, I hope you not only take my own words and lessons to heart, but also that you have found ways to become more self-aware in your own ability to course correct.

Furthermore, I am arguing for you to not just take my word but also to examine these stories through your own lens and view of the world. I hope you can come to understand the importance of having an open mind, questioning what you take as fact, and finding a desire to remap and course correct your beliefs, your dreams, and your relationships when appropriate. This is your life, and I want you to step out of the daily grind and routine and focus on what is really important, what really moves the needle for you and what gets you up and moving. But you can't take it from me; you have to go out and solve your own questions, discover your own purpose. It is often happiness that you seek in your life, and as Mark Manson describes in his book *The Subtle Art of Not Giving a #@%!*, "Happiness is not a solvable equation. It is not passively bestowed on you from discovering something from a self-help book. It's a constant work in progress because you are constantly solving problems."[125] What Mark is arguing for is that while we can't choose all of our struggles in life, there are many we can choose. And if you are not careful about which pursuit in life you choose, or which struggle to grapple with, your mind will automatically pick a struggle, usually a less worthy struggle. Mark continues, "Happiness comes from solving worthwhile problems, such as developing better friendships, becoming a better son." It is in the act of choosing to solve worthy problems that you realize happiness." Mark suggests, "The more interesting question is not what do you want in life, but what pain are you willing to endure and choose to endure?"[126]

While the internal search for a worthy cause in life to struggle for is heroic, it can be juxtaposed and balanced with a healthy dose of letting go. While it is important to take your life's purpose seriously, it is equally necessary to balance your passionate pursuits by releasing the pressure valve on the stress gauge. Alan Watts's discovery of the Backwards Law tells us the more we pursue something, the more we achieve the opposite of what we truly want and the more disappointed we feel. For example, when you try to stay on the surface of the water, you sink, and when you try to sink, you float. Origins of this law come from Tao Te Ching or Zen Buddhism. The constant striving to be happy makes people unhappy. The more you try to get people to love you and respect you, the fewer people often will. As with anxiety, the more anxious you are, the more you try to control every aspect of your life. The more you try to control your feelings, the less in control you feel. Only with self-acceptance with what you feel and who you are can you feel more in control of your lives. In other words, don't just reject your thoughts and feelings; accept them. Accept your anxiety and your missteps in life; accept that happiness is a journey and not a destination.

David Epstein, author of *The Sports Gene*, comments on how some of the greatest musicians were self-taught or never learned to read music.[127] He wasn't saying one way is the best, but he hears about a lot of students from schools that are teaching jazz, and they all sound the same. They don't seem to find their own voice, and that could be because when you are self-taught you experiment more, trying to find the same sound in different places, learning how to solve problems. Like the baseball card story and how we should take pride in our cards, remember to take pride in your journey, in your experiences, in your failures, and find your own voice along the way. Don't follow someone else's playbook for life, but design and go after the one you want to follow. Having classical training is probably important if you want to be an astronaut, an attorney, an accountant, or a doctor, but the route you take to get there and the experiences you fill your life with to become even better than the standard textbook astronaut or doctor becomes your own unique playbook and your own edge. Be greater than a textbook, resume, or research paper. Play around with life, and remember to try different things, experiment, and fail quickly. And when you find that one thing you love, stick to it and commit.

Steve Jobs once said, "You can't connect the dots looking forward; you can only connect them looking backward. So you have to trust that the dots will somehow connect in your future."[128]

Yes, take action now, but remember that action taken today leads to results tomorrow, and nothing is won immediately. In the meantime, let's try to eliminate the "afters." "I'm doing it after," "I'll say it after," "I'll think about it after." We leave everything for later as if "after" is ours. What we don't understand is that afterward, the coffee gets cold. Afterward, priorities change. Afterward, the charm is broken. Afterward, health passes. Afterward, the kids grow up. Afterward, parents get old. Afterward, promises are forgotten. Afterward, the day becomes the night. Afterward, life ends. And then it's often too late. So let's leave nothing for later, because waiting to see later, we can lose.

Most producers understand that filmmaking is all about knowing your ending. If the actors and actresses understand the plot and thematic endpoints, they can create a concise journey for the audience to follow. When I think back on some of the chapters that introduced embarrassment, failure, and lessons learned, I realize that you can't please everyone. It is not only normal but also important to fail, and at the end of the day, we don't know how our story will end. However, we can make the necessary course corrections along the way as long as we are aware and attuned to our surroundings, habits, and internal dialogue with ourselves. In his book *Will*, Will Smith details the idea that you are going to stumble and get ridiculed, sometimes you are going to be cheered and celebrated, but ultimately no one is destined for a life of perfection. No one escapes unscathed. "Life is similar to a film; You're born into a bunch of characters, everyone's looking at you, you can't communicate, you can't walk, you can't feed yourself, yet everybody seems to be excited to see what you're going to end up doing. So, you begin telling your joke, with no fucking clue what the punch line is going to be. You're watching the audience, sometimes they chuckle, sometimes they book, but deep down inside they hope you land the punch line. Some of us are born into loving and supportive audiences, and some of us land onstage in front of a crowd of hecklers. Most of us land somewhere in between."[129]

Life is not about aging; it's about living. Do you have regrets? Of course, you wouldn't be human if you didn't. Although you never lose that, the intensity of pain softens and becomes part of the landscape of your life. It becomes more level. Its life is the process of seasons, as my wife says. You will be taken by surprise at how full of purpose anyone's life can become when they have gratitude for the day at hand. Anyone looking forward to retirement has got the wrong end of the stick, in my opinion. It should be the beginning of life starting, not the end.

Until you open that part of you that has been shut down for so long because of the necessities of life, it's not going to happen. It will become a self-enlarging process, and you will grow with it.

Youth has so much potential for loving and living and being and creating. The potential of life is so extreme and so powerful, and so few people are conscious of it, especially youth. If you don't note with satisfaction the good things in life, you will become a grumpy old man or woman. I urge you to be very conscious of the gifts around you and to arm yourself against what the band Dispatch warns us about: a passerby.

As you go about your life in search of your own identity, don't be afraid to go after something, to show your vulnerability, to find balance between introspection and action, and to leave it all out on the line when it comes to love. Chase something worthy of the struggle, ask yourself important questions, remain committed to your values, and always remember you are only a small course correction away from wherever you want to be, no matter how off-track you might have gone.

Be you. Be different.

Notes

1. Alex Haley, *The Autobiography of Malcolm X* (New York: Ballantine Books, 1965).

2. Découvertes (1970), as quoted by Stuart Wells in *Choosing the Future: The Power of Strategic Thinking* (Boston: Butterworth-Heinemann, 1997), 15.

3. David Brooks, *The Road to Character* (London: Penguin Books, 2016), 9.

4. Harry Emerson Fosdick, *On Being a Real Person* (New York: Harper and Brothers, 1943), 25.

5. David Carr, as quoted by Austin Kleon, *Show Your Work!* (New York: Workman Publishing Company, 2014), 1–163.

6. Seyda Noir, "When Nothing Else Makes Sense, Read This," Medium.com, June 28, 2022, https://medium.com/@seydanoir/when-nothing-else-makes-sense-read-this-prose-b7ee1ed6baab.

7. Jordan Kutzer, X corporation post, October 24, 2022, 10:39 a.m., https://twitter.com/JordanKutzer/status/1584570218541875201.

8. John Soforic, *The Wealthy Gardener: Life Lessons on Prosperity between Father and Son* (New York: Portfolio/Penguin, 2020).

9. Maharishi International University, "Jim Carrey at MIU: Commencement Address at the 2014 Graduation (EN,

FR, ES, RU, GR, . . .)," YouTube video, May 30, 2014, www.youtube.com/watch?v=V80-gPkpH6M.

10. Shakti Gawain, *Creative Visualization* (Novato, CA: New World Library, 2008).

11. Shakti Gawain, *Creative Visualization*, (Novato, CA: New World Library, 2008).

12. Bob Burg and John David Mann, *The Go-Giver: A Little Story about a Powerful Business Idea* (London: Portfolio/Penguin, 2015).

13. David Brooks, *The Road to Character* (London: Penguin Books, 2016).

14. David Brooks, *The Road to Character* (London: Penguin Books, 2016).

15. Rich Roll, "The Art of Transformation: How to Make Lasting Change | Rich Roll Podcast," YouTube video, May 11, 2023, www.youtube.com/watch?v=A98s9CqUM0w.

16. Jenny Gross, "Goodfellas (1990) with Ray Liotta, Robert de Niro, Lorraine Bracco, Paul Sorvino, Joe Pesci Movie," YouTube video, October 12, 2016, www.youtube.com/watch?v=VNKlNGTaxbQ.

17. "Transcript: Michelle Obama's Convention Speech," NPR.org, September 4, 2012, https://www.npr.org/2012/09/04/160578836/transcript-michelle-obamas-convention-speech.

18. Peacock TV, "The Godfather | Don Corleone," Facebook post, January 13 2023, www.facebook.com/PeacockTV/videos/the-godfather-don-corleone/685529699879296/.

19. David Brooks, *The Road to Character* (London: Penguin Books, 2016).

20. Will Smith and Mark Manson, *Will* (New York: Penguin Press, 2021).

21. Will Smith and Mark Manson, *Will* (New York: Penguin Press, 2021).

22. Will Smith and Mark Manson, *Will* (New York: Penguin Press, 2021).

23. Carla A. Harris, *Lead to Win: How to Be a Powerful, Impactful, Influential Leader in Any Environment* (New York: Avery, 2022).

24. Daniel Kahneman, *Thinking, Fast and Slow* (New York: Farrar, Straus and Giroux, 2011).

25. "Dwight Eisenhower and Responsibility Narrative," Bill of Rights Institute, billofrightsinstitute.org/activities/ dwight-eisenhower-and-responsibility-narrative (Accessed October 4, 2023).

26. Carla A. Harris, *Lead to Win: How to Be a Powerful, Impactful, Influential Leader in Any Environment* (New York: Avery, 2022).

27. John Mack, *Up Close and All In* (New York: Simon and Schuster, 2022).

28. Rachel Looker, "General Colin Powell Shares Leadership Skills," *National Association of Counties*, March 3, 2020, www.naco.org/articles/general-colin-powell-shares-leadership-skills.

29. Rachel Looker, "General Colin Powell Shares Leadership
    Skills," *National Association of Counties*, March 3, 2020,
    www.naco.org/articles/general-colin-powell-shares-
    leadership-skills.

30. Rachel Looker, "General Colin Powell Shares Leadership
    Skills," *National Association of Counties*, March 3, 2020,
    www.naco.org/articles/general-colin-powell-shares-
    leadership-skills.

31. Alex Banayan, *The Third Door: The Wild Quest to Uncover
    How the World's Most Successful People Launched Their
    Careers* (New York: Currency, 2018).

32. InsideBamaRecruiting Alabama Football, X Corporation
    post, August 27, 2019, 12:22 p.m., twitter.com/RTRnews/
    status/1166400619684478979?lang=en.

33. Adam Grant, X Corporation post, September
    28, 2022, 10:31 a.m., twitter.com/AdamMGrant/
    status/1575146105716744195?lang=en.

34. David Epstein, *Range: Why Generalists Triumph in a
    Specialized World* (New York: Riverhead Books, 2019).

35. David Brooks, *The Road to Character* (London: Penguin
    Books, 2016).

36. Search results for "Short Term Planning," Seth's Blog,
    seths.blog/?s=short+term+planning (accessed August 17,
    2023).

37. Bobby Orr, *Orr: My Story* (Toronto: Penguin Canada,
    2013).

38. David Epstein, *Range: Why Generalists Triumph in a Specialized World* (New York: Riverhead Books, 2019).

39. Austin Kleon, as quoted by Jory MacKay, "Get Out of Your Damn Bubble," TNW Lifehacks, July 31 2016, thenextweb.com/news/get-damn-bubble.

40. Socio Empath, "Charles Cooley: I Am What I Think You Think I Am," SmartCasualSG, April 28, 2018, smartcasualsg.com/charles-cooley-sociology-quotes.

41. Focus+, "My Favorite Quote "Attitude" by Charles Swindoll," FocusPositives, www.focuspositives.com/my-favorite-attitude-quote/.

42. "A Quote by Jerry Garcia," Goodreads.com, www.goodreads.com/quotes/10845286-it-s-not-enough-to-be-the-best-at-what-you.

43. Kobe Bryant, *The Mamba Mentality* (New York: MCD, 2018).

44. Kobe Bryant, *The Mamba Mentality* (New York: MCD, 2018).

45. Laura Huang, *Edge: Turning Adversity into Advantage* (New York: Portfolio/Penguin, 2020).

46. Peter Sims, *Little Bets: How Big Ideas Emerge from Small Discoveries* (London: Random House Business, 2012).

47. Peter Sims, *Little Bets: How Big Ideas Emerge from Small Discoveries* (London: Random House Business, 2012).

48. Peter Sims, *Little Bets: How Big Ideas Emerge from Small Discoveries* (London: Random House Business, 2012).

49. David Goggins, *Can't Hurt Me: Master Your Mind and Defy the Odds* (Carson City, NV: Lioncrest Publishing, 2019).

50. Peter Sims, *Little Bets: How Big Ideas Emerge from Small Discoveries* (London: Random House Business, 2012).

51. NFL Films, "The Brady 6: Journey of the Legend No One Wanted!" YouTube video, March 5, 2020, www.youtube.com/watch?v=o5fdhfVrg1I.

52. Kobe Bryant, *The Mamba Mentality* (New York: MCD, 2018).

53. Kobe Bryant, *The Mamba Mentality* (New York: MCD, 2018).

54. David J. McGillivray, *The Last Pick* (Emmaus, PA: Rodale Books, 2006).

55. David J. McGillivray, *The Last Pick* (Emmaus, PA: Rodale Books, 2006).

56. "Mike Tyson Quotes," BrainyQuote, www.brainyquote.com/quotes/mike_tyson_382439 (accessed October 4, 2023).

57. Paraphrased from Caitriona Loughrey, as quoted by Dr. Denise Taylor, "Barely the Day Started And . . ." The50pluscoach, www.the50pluscoach.co.uk/barely-the-day-started-and/ (accessed October 4, 2023).

58. Paraphrased from Caitriona Loughrey, as quoted by Dr. Denise Taylor, "Barely the Day Started And . . ." The50pluscoach, www.the50pluscoach.co.uk/barely-the-day-started-and/ (accessed October 4, 2023).

59. Rich Roll, *Finding Ultra: Rejecting Middle Age, Becoming One of the World's Fittest Men, and Discovering Myself* (New York: Harmony Books, 2018).

60. Michael A. Singer, *The Untethered Soul: The Journey beyond Yourself* (Oakland, CA: New Harbinger Publications/Noetic Books, 2013).

61. Alp Mimaroglu, "The Best Advice Steve Jobs Ever Gave," *Entrepreneur*, January 21, 2021, www.entrepreneur.com/leadership/the-best-advice-steve-jobs-ever-gave/362596.

62. John Soforic, *The Wealthy Gardener: Life Lessons on Prosperity between Father and Son* (New York: Portfolio/Penguin, 2020).

63. Michael A. Singer, *The Untethered Soul: The Journey beyond Yourself* (Oakland, CA: New Harbinger Publications/Noetic Books, 2013).

64. "June Jordan Quotes," Quotefancy.com, quotefancy.com/quote/1262132/June-Jordan-As-a-child-I-was-taught-that-to-tell-the-truth-was-often-painful-As-an-adult (accessed August 17, 2023).

65. Carlos Castaneda, *The Art of Dreaming* (Shaftesbury, UK: Element Books, 2004).

66. Carlos Castaneda, *The Art of Dreaming* (Shaftesbury, UK: Element Books, 2004).

67. Alan C. Greenberg, *Memos from the Chairman* (New York: Workman Publishing Company, 1996).

68. Adam Grant, X Corporation post, March 27, 2022, 10:52 a.m., twitter.com/AdamMGrant/status/1508109675421700098?lang=en.

69. David Brooks, *The Road to Character* (London: Penguin Books, 2016).

70. "John Bytheway Quotes," Goodreads.com, www.goodreads.com/quotes/321104-inch-by-inch-life-s-a-cinch-yard-by-yard-life-s (accessed October 4, 2023).

71. James Clear, "The 3-2-1 Newsletter," JamesClear.com, August 17, 2023, jamesclear.com/3-2-1.

72. Kerry Patterson et al., *Crucial Conversations: Tools for Talking When Stakes Are High* (New York: McGraw Hill, 2012).

73. Morgan Housel, *The Psychology of Money* (Petersville, UK: Harriman House Limited, September 8, 2020.

74. Sara Moore, "Amy Cuddy TED Talk—Fake It till You Make It" YouTube video, July 7, 2016, www.youtube.com/watch?v=RVmMeMcGc0Y.

75. Adam Grant, X Corporation post, July 25, 2022, 10:06 a.m., twitter.com/AdamMGrant/status/1551584622420672513.

76. Alex Banayan, *The Third Door: The Wild Quest to Uncover How the World's Most Successful People Launched Their Careers* (New York: Currency, 2018).

77. MangaFX, "President Barack Obama: Just Learn How to Get Stuff Done," YouTube video, June 27, 2023, www.youtube.com/watch?v=YNY4UFaHbP4.

78. MangaFX, "President Barack Obama: Just Learn How to Get Stuff Done," YouTube video, June 27, 2023, www.youtube.com/watch?v=YNY4UFaHbP4.

79. MangaFX, "President Barack Obama: Just Learn How to Get Stuff Done," YouTube video, June 27, 2023, www.youtube.com/watch?v=YNY4UFaHbP4.

80. "Upton Sinclair Quotes," Goodreads.com, www.goodreads.com/quotes/21810-it-is-difficult-to-get-a-man-to-understand-something (accessed October 4, 2023).

81. Wei Dai, as quoted by James Clear, "3-2-1: Judging Potential, Negotiating, and Balancing Life" JamesClear.com, June 22, 2023, jamesclear.com/3-2-1/june-22-2023#:~:text=%E2%80%9COnce%20you%20achieve%20high%20status.

82. Alex Banayan, *The Third Door: The Wild Quest to Uncover How the World's Most Successful People Launched Their Careers* (New York: Currency, 2018).

83. Paraphrased from "Harvey Specter Always Specifically Mentions '146' Things You Can Do When Someone Holds a Gun to Your Head. Is There a Reason for the Number 146?" Quora, www.quora.com/Harvey-Specter-always-specifically-mentions-146-things-you-can-do-when-someone-holds-a-gun-to-your-head-Is-there-a-reason-for-the-number-146 (accessed October 4, 2023).

84. Paraphrased from Courtney Carver, "The Story of the Mexican Fisherman," Be More with Less, May 24, 2010, bemorewithless.com/the-story-of-the-mexican-fisherman/.

85. QuoteResearch, "I Think Everybody Should Get Rich and Famous So They Can See That That's Not the Answer," Quote Investigator, November 9, 2022, quoteinvestigator. com/2022/11/09/rich-famous/.

86. Joe Taysom, "Dave Grohl Reveals His Cheesy Pop Music "Guilty Pleasure" Song," *Far Out*, October 14, 2020, faroutmagazine.co.uk/foo-fighters-dave-grohl-embarassing-guilty-pleasure-spice-girls/.

87. Mark Groves, "Mark Groves Home Page," MarkGroves. com, markgroves.com (accessed October 4, 2023).

88. James Clear, "3-2-1: Acting Your Age, Financial Advice from a Grandmother, and Forgiveness," JamesClear.com, June 16, 2022, jamesclear.com/3-2-1/june-16-2022.

89. Light Watkins, as quoted by James Clear, " 'People Usually Judge You Based on Where You Are at Currently, Not What You Could Become Eventually. Don't Let One Comment Stop You from Trying. File It Away or Use It as Fuel. Focus on Getting Better. Someone Else's Analysis of Your Current Position Doesn't Tell You Anything about Your Current Potential,' " JamesClear.com, jamesclear. com/quotes/people-usually-judge-you-based-on-where-you-are-at-currently-not-what-you-could-become-eventually-dont-let-one-comment-stop-you-from-trying-file-it-away-or-use-it-as-fuel-focus-on-getting-bett (accessed August 17, 2023).

90. Angela Duckworth, *Grit: The Power of Passion and Perseverance* (New York: Scribner, 2016).

91. Angela Duckworth, *Grit: The Power of Passion and Perseverance* (New York: Scribner, 2016).

92. Will Smith and Mark Manson, *Will* (New York: Penguin Press, 2021).

93. Catherine Versfeld, "Robin Williams—Perfect Imperfections Super Philosophy (Good Will Hunting)," YouTube video, August 23, 2014, www.youtube.com/watch?v=9H43uP01PyQ.

94. Mind & Mood, "Train Your Brain," Harvard Health, February 15, 2021, www.health.harvard.edu/mind-and-mood/train-your-brain#:~:text=Your%20brain%20has%20the%20ability.

95. Brené Brown, *Daring Greatly: How the Courage to Be Vulnerable Transforms the Way We Live, Love, Parent, and Lead* (New York: Avery Publishing Group, 2015).

96. Guy Raz, "Spanx: Sara Blakely" Apple Podcasts: How I Built This with Guy Raz, podcasts.apple.com/si/podcast/spanx-sara-blakely/id1150510297?i=1000396023160 (accessed August 17, 2023).

97. Lexi Alexander, et al. "Green Street Hooligans," IMDb.com, September 9, 2005, www.imdb.com/title/tt0385002/.

98. Liz Mineo, "Good Genes Are Nice, but Joy Is Better," *The Harvard Gazette*, April 11, 2017, news.harvard.edu/gazette/story/2017/04/over-nearly-80-years-harvard-study-has-been-showing-how-to-live-a-healthy-and-happy-life/.

99. Liz Mineo, "Good Genes Are Nice, but Joy Is Better." *The Harvard Gazette*, April 11, 2017, news.harvard.edu/ gazette/story/2017/04/over-nearly-80-years-harvard-study-has-been-showing-how-to-live-a-healthy-and-happy-life/.

100. Bob Burg, and John David Mann, *The Go-Giver: A Little Story about a Powerful Business Idea* (London: Portfolio / Penguin, 2015).

101. John C. Maxwell, *The 21 Indispensable Qualities of a Leader* (New York: HarperCollins Leadership, 2007).

102. Naked Treaties, Facebook post, August 22, 2016, https:// www.facebook.com/nakedtreaties/photos/a.1141010852 98220/1193584790683172/?type=3 (accessed October 6, 2023).

103. Free Souls, Instagram post, January 13, 2023, https://www. instagram.com/p/CnXN1QnMpr3/ (accessed October 6, 2023).

104. Michael A. Singer, *The Untethered Soul: The Journey beyond Yourself* (Oakland, CA: New Harbinger Publications/Noetic Books, 2013).

105. David Brooks, *The Road to Character* (London: Penguin Books, 2016).

106. Kobe Bryant, *The Mamba Mentality* (New York: MCD, 2018).

107. Martin O'Toole, "10 Yung Pueblo Quotes to Inspire Your Healing Journey" Medium, February 2, 2020,

martinotoole.medium.com/10-yung-pueblo-quotes-to-
inspire-you-on-your-healing-journey-d12ee5d1e458.

108. David Brooks, *The Road to Character* (London: Penguin
Books, 2016).

109. M. Scott Peck, *The Road Less Traveled* (London: Rider
Books, 2020).

110. Lois Greiman, *Finding Home* (New York: Kensington
Publishing, 2012).

111. "'Peace Comes from Within. Do Not Seek It Without,'"
Fake Buddha Quotes, June 19, 2012, fakebuddhaquotes.
com/peace-comes-from-within-do-not-seek-it-without/.

112. Michael A. Singer, *The Untethered Soul: The Journey
beyond Yourself* (Oakland, CA: New Harbinger
Publications/Noetic Books, 2013).

113. Michael A. Singer, *The Untethered Soul: The Journey
beyond Yourself* (Oakland, CA: New Harbinger
Publications/Noetic Books, 2013).

114. Michael A. Singer, *The Untethered Soul: The Journey
beyond Yourself* (Oakland, CA: New Harbinger
Publications/Noetic Books, 2013).

115. Will Smith and Mark Manson, *Will* (New York: Penguin
Press, 2021).

116. M. Scott Peck *The Road Less Traveled* (London: Rider
Books, 2020).

117. "Kirsten Corley Quotes," The Minds Journal, December
31, 2020, themindsjournal.com/quotes/i-think-the-key-to-
staying-in-love-is-staying-grateful/.

118. Neal Brennan, et al., "Seth Meyers: Lobby Baby." IMDb.com, November 5, 2019, www.imdb.com/title/tt11168100/.

119. "Wes Angelozzi Quote," Quotecatalog.com, quotecatalog.com/quote/wes-angelozzi-go-and-love-som-EpREGm7/ (accessed August 17, 2023).

120. Julia Cameron, *The Artist's Way: A Spiritual Path to Higher Creativity* (London: Profile Books, 2021).

121. Julia Cameron, *The Artist's Way: A Spiritual Path to Higher Creativity* (London: Profile Books, 2021).

122. Julia Cameron, *The Artist's Way: A Spiritual Path to Higher Creativity* (London: Profile Books, 2021).

123. Bruce Springsteen, *Born to Run* (New York: Simon & Schuster Paperbacks, 2017).

124. Bruce Springsteen, *Born to Run* (New York: Simon & Schuster Paperbacks, 2017).

125. Mark Manson, *The Subtle Art of Not Giving a #@%!: A Counterintuitive Approach to Living a Good Life* (New York: HarperOne, 2016).

126. Mark Manson, *The Subtle Art of Not Giving a #@%!: A Counterintuitive Approach to Living a Good Life* (New York: HarperOne, 2016).

127. David J. Epstein, *The Sports Gene: Talent, Practice and the Truth about Success* (London: Yellow Jersey Press, 2014).

128. " 'You've Got to Find What You Love,' Jobs Says," *Stanford News*, June 12, 2005, news.stanford.edu/2005/06/12/ youve-got-find-love-jobs-says/.

129. Will Smith and Mark Manson, *Will* (New York: Penguin Press, 2021).

THE 'REAL' BIOGRAPHY

Besides for being a husband and dad, Kevin is most proud of all his failures throughout his childhood, adolescence and yes, adulthood. His younger sister by 3 years learned the alphabet before he did, his doctor required him to wear reverse headgear in middle school, and his dream of becoming a naval officer was abruptly ended. Kevin did not win any Olympic gold medals, solve any rare diseases, and definitely was not voted prom king. Kevin holds a rejection letter from Harvard Business School, received a handful of D's in undergraduate school, and was chewed out in his first internship. Kevin does not look at his life as the paragon for others to follow, but as a series of common missteps and mishaps, of which requires course correcting, leading him to further self-examination and freedom from the fear of failure. Making tiny adjustments along the way has proved to be an integral life design framework. Kevin carries two resumes, and the one he attributes to his grounding and earnest outlook on life, is his failure resume.